A Student's Guide to Communication Arts

Bryan M. Johnson • Lynette M. Sandley • David W. Chapman

KENDALL/HUNT PUBLISHING COMPANY
4050 Westmark Drive   Dubuque, Iowa 52002

Contents

Acknowledgments

One of the goals of the Communication Arts program is providing students with a community of listeners and readers who have a commitment to helping students write and speak with more confidence. This guide is a product of such a community.

The exercises, sample essays, and resources also reflect a community of instructors and past students who clearly understand that good writing and speaking are hard work, work that requires discipline, effort, and dedication. We are grateful to the students and instructors who have contributed to this effort.

Communication Arts is also made the richer by instructors in a variety of fields: literature, writing, history, journalism, speech, and theatre. Each of these Communication Arts instructors has contributed in some way to this guide: Dana Basinger, Jonathan Bass, Amanda Borden, Martha Clark, Jon Clemmensen, Ben Coulter, Sonya Davis, Dave Dedo, Gary Greene, Marcia Hotchkiss, Ken Kirby, Kathy Parnell, Patrick Pittman, Mary Rees, David Roberts, Bill Self, David Shipley, Melissa Tate, and Julie Williams.

This guide has also been made possible by the conscientious contributions of other administrators, faculty, and staff who care deeply about the success of our students: Dean Rod Davis, Ginger Frost in history, David Pridemore in the Technology Learning Center, Donna Fitch and Olivia Davis in Davis Library, and Gwen McKenzie in the Core Curriculum office. In addition, we would like to thank Margaret Whitt from the University of Denver for her assistance.

Bryan Johnson
Assistant Professor of English

Lynette Sandley
Instructor of English

David Chapman
Associate Dean, Arts and Sciences

COURSE GUIDE

Introduction

HOWARD COLLEGE OF ARTS AND SCIENCES
Office of the Dean

RODERICK DAVIS
Dean

Welcome to a very different course than you might have encountered before. Instead of your taking separate courses in English composition, oral communication, and such computer programs as PowerPoint, at Samford we fold the basic elements of each into one interdisciplinary course, Communication Arts I and II.

We have done this because, despite communication having the different facets of writing, speaking, and illustrating, as well as being both a skill and an art, it is fundamentally one kind of activity with similar basic principles that broadly apply. It therefore makes sense to us to study these basics and their various applications in the more coherent form of one course. In this format, we can better see the connections between what, in the past, were treated as separate elements.

Making connections and relationships, synthesizing our learning, is more important than ever in a world where there is so much now to learn. This interconnectedness was seen, however, even four centuries ago by one of the most multidisciplinary scholar-writer-scientist-statesmen of his time, Sir Francis Bacon, who recognized then that reading makes a "full" person, writing an "exact" one, and conversation a "ready" one.

Ultimately, we hope that learning how each of the elements of this course feed each other will make your college experience a more coherent one for you as a more articulate and fully rounded person. For how you use this and all your courses to help make your own life a more focused one is what is most important of all.

Roderick Davis
Dean of Arts and Sciences

Communication Arts Staff and Support

CHAPMAN, David, Ph.D. 726-2949
Associate Dean, Howard College of Arts and Sciences

JOHNSON, Bryan, Ph.D. 726-4036
Communication Arts Course Coordinator

MCKENZIE, Gwen 726-2071
Secretary, Core Curriculum

DEDO, David, Ph.D. 726-2137
Director, Communication Resource Center

BASINGER, DANA 726-2137
Assistant Director, Communication Resource Center

PRIDEMORE, David 726-2108
Computer Labs Manager

University Mission

The mission of Samford University is to nurture persons, offering learning experiences and relationships in a Christian community, so that each participant may develop personal empowerment, academic and career competency, social and civic responsibility, and ethical and spiritual strength; and continuously to improve the effectiveness of the community.

At Samford we expect to develop personal empowerment as we:

- work, participate, cooperate, and serve because we are accountable for our own actions.
- think, listen, speak, and write because the ability to communicate is a responsibility as well as a gift.
- encourage physical and mental well-being, sharing our triumphs and tragedies, because there is strength in community.

At Samford we expect to develop academic and career competency as we:

- read books, utilize technology, experience the arts, discuss ideas, and develop ideals.
- reason, measure, and research to engage the issues of our time and our world.
- identify and cultivate our talents, develop career goals, and participate in meaningful work.

At Samford we expect to develop social and civic responsibility as we:

- exercise civility, tolerance, fairness, and compassion by respecting both individual convictions and cultural differences.
- become good stewards of the opportunities entrusted to us.
- act with global awareness, use resources responsibly, and practice peacemaking.

At Samford we expect to develop ethical and spiritual strength as we:

- forge personal integrity in classroom and community life, in relation to God and to persons.

- discern right and wrong, good and evil, the consequences of actions and words, and shape a purpose in life that includes but exceeds "making a living."

- grow in grace and in the knowledge of Jesus Christ.

Core Curriculum Mission

Samford's **Co-Nexus** program was designed to meet the needs of a diverse student population as they prepare for life beyond college. The word **"Co-Nexus"** was coined to define the two essential attributes of the program: **co**mmunity (mutual learning) + **nexus** (place of coming together). Through **Co-Nexus**, students will come together to learn from the past and to prepare for the future. The **Co-Nexus** program begins with a core curriculum that shows the interconnectedness of art, history, literature, and philosophy; that develops the ability to read, write, and reason; and that promotes healthy living and enduring values. Students actively participate in the educational experience as they make multimedia presentations, participate in e-mail discussion groups, work through problem-solving scenarios, and carry out service-learning projects. **Co-Nexus** is premised on the idea that an education is not only what you know, but what you can do.

Communication Arts Mission

If students are to succeed in their college work, they must be able to write and speak effectively. After graduation, these skills will be continually in demand in the job market. Employers consistently rate good communication skills among the most desirable qualities of their employees. The Communication Arts courses are designed to help students develop and refine these vital skills. In the first semester, students will read and analyze sophisticated texts of various kinds. They will learn to develop a clear and interesting thesis, collect supporting materials, organize ideas effectively, and express their thoughts in vivid and appropriate language. Students will learn how to adapt a written document for oral presentation with a particular audience, purpose, and setting in mind. They will learn to use the computer for collecting information (e.g., Internet and online databases), communicating with others (e.g., Simeon mail), and preparing documents (word processing applications). In the second semester, students will develop the advanced rhetorical skills necessary for persuasive communication, including understanding the structure of a logical argument and the ability to recognize logical fallacies. They will develop small group and interpersonal communication skills and learn to use computers for presentation of information such as through PowerPoint presentations.

The impetus for the Communication Arts format came from an awareness that technology has radically changed communication strategies. The boundaries between oral, written, and visual communication were more clearly defined in the past. Media and computer technology have blurred many of these boundaries. The faculty who teach the course are drawn from literature, writing, speech, theatre, and journalism backgrounds, each contributing to the course design from their areas of expertise. This course allows us to establish the proficiency of all Samford students in these vital skills and prepare them for the speaking, writing, and computing demands of their upper division courses.

Communication Arts Requirement

The Core and General Education curricula are designed to provide an academic foundation for work toward the major field of study and should be completed as early as possible. All freshmen are required to take the core curriculum at Samford. All students should be registered for UCCP 101 in their first semester. They should also register for UCCA 101 or UCCA 102, depending on their placement. Students should consult their academic advisors for recommended scheduling. The prerequisite for UCCA 102 is UCCA 101. **Students must make at least a C- to pass both courses, and students do not qualify for UCCA 102 until they pass UCCA 101. Making a C- in UCCA 102 meets the requirement for writing proficiency**.

The UCCA/UCCP Connection

It is very easy to think that what you learn in one class has no bearing on other course work. But Cultural Perspectives and Communication Arts are designed precisely to remedy such thinking. It will help you in both courses to understand that Communication Arts and Cultural Perspectives are companion courses. They are both required in the first year because the material in each course distinctively supports the other. Both courses, for example, teach you to read and think critically about a broad range of materials. Both courses expect you to synthesize a lot of new and potentially challenging ideas. Though you are reading classical works in Cultural Perspectives, and contemporary prose essays in Communication Arts, the skills you are developing are exactly the same. When you are writing your essays in Communication Arts, it will help you to consider the material you read in Cultural Perspectives. For instance, if you are writing a position essay on higher education for Communication Arts, you might be influenced by Plato (who doubted if all people were suited for advanced learning); by Augustine (who doubted if education made people better); or by Locke (who thought that education was the basis of human liberty). Although these writers did not address nuclear disarmament, e-mail privacy, or other contemporary issues, they did address issues of justice, goodness, temperance, and charity. Strong writers make an attempt to place their experiences in a context; it is important as a young writer to remember that others have gone before you, that other, more experienced writers can help to illuminate your experiences. Similarly, all of the writing and speaking skills you learn in Communication Arts transfer to your other classes, including Cultural Perspectives. Your Cultural Perspectives instructors will expect you to write clear, well-reasoned, fully developed, responsibly researched essays. The materials you read and the skills you learn in each course are not intended to simply help you pass those courses. Both courses seek to teach you how to be a better, more broad-minded student.

Placement and Substitute Credit

**University Policies Regarding Transfer Credit,
Credit by Examination, and Transient Credit for Courses**

The policies for transfer credit, transient credit, and credit by examination were developed by an ad hoc committee formed for this purpose in December 1996. The committee was made up of the deans of the undergraduate schools and various faculty and student representatives. The recommendations of the ad hoc committee were voted on by the university faculty and adopted on February 14, 1997.

Entering Freshmen (EFR)

Any student who enrolls with fewer than 18 hours of transfer credit is classified as an entering freshman. All freshmen are required to take the core curriculum at Samford. All students should be registered for Cultural Perspectives 101 in their first semester at Samford. They should also register for Communication Arts 101 or Communication Arts 102, depending on their placement. Students are eligible for Communication Arts 102 if they meet any of the following criteria:

1. a score of 4 or 5 on the Advanced Placement exam in English Language or English Literature

2. an SAT score of 630 or above

3. an ACT score of 30 or above on English and Social Science

4. successful completion of an English composition course at an accredited college or university

Credit-by-Examination

Entering freshmen may present advanced placement or CLEP examination credit for any core or general education requirement except Cultural Perspectives 101 and 102 and Communication Arts 102. Students who earn AP credits for literature or history may apply these as elective credits, but they will not be exempted from the Cultural Perspectives course requirements. Similarly, students who earn AP credit on the English Language or Literature examination may receive credit for UCCA 101, but they will be required to take UCCA 102.

Transfer Credit

Samford University strives to offer a distinctive curriculum that challenges students to their fullest potential and which employs innovative teaching techniques. All students should complete their general education requirements in residence whenever possible.

However, students who are transferring to Samford from another university should not feel that the core and general education requirements form a roadblock to their normal progress toward the degree. In general, the university will accept courses of equivalent content and objectives as satisfying the general education requirements. Courses do not have to be an exact match in credit hours, but should be at least 75% (i.e., a 3-hour course could satisfy a 4-hour requirement). Students will only receive the credit they earned (not the credit of the course being replaced). Students will still need to meet the total number of hours required for their degree program (128 minimum).

Transfer students may substitute more traditional courses that they have taken elsewhere for the interdisciplinary courses of the core curriculum. For instance, courses in literature or history may be substituted for the Cultural Perspectives courses. Courses in English composition may be substituted for the Communication Arts sequence. However, students who substitute another course for UCCA 102 will be required to take the writing proficiency examination.

Transient Enrollment for Core Curriculum and General Education[1]

Core curriculum requirements cannot be met through transient enrollment.

Samford students will continue to be required to complete transient enrollment forms before taking courses at other institutions. Transient forms must be signed by the head of the administrative unit responsible for the course.

---

1 Technically, transient enrollment refers to students from other institutions who are taking courses at Samford. Credit Samford students earn at other institutions should be referred to as transfer credit, but the more familiar term is used here.

Students may transfer two general education courses from another accredited institution or from the Samford Metro College for fewer credits than the courses being replaced.

If a student wishes to take more than two courses for general education credit, the courses must be equal to or greater than the number of credit hours being replaced. Any credit beyond the requirement will be shown as elective credit. For instance, if a student takes two three-credit courses to meet a four-credit requirement, the additional credits will count as electives toward the total required for graduation.

Transient Enrollment for Elective Courses and Major Requirements

Students enrolled at Samford may also transfer additional courses to be applied as electives or as major courses from another accredited institution or from the Samford Metro College for fewer credits than the courses being replaced. Permission to take courses at another institution that apply toward the major must be given by the department chair or dean of the school in which the major is offered.

1. 1

Section Review

1. According to Dean Roderick Davis, what is the rationale behind the Communication Arts curriculum?

   _____

   _____

2. Who claimed that reading makes one a "full" person, writing an "exact" one, and conversation a "ready one"?

   _____

   _____

3. In what ways is Communication Arts consistent with Samford's mission?

   _____

   _____

4. From which two words does the term Co-Nexus originate?

   _____

   _____

5. What are some differences between Communication Arts 101 and Communication Arts 102?

   _____

   _____

6. What grade must you make to pass Communication Arts?

   _____

   _____

7. What is the relationship between Communication Arts and Cultural Perspectives?

   _____

   _____

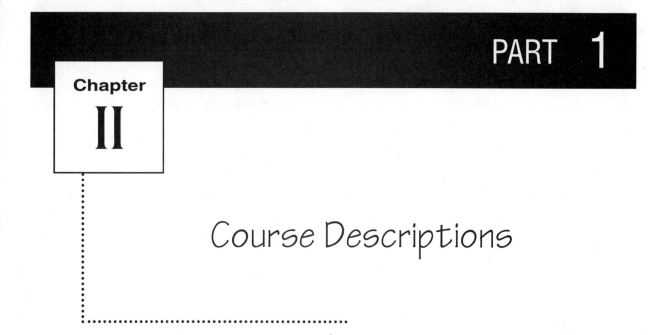

Course Descriptions

Communication Arts General Requirements

Every Communication Arts course requires students to write a minimum of 16–20 pages or 3600 to 4500 words in four essays, to deliver a variety of speeches, to read non-fiction essays, to develop computer skills, and to take a final exam (UCCA 102). In-class writing and group exercises are also required.

UCCA 101 Communication Arts

One of the most valuable skills you will develop in college is the ability to communicate effectively. Such skills will be prized by all your college teachers and by your eventual employers. Communicating effectively involves four related activities: speaking, listening, writing, and reading. You will also need to be able to retrieve information through electronic and print sources. You will use the computer to prepare documents and to analyze information. When you complete this course, you should feel more confident of your abilities in all these areas. Specifically, you should be able to:

1. Use word processing for preparation of essays and outlines

2. Use a Web browser and electronic databases

3. Demonstrate proper interviewing skills

4. Communicate information concisely, directly, and clearly

5. Demonstrate confidence in various oral communication settings

6. Listen for specific purposes

7. Read and analyze sophisticated texts of various kinds

8. Develop a clear and interesting thesis, collect supporting materials, organize ideas effectively, and use vivid, appropriate language

9. Adapt a message for a specific audience, occasion, and purpose

10. Use appropriate methods of rhetorical invention

11. Make appropriate inferences

12. Select and evaluate sources carefully

13. Practice both global revision and surface editing for clarity and correctness

UCCA 102 Communication Arts

In Communications Arts 101 you concentrated on writing and speaking about experiences, observations, and readings. In this course, you will emphasize the ability to collect and synthesize information from a variety of sources and to write and speak persuasively. You will also extend your use of computers, understanding a variety of functions that they can perform. Specifically, you should be able to:

1. Conduct a bibliographic search using electronic and print resources

2. Prepare a graph or table using the appropriate computer software

3. Follow ethical guidelines for computer use

4. Analyze television news and commercial advertising

5. Develop small group communication skills

6. Develop interpersonal communication skills

7. Employ referential communication skills

8. Develop an appropriate interview agenda

9. Use concrete and vivid language

10. Recognize the structure of logical argument

11. Make appropriate inferences from a text

12. Recognize and avoid logical fallacies

13. Support a claim with appropriate evidence

Honors Courses

All Honors students should enroll in one of the UCCA 102 Honors sections during the fall of their freshman year. Honors students must have an ACT score of 26 or an SAT-I score of 1155 and a high school GPA of 3.5 (B+) or higher. Additional information about eligibility and requirements can be obtained from the Honors Program Director.

The Honors sections of Communication Arts are taught in small seminar classes with enrollment limited to fifteen students. Although the Honors sections have the same high standards as the other Communication Arts courses, they devote less time to basic skills, allowing students to concentrate on advanced rhetorical strategies. One of the best features of the Honors sections is the rich dialogue that goes on between students and faculty about the works they are reading and the ideas they are developing in their own writing and speaking. Participating in the Honors Program is an excellent way to make the most of your educational experience at Samford.

Writing Component

In UCCA 101 students write four essays: an autobiography essay that focuses on personal experiences, a reflection essay that asks students to reach conclusions about the external world, an observation essay that helps students develop their descriptive skills, and a concept essay that requires students to explain abstract ideas. The techniques of research and documentation will be emphasized to prepare students for academic writing.

UCCA 102 focuses on writing research-based persuasive arguments: an evaluation essay reviewing some form of media (film, news, art, etc.), a proposal essay advocating a solution to a problem, a cause/effect essay establishing a causal argument, and a position essay taking a stand on a significant issue.

Speech Component

Speeches in Communication Arts are intended to support your writing activities. Most of your essays will be accompanied by an oral activity. You will deliver two individual speeches in UCCA 101, an autobiography speech and concept speech. You will also participate in a panel presentation speech for the observation essay and deliver some shorter special occasion speeches. You will deliver two individual speeches in UCCA 102, an evaluation speech and a proposal speech. You will also participate in a public interview with one of your classmates.

Computer Component/E-Mail

You are required to use a word processor for out-of-class essays. All Communication Arts instructors will make use of Samford's computer labs, instructing students in word processing skills, e-mail and Web use, graph and table software, and PowerPoint. All Communication Arts instructors will make use of e-mail to support classroom activity. You should take responsibility for communicating with your instructor by e-mail as well.

1. How much writing should you expect to do in your Communication Arts courses?

    _____

    _____

2. Identify at least three of the goals in Communication Arts 101 that are of particular importance to you.

    _____

    _____

3. Identify at least three of the goals in Communication Arts 102 that are of particular importance to you.

    _____

    _____

4. What distinguishes Communication Arts Honors courses from other Communication Arts courses?

    _____

    _____

5. Identify one of the essays you will be expected to write in Communication Arts 101. What does that assignment attempt to teach?

    _____

    _____

6. Identify one of the essays you will be expected to write in Communication Arts 102. What does that assignment attempt to teach?

    _____

    _____

7.   How many individual speeches will you deliver in each Communication Arts course?

_____

_____

8.   Identify two of the computer activities you will learn in Communication Arts.

_____

_____

Opportunities for Writing and Tutorial Assistance

Communication Resource Center (CRC)

The Communication Resource Center (CRC) is a small suite packed with equipment, including computers, printers, videotape cameras, and an LCD projector, staffed by consultants specially trained to help you improve your communication skills. The CRC consultants will focus on the practical issues of conveying ideas effectively. They can help you become comfortable with e-mail, Web browsers, search engines, word processors, spreadsheets, and PowerPoint.

CRC consultants will also help you to read more critically, to write more coherently, to speak more fluently. While they will not simply correct your essays or do your work, they will teach you how to develop your ideas, organize your thoughts, and recognize flaws in your reasoning, errors in your usage, and awkwardness in your style. To make an appointment with a CRC consultant you can stop by UCA 309—on the third floor above the journalism and geography departments—or call David Dedo or Dana Basinger at 726-2137.

The SALT Center
(Student, Advising, Learning, Tutoring)

The SALT Center offers the following to freshmen:

1. Academic advising and guidance toward a major for all undeclared majors.

2. Administration of the S.U.ccess Program, which mentors freshmen who feel they may have academic difficulty.

3. Early identification and intervention with freshmen having academic difficulty in the first semester of their freshman year.

4. Administration of a program in the spring semester of the freshman year for students placed on probation after the fall semester.

5. Assistance in securing tutors for students having academic difficulty.

The SALT Center is administered by the Dean of Freshmen, the Center secretary, and several people from various departments in the university who will assist with mentoring and advising students involved in the Center's programs. For information about the SALT Center, you can call Amanda Borden at 726-2511.

Conferences

Students are expected to have at least two conferences with their instructor during each Communication Arts course. These conferences are valuable for discussing your writing and speaking in more detail than class time permits. Moreover, you can bring up questions you might hesitate to ask during class. Be sure to show up for your conference on time and bring all your class work with you when you meet. Your instructor will announce a conference schedule after the semester has begun.

Electronic Mail

All faculty and students have access to e-mail accounts. Problems with your e-mail account are handled by the Computer Support Desk (2662). Instructors will respond to students within a reasonable amount of time, though you should remember that not all faculty are on campus every day.

Office Hours

All Communication Arts instructors will hold office hours for a minimum of four hours a week. If these office hours conflict with your class schedule, you may request an appointment at a time that is mutually convenient. If you are having difficulty with the class or are considering dropping the course, you should make an appointment to meet with your instructor.

1. In addition to help with your writing, what other services are offered by the Communication Resource Center?

   _____

   _____

2. What does the SALT Center do for freshmen?

   _____

   _____

3. How many conferences should you have with your Communication Arts instructor?

   _____

   _____

4. In addition to scheduled conferences, what are a couple of ways you can get assistance from your Communication Arts instructor?

   _____

   _____

Library

The Harwell G. Davis Library is the primary library for all students, faculty, and staff. There are over a half million volumes available for access by the Online Public Access Catalog. In addition to the book and periodical collections, the library houses a government document collection, a Special Collection, and a multimedia collection. Complementing the strong collection of print, microform, and multimedia items are the library's technological tools: CD and online databases, World Wide Web access, a computer lab, and a technology learning center are among the technology services available to patrons.

Library Hours (subject to change)

Regular Hours

Monday–Thursday	7:45 a.m. to 12 a.m.
Friday	7:45 a.m. to 5 p.m.
Saturday	9 a.m. to 5 p.m.
Sunday	2 p.m. to 12 a.m.

Summer Hours

Monday–Thursday	7:45 a.m. to 8 p.m.
Friday	7:45 a.m. to 4:30 p.m.
Saturday	12 p.m. to 4 p.m.
Sunday	CLOSED

Jan Term Hours

Monday–Thursday	7:45 a.m. to 8 p.m.
Friday	7:45 a.m. to 4:30 p.m.
Saturday	12 p.m. to 4 p.m.
Sunday	2 p.m. to 6 p.m.

A Tour of Harwell G. Davis Library

Lower Level

Special Collection
The Special Collection houses research materials in Alabama and Southeastern history, Baptist records, Irish history, and Samford University archives.

Computer Lab and Computer Teaching Classroom
Both the computer lab and the computer teaching classroom are open labs except when a class is in session in the teaching classroom.

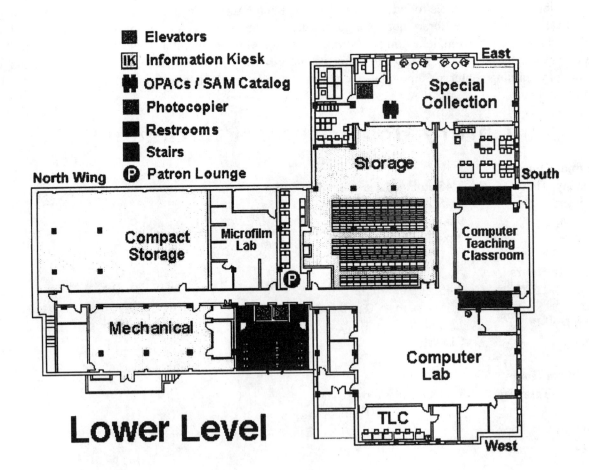

First Floor

The first floor is designated for group study.

Circulation Desk
Book check out, recall, change for photocopiers, fine payments, reserve materials. Undergraduate students may borrow books for four weeks. A validated I.D. is required. If you cannot locate a book, inquire to see if it is waiting to be reshelved or is checked out to another borrower. Books may be recalled for use by another borrower. A fine schedule for overdue books is available at the circulation desk. Library conference rooms may be reserved with a student I.D. by signing up at the desk. For further information about circulation procedures, ask at the circulation desk or call 726-2748.

Periodicals
Bound and unbound journals and recent issues of newspapers are housed in this area. There are blue binders located on desks throughout the library which list the library's periodical subscriptions. Microfilm periodicals are housed west of the circulation desk. Online periodicals are available at any computer station.

Multimedia
Compact discs, videos, music scores, and media equipment are housed west of the circulation desk. Listening rooms are available throughout the library.

Book Stacks
Books with call numbers A, C-G are shelved on the east side.

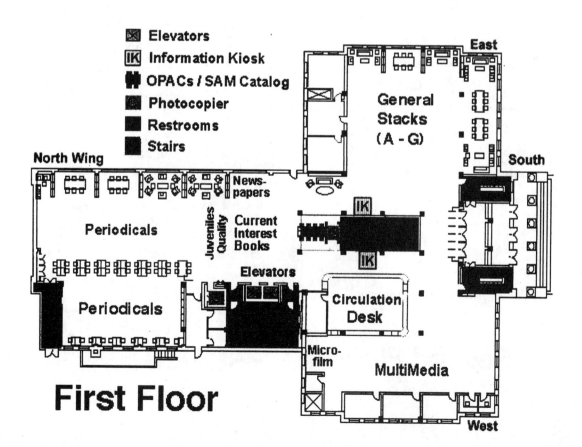

Second Floor

The second floor is designated for quiet small group study and quiet conversation. In addition, there are group study rooms available on a first come/first serve basis.

Reference Desk

Librarians are on duty during normal business hours, evenings, weekends, and by appointment (726-2196). Reference librarians provide instruction for library resources, the online public access catalog, indexes, and other materials in the reference collection. They are prepared to instruct you in designing search strategies and in selecting sources of information. If you have questions you can ask one of several reference librarians.

Government Document Stacks

Samford University is a selective depository of U.S. government documents. These materials are arranged by the Superintendent of Documents classification system.

Book Stacks

Books with call numbers B are shelved on the west side.

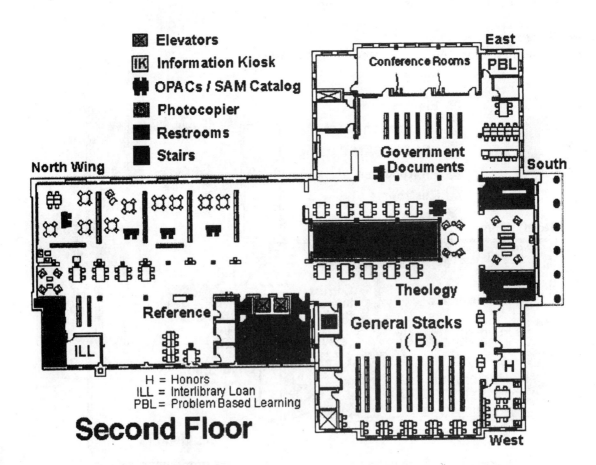

Third Floor

The third floor is designated for quiet study. Please do not use for group study or conversation. In addition, there are individual study rooms available on a first come/first serve basis.

Book Stacks

Books with call numbers H-N are shelved on the east side, P on the west side, and Q-Z on the west side in the north wing.

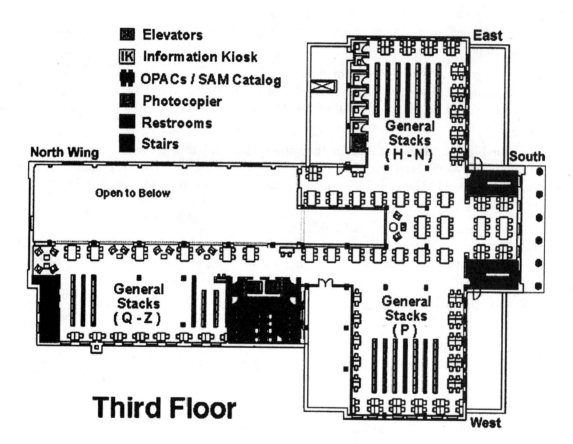

Frequently Asked Library Questions

1. **Can patrons renew books over the phone?**
   No. Part of the renewal process is making sure the materials checked out are kept in the best possible condition.

2. **Does the library have a "lost and found?"**
   Yes. It is located at the main circulation desk at the front entrance of the library.

3. **Does the library have a back entrance/exit?**
   Yes. But it is for handicapped patrons and deliveries to the library only.

4. **How do I get material that is located in storage?**
   If you bring your request to the main circulation desk, one of the staff members will be glad to assist you in retrieving the material.

5. **How do I get help with the computer labs?**
   Although the circulation staff is here to help you in any way possible, they are not experts in the computer lab nor do they maintain the labs. For the best possible help seek out a computer lab assistant or the computer lab manager.

6. **Does the library sell copy cards for the copiers that only take a card?**
   Yes, the library sells copy cards in a vending machine on the first floor. The minimum amount to buy a card is $5.00. However, if you already have a card, you may add credit in $1.00 increments.

7. **Does the library have change if I don't have a copy card?**
   Yes. The circulation unit has change to help patrons who don't have copy cards. They don't, however, in most cases, make change for more than a $10 bill (Unless a patron is paying for a fine).

8. **What are the overdue fine rates?**
   For:
   - A. Regular circulation materials—20 cents/day
   - B. CIB's (Current Interest Books)/Quality Collection—25 cents/day
   - C. ILL (InterLibrary Loan)—50 cents/day
   - D. Reserve—10 cents/hour
   - E. Reserve removal-one time, per item—$10 fine
   - F. Replacement Cost—value of the material
   - G. Processing Fee (when material has to be replaced)—$10 per item replaced

9. **What happened to my fines at the library?**
   At the beginning of each month the automation librarian runs a program to clear all patron accounts in the VTLS systems. At that time the current fines accumulated on each patron's account are transferred to the Bursar's Office and must be paid there.

10. **Can I check out materials at other university libraries in the area?**
    Yes. Samford has a cooperative agreement with other universities in the Birmingham area. With a student I.D. you can go and use their libraries as well. The libraries Samford has an agreement with are:

    1. Bessemer State Tech
    2. Birmingham Southern College
    3. Daniel Payne College
    4. Jefferson State
    5. Judson College
    6. Faulkner University
    7. Lawson State Jr. College
    8. Lee College
    9. Miles College
    10. New Orleans Seminary Extension Center
    11. Samford Extension Division-Tuscaloosa
    12. Southeastern Bible College
    13. Spring Hill College
    14. University of Alabama-Birmingham

11. **How many books can I have on my account at a time?**
    Samford students may have 99 books on their account at one time.

12. **What can I do if material that I need is checked out?**
    The circulation unit can put a hold on that material. When the material is returned you will get the first opportunity to check the material out. The material will be placed on the hold shelf at the circulation desk and you will be called to come and retrieve it. The material stays on the hold shelf for seven days, then it is returned to the stacks. If you are in dire need, the circulation unit can recall material. The circulation unit will send a letter to the patron who has the material and request an early check-in of that material if possible. A recall is a request to a patron, not a demand.

13. **If something is on reserve where do I get it?**
    All main-reserve items are located at the main circulation desk and may be retrieved from there. All media reserve items are located in the multimedia desk and may be retrieved from there.

Library of Congress Classification

A	General Works
B	Philosophy and Religion
C–D	General
E–F	History: Americas
G	Geography and Anthropology
H	Social Sciences
J	Political Science
K	Law
L	Education
M	Music
N	Fine Arts
P	Literature
Q	Science
R	Medicine
S	Agriculture
T	Technology
U–V	Military and Naval Science
Z	Bibliography and Library Science

Laptop Computer Loan Program

Program Description

The Davis Library provides laptop computers for loan to students. The computers may be checked out from the library in a manner similar to other resources.

Purpose

The purpose of this program is to provide laptop computers for loan to students for University-related use. All policies that normally govern the use of Samford-owned resources apply to this program.

Borrowing Procedures

Computers may be checked out from the circulation desk in the Davis Library. Computers are due by 2 p.m. on the due date so that they can be properly prepared for the next borrower. Every attempt will be made to assure that all available units are ready for checkout by 4 p.m. Borrowers will be expected to sign a checklist indicating receipt of each part of the computer system, and this checklist will be used to verify proper return of the equipment.

Loan Duration

Ten computers are available for a three-day loan. Thirty computers are available for a seven-day loan. The relative size of these two pools may change in response to demand.

Renewals, Reservations, and Holds

No renewals are permitted. Computers may not be reserved in advance but a request can be made to hold the next available unit. A hold request will be honored until 6 p.m. on the day a computer becomes available. If the borrower requesting the hold has not checked out the computer by that time, the hold will be released and the computer will be made available to the next person requesting it.

Late Returns

Fines for overdue computers will be charged to the borrower's account at the rate of $25.00 per day.

Loss or Damage

The borrower assumes full responsibility for any loss or damage to the computer. The cost of repair or replacement of damaged, lost, or stolen computers will be charged to the borrower.

Restrictions

As previously stated, the loan program is for the benefit of Samford students and their use should be consistent with this purpose. To help ensure maximum availability of computers to all students, the following restrictions apply:

- All use of the computer must be for a Samford-related activity.

- The computer may not be loaned to another party but must be for the use of the person to whom it is checked out.

- Due to the variation in electric power in other countries, international travel with a laptop must be pre-approved.

Online Research Resources Available Through Davis Library

You will find much of your information for speeches and essays in databases. A database is an organized index of information and sources in electronic form. Although they both appear in a Web-based format, databases should not be confused with Internet sources. In the following list of databases, those marked public can be accessed through any on-line service. Those marked on-campus are only accessible through the on-campus network.

Business

Accounting, Auditing, & Tax **via Academic Universe**	on-campus
ABI/INFORM Global	on-campus
Business Source elite **via EBSCOHost**	on-campus
Company Financial Information **via Academic Universe**	on-campus
Company News **via Academic Universe**	on-campus
EconLit	on-campus

Entrez (GenBank)	public
General BusinessFile ASAP **via InfoTrac**	on-campus
Industry & Market News **via Academic Universe**	on-campus
Standard and Poor's Net Advantage	on-campus
Vocational Search	on-campus
Wall Street Journal	on-campus

General Research

Academic Search FullTEXT **via EBSCOHost**	on-campus
Academic Universe **via Lexis-Nexis**	on-campus
AP Photo Archive	on-campus
Area Libraries	public
ArticleFirst	on-campus
Biographical Information **via Academic Universe**	on-campus
Biography and Genealogy Master Index	on-campus
Books in Print with Book Reviews **via InfoTrac**	on-campus
Britannica Online	on-campus
College Source—College Catalogs Online	on-campus
Contents First	on-campus
Dissertation Abstracts	on-campus
EBSCOhost	on-campus
Electric Library	on-campus
Electronic Collections Online	on-campus
Encyclopedia Americana	on-campus
ERIC **via EBSCOHost**	on-campus
ERIC **via Syracuse University**	public
Expanded Academic ASAP **via InfoTrac**	on-campus
Funk & Wagnalls New Encyclopedia **via EBSCOHost**	on-campus
General News Topics **via Academic Universe**	on-campus
Grolier Multimedia Encyclopedia	on-campus
InfoTrac	on-campus
Library Literature	on-campus
Library Resource Guides & Instruction Tools	public
MAS FullTEXT Ultra **via EBSCOHost**	on-campus
MasterFILE Premier **via EBSCOHost**	on-campus
The New Book of Knowledge Encyclopedia	on-campus
News Transcripts **via Academic Universe**	on-campus
Online Citations **via EBSCOHost**	on-campus
Papers First	on-campus
Periodicals Contents Index	on-campus
Periodical Holdings (Samford University Library)	public
Primary Search **via EBSCOHost**	on-campus
Proceedings First	on-campus
Reference & Directories **via Academic Universe**	on-campus
The Reference Shelf	public
Samford Libraries Catalog	public
Samford University Library Periodical Holdings	public
Top News **via Academic Universe**	on-campus
Union List of Periodicals	on-campus
Worldcat (OCLC)	on-campus

History

America: History and Life	on-campus
Historical Abstracts	on-campus

Literature and Languages

Contemporary Authors	on-campus
Contemporary Literary Criticism	on-campus
Dictionary of Literary Biography **via Gale**	on-campus
Foreign Language News **via Academic Universe**	on-campus
Gale Literary Databases	on-campus
Literary Research **via Gale**	on-campus
MLA Bibliography	on-campus
Scribner Writers Series **via Gale**	on-campus
Twayne Authors Series **via Gale**	on-campus

Music

RILM Abstracts of Musical Literature	on-campus

Philosophy and Religion

Alabama Baptist Index	public
ATLA Religion Database	on-campus
Philosopher's Index	on-campus

Science and Medicine

BasicBIOSIS	on-campus
CANCERLIT	public
CINAHL (Cumulative Index to Nursing and Allied Health)	on-campus
Clinical Reference Systems **via EBSCOHost**	on-campus
EBSCO Animals **via EBSCOHost**	on-campus
Environmental Law Reporter (ELR)	on-campus
General Medical & Health Topics **via Academic Universe**	on-campus
Health Reference Center **via InfoTrac**	on-campus
Health Source Plus **via EBSCOHost**	on-campus
Internet Grateful Med	public
Medical Abstracts (MEDLINE) **via Academic Universe**	on-campus
MEDLINE via National Library of Medicine	public
PsycINFO	on-campus
USP DI Vol. II Advice for the Patient **via EBSCOHost**	on-campus

Social Sciences—Education, Geography, Government, Law, and Sociology

Child Abuse and Neglect Database	on-campus
Country Profiles **via Academic Universe**	on-campus
Family Studies Database	on-campus
Federal Case Law **via Academic Universe**	on-campus
GEOBASE	on-campus

Government & Political News **via Academic Universe**   on-campus
Law Reviews **via Academic Universe**   on-campus
Legal News **via Academic Universe**   on-campus
LegalTrac **via InfoTrac**   on-campus
PAIS International   on-campus
Professional Development Collection **via EBSCOHost**   on campus
Sociology Abstracts: Abridged Edition   on-campus
State Legal Research **via Academic Universe**   on-campus
State Profiles **via Academic Universe**   on-campus
Thomas, Legislative Information **via Library of Congress**   public
U.S. Code, Constitution & Court Rules **via Academic Universe**   on-campus

Library Exercises

The following exercises are intended to acquaint you with some of the practices of collecting library research in a variety of disciplines. Learning how to track down information, weigh evidence, evaluate sources, and draw conclusions from research are all important aspects of becoming a responsible student scholar. For each answer, write the source of the information and the page number or Web address.

1. What is "duende?"

2. Find a poem written in dimeter quatrains with alternating rhymes.

3. Identify: Halichondroid, lenticel, cotunnite, cotzooks, ogdoad.

4. Where would you go to be vaccinated for smallpox?

5. Who is the preeminent scholar on "orientalism?"

6. Find an account (newspaper, diary, etc.) of pre-twentieth century millenial fear.

7. Summarize the original critical reception of *Citizen Kane*.

8. Who invented the geodesic dome?

9. Where did the expression "saved by the bell" originate?

10. How did the practice of funeral wakes begin?

11. What is the Andromeda strain?

12. How would you find out which countries are currently under travel advisories?

13. Who delivered the "Checkers Speech" and what was the occasion?

14. What is ironic about the following phrase: "Peace in our time."

15. Who is fifth in line for the U.S. presidency?

16. What is the College of Cardinals?

17. What are Internet cookies?

18. Route a trip to Cochabamba, Bolivia, by road only.

19. On the WWW what is an OWL?

20. On what day is the Feast of St. John the Baptist celebrated?

21. Identify: Ordinary Time, Aymara, Gaius Suetonius Tranquillus, Kimchi, Orville Knapp.

22. What is a fourteener?

23. To what do the "disappearances" refer?

24. What is an antonym for synonym?

25. Where would you find the *Gospel of the Egyptians*? Whose life does it present?

26. Who wrote the music to John Gay's serenata *Acis and Galatea*?

27. What are the differences between a burlesque, a farce, a satire, and a parody?

28. Identify: Harry Paddington, future noir, Dr. Benjamin Rush, Mary Ellmann, maitake, goetist, Peter Martyr.

29. Find a post-seventeenth century account of a witchcraft trial in the American colonies.

30. What are the dangers of partially-hydrogenated oils?

31. What is the Dogma style of filmmaking?

32. What are the requirements for entry in the LPGA Hall of Fame?

33. Several books attempt to explain the psychology of President Clinton. Looking at one of these, how reliable is the factual evidence the author uses to make his or her case? What scientific evidence does the author use?

34. Find an editorial in a national newspaper written the day you were born. What does it tell you about the social, political, or cultural climate of the time?

35. What is the difference between a wide-screen and a pan-and-scan film?

36. Find a newspaper account of Hitler's reaction to Jesse Owens in the 1939 Berlin Olympics.

37. Where would you find Mark Tansey's painting, *Myth of Depth*?

38. Using a library source, identify the political biases of the following magazines:
    a. *The New Republic*
    b. *Newsweek*
    c. *The Christian Science Monitor*
    d. *Time*
    e. *U.S. News and World Report*

39. What authority is there for the following statements? Which can you prove to be untrue or inaccurate?
    a. Thomas Jefferson believed that nature would not allow animals to become extinct.
    b. Edgar Allan Poe was found dead in a gutter.
    c. If a college professor is more than fifteen minutes late to class it is acceptable for students to leave.
    d. FDR knew of the Japanese plans to attack Pearl Harbor.
    e. The Catholic monk and mystic Thomas Merton committed suicide.
    f. Cassius Clay threw his Olympic gold medal in the Ohio River.
    g. An outside source can steal or change files on your hard drive through an Internet connection.
    h. In early nineteenth-century Massachusetts, widows remarried in the nude so their dead husbands' debts wouldn't be transferred to the new spouses.

40. What are some differences between a masque and a play?

41. Find a newspaper editorial criticizing Lyndon Johnson's handling of the Vietnam War.

42. Identify: Chelsea Hotel, dodger, cenobite, H.D.

43. How was ink made in the eighteenth century?

44. Identify: mutual fund, individual retirement account, blue chip, ammortization table, bulls and bears, Nasdaq, Allen Greenspan.

45. Find a reliable and scientific source of information on the benefits and dangers of acupuncture.

46. Write a complete filmography of the director Wim Wenders.

47. Find the names of support groups for the following: lupus, post-traumatic stress disorder, amnesia, domestic abuse.

Section Review

1. Where would you find the Special Collection at Harwell G. Davis Library?

   _____

   _____

2. What types of study are designated for each floor?

   _____

   _____

3. On which floor are bound periodicals housed?

   _____

   _____

4. On which floor is the reference desk located?

   _____

   _____

5. What does ILL stand for and how do you access it?

   _____

   _____

6. Is it true that Samford is not allowed to house government documents because it is a religious institution?

   _____

   _____

7. Where can you access Samford's online catalog?

   _____

   _____

8. What are the overdue fine rates for regular circulation materials?

_____

_____

9. What do you do if you can't find a book or periodical in Samford's library?

_____

_____

10. Where do you get works put on reserve?

_____

_____

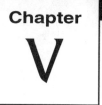

Chapter

V

Computer Labs and Resources

Computer Labs

Seven general access computing laboratories are available to every student on campus, except during times when one or more of the labs may be scheduled for classes. Several departments also have computing labs that support their specialized needs. Computers in the general access labs offer word processing and PowerPoint software that you will need to process your assignments for Communication Arts. The labs are staffed by student assistants who can help with the use of the resources located in the labs. Help is also available from User Services in Computing and Telecommunication Services at 726-2662.

- **Chapman Hall,** Room 212, 726-2318

Hours:		
	Monday–Thursday	8 a.m. to 10 p.m.
	Friday	8 a.m. to 5 p.m.
	Saturday	Closed
	Sunday	Closed

- **Brooks Hall,** Room 105, 726-2314

Hours:		
	Monday–Thursday	8 a.m. to 12 a.m.
	Friday	8 a.m. to 5 p.m.
	Saturday	10 a.m. to 10 p.m.
	Sunday	2 p.m. to 12 a.m.

- **Davis Library,** Lower Level, 726-2316

Hours:		
	Monday–Thursday	8 a.m. to 12 a.m.
	Friday	8 a.m. to 5 p.m.
	Saturday	9 a.m. to 5 p.m.
	Sunday	2 p.m. to 12 a.m.

- **Journalism Lab,** Room 113 University Center Annex, 726-2311

Hours:		
	Monday–Thursday	8 a.m. to 12 a.m.
	Friday	8 a.m. to 5 p.m.
	Saturday	10 a.m. to 5 p.m.
	Sunday	2 p.m. to 12 a.m.

- **Composition**, Room 309, University Center Annex, 726-2319
  Hours: Monday–Thursday 8 a.m. to 10 p.m.
  Friday 8 a.m. to 5 p.m.
  Saturday Closed
  Sunday Closed

- **Orlean Bullard Beeson Hall,** Room 322, 726-2315
  Hours: Whenever the Curriculum Materials Center is open.

- **Center for Healing Arts,** Room 103-C, 726-2317
  Hours: Monday–Thursday 8 a.m. to 10 a.m.
  Friday 8 a.m. to 5 p.m.
  Saturday 10 a.m. to 5 p.m.
  Sunday 2 p.m. to 12 a.m.

Computer Lab Etiquette

It is important to remember that the computer labs on campus are available for all students. Many instructors use them for classes, and some students depend on them for their school work. To show respect for this community property and respect for other students, you should adhere to the following guidelines:

- Food and drinks are not allowed in computer labs.

- Students are not allowed to load software on school computers.

- Lab computers may not be used for off campus business, computer gaming, or illegal activity.

- Be careful about excessive printing; print only what you need for school work.

E-mail Etiquette

Electronic mail, or the ability to send and receive messages over a computer network, is one of the simplest, and yet one of the most transformational, technological changes of our time. Like the telephone, e-mail allows rapid communication with people at great distances. Like a traditional letter, e-mail provides a written record of a message, which can be read carefully and then kept for future reference. It can also be—and frequently is—quickly discarded. Because e-mail has some of the qualities of both oral and written discourse, new users of this technology are sometimes unsure of the proper protocol to follow when writing e-mail messages. Although the following suggestions are not hard-and-fast rules, they do provide some general principles for e-mail use.

1. Consider your e-mail message to be a public document.

   Although you may intend your message to be a private correspondence with a trusted friend, you cannot be sure who will ultimately read your words. Many computers are shared by more than one person; and therefore, others may have access to the "private" message you have sent. Sometimes your message will be forwarded, intentionally or inadvertently, to other readers. A good question to ask before sending the message is, "How would I feel if someone other than the intended audience were to read this?" This question is particularly important to consider in the workplace where all messages produced on a company-owned machine are considered to be the property of the firm.

2. Use good judgment in sending e-mail to others.

   Many people feel greater freedom to send e-mail than they would to make a personal call. However, no one likes to receive junk mail, whether it is your favorite recipe for chocolate chip cookies, an advertisement about your '88 Buick for sale, or a chain letter you've been asked to forward to ten of your friends. Sending e-mail to hundreds of people via listserv (a practice frequently known as "spamming") is particularly obnoxious.

3. Maintain the right tone in your messages.

   E-mail users sometimes fall prey to using inflammatory or abusive language in their replies. Avoid the use of all capital letters in a reply, which is the e-mail equivalent of shouting. The distance, and sometimes anonymity, of the Internet is no excuse for abandoning the standards of polite conversation. A business-like tone stating the facts of the case is more likely to merit an appropriate response than a stream of invective. And remember, unlike the spoken word, e-mail messages are a permanent reminder of your temperamental or uncivil behavior.

4. Use the "Copy" or "cc" command to keep others informed of decisions that are being made.

   One of the helpful features of e-mail is the ability to send complimentary copies of your e-mail message to those who should be aware of your directives or inquiries. For instance, you might want to copy the other members of your writing group when asking your professor a question about the group's assignment. However, be aware that a copy of a message sent to an employee's manager would be considered threatening, not just informative.

5. Always check the e-mail address or addresses in the "To:" box before sending a message.

   Nearly everyone can share an embarrassing story of someone who meant to send a private message, but inadvertently sent the message to a large group of people. This is particularly true when replying to listserv messages. You can lessen your chances of having this problem if you always check the addresses before sending a message.

6. Be ethical in the way you treat the messages you receive from others.

   Generally, you should ask permission before forwarding a message you've received from someone else. This is especially true for messages being forwarded to a large group of people, or if the message is likely to create embarrassment or hostility.

7. Make sure you keep your e-mail and your password secure.

   Your password protects you from anyone accessing your e-mail account without permission. Some students have carelessly left their e-mail account open on a lab computer and then been victimized by someone sending an embarrassing memo in the name of the student who owns the account. Always exit from your e-mail before leaving the computer.

   You should also exercise caution in giving out personal information to those on the Internet. Many e-mail users have a setup file that automatically appends their names, e-mail addresses, and phone numbers to the message. Some even include their mailing address. Such information may invite unwanted attention, or even stalking, from another Internet user.

8. Choose a level of formality appropriate to the audience, purpose, and occasion.

   The formality of the e-mail is indicated by verbal features such as the salutation ("Dear Sir" v. "Hey Baby"), your diction ("relocating to another venue" v. "I'm outta here"), and your organization ("In light of these factors, I recommend . . ." v. "Bama rules! You got tickets? Me neither.") Of course, family and friends will be more tolerant of spelling and punctuation errors, but messages sent to teachers, co-workers, etc., should be clear, correct, and concise.

1. If you leave your e-mail account open in a public place, are you responsible if someone else uses the account?

   _____

   _____

2. What is spamming?

   _____

   _____

3. What are you not allowed to bring to computer labs?

   _____

   _____

4. What advice would you give a novice e-mail user about e-mail etiquette?

   _____

   _____

   _____

   _____

   _____

   _____

   _____

5. What is the difference between databases and Internet sources?

   _____

   _____

Plagiarism and Academic Integrity

Academic Integrity

The academic community of students and faculty at Samford University strives to develop, sustain, and protect an environment of honesty, trust, and respect through Academic Integrity as stated in the Code of Values. *We value a campus community that encourages personal growth and academic development in an atmosphere of positive Christian influence. We affirm the necessity of academic standards of conduct that allow students and faculty to live and study together. These values can be violated by academic dishonesty and fraud (Samford University Student Handbook).*

An academic integrity values violation is defined as the act of lying, cheating, or stealing academic information with the intent to gain academic advantage for one's self or another. Additional information about the process followed when a Code of Values violation is believed to have occurred may be found in the *Student Handbook.*

Plagiarism and Other Academic Integrity Issues

Q: What is plagiarism?

A: Plagiarism is the use of words, ideas, images, or data generated by another writer or speaker without properly acknowledging the source material.

Q: Does plagiarism require an intent to deceive the reader?

A: No. Plagiarism may be intentional or unintentional. Some of the most notorious cases of plagiarism have occurred when writers, composers, and other artists have picked up ideas from someone else almost unconsciously.

Q: What is the penalty for plagiarizing another writer's work?

A: Plagiarism is a violation of academic integrity, which is one of the five principal values of Samford University. The minimum sanction for a first offense is an "F" in the course for which the plagiarized work was submitted and academic probation.

Q: If I paraphrase another writer's ideas, can I still be guilty of plagiarism?

A: Yes. The idea, as well as the verbatim expression of the idea, must be acknowledged. If a writer suggests several causes for the rising rate of suicide among young people, you must give credit to the author—even if you use your own words to describe those causes.

Q: How do I properly acknowledge the source of the words and ideas I have used in my essay?

A: The acknowledgment has two parts: a bibliographic reference, which usually appears at the end of your document, and an in-text citation. In-text citations were once commonly made with raised numbers in the text that referred to footnotes or endnotes. Now, most style manuals use parenthetical citations that include the author's last name or some other means of referring to the complete bibliographic reference at the end of the essay.

Q: How do I know the exact information that is required in my bibliography and in-text citations?

A: Several style manuals are in common use for this purpose. The Modern Language Association (MLA), the American Psychological Association (APA), and the Council of Biological Editors all publish style manuals. Another well-known style manual is the *Chicago Manual of Style* (also known as "Turabian"). Each of them provides detailed information about properly citing sources.

Q: Is it important to follow the exact form for a bibliographic citation as long as I am careful to include all the necessary information?

A: Following the exact form of a style manual is important. Although most manuals require nearly the same information (title, author, publisher, etc.), the arrangement of the information makes it possible to tell at a glance if any information has been omitted.

Q: How can I cite information from the Internet since many websites don't have an author or publisher in the traditional sense?

A: The style manual you are using should contain information about documentation of information taken from online sources. In general, you should be cautious about using information that is unrefereed (that is, not reviewed by scholars in that discipline). Because many false and misleading claims have been made on websites, it is absolutely essential that you provide a citation that will allow your readers to review and substantiate the information you have obtained from such sources.

Q: Why doesn't Samford agree on one style manual to be used in all classes?

A: Different disciplines have special needs that determine how information should be organized. For instance, the date of material is more important in the sciences than in the humanities, so it takes a more prominent place in APA style than in MLA style.

Q: Where can I get information about the different forms of manuscript style?

A: All students are required to have a handbook (currently, *A Writer's Reference* by Diana Hacker) in their Cultural Perspectives and Communication Arts courses that includes several of the most commonly used style guides. Style guides are also available for purchase in the campus bookstore.

Q: How can I get individual help in learning how to cite sources properly?

A: All students will receive instruction on the use of sources in their Communication Arts classes. One-on-one tutoring on the use of sources is provided by the Communication Resource Center in the University Center Annex.

Q: Isn't some information such common knowledge that the source doesn't need to be acknowledged?

A: Yes. Common knowledge is not necessarily what everyone knows, but information that is readily available in reference sources and is beyond dispute. For instance, the date that the Battle of Bunker Hill was fought would be considered common knowledge even though most people might not actually know this date. In general, information that can be looked up in standard reference sources is common knowledge. However, even common knowledge is sometimes subject to interpretation. For instance, the Battle of Bunker Hill was actually fought on Breed's Hill and some scholars prefer the latter designation. If an educated person would have to use a catalog or database to look up the information you are using, you should include the bibliographic information.

Q: If I have to acknowledge every source that I use, won't I have to provide an in-text citation after every sentence?

A: Research is more than simply reciting the facts and ideas that you have found in other sources. In most assignments, your professors will be asking you to weave together information from various sources to support a case that you are making. This will require you to analyze and interpret the data or texts you are studying and to explain how they support your own contentions. An essay that consisted entirely of snippets from various sources would show very little thought on the student's part.

Q: Is it permissible to borrow ideas and expressions without acknowledgment if the sources are unpublished or uncopyrighted?

A: No. Copyright establishes a legal ownership to a writer's work, but it has no direct bearing on the issue of plagiarism. Sources must be acknowledged even if they have not been published or copyrighted. If, for instance, a student borrows ideas or expressions from another student's essay, that borrowing must be acknowledged.

Q: Is it a violation of academic integrity for students to loan documents they have written to other students?

A: If the student loans the document with the intent of allowing that student to copy the document and present it as his or her own work, then it is a values violation. On the other hand, students are encouraged to share ideas with one another and to learn from one another. As noted above, when students do borrow ideas from another student's essay, they must acknowledge this source just as they would published information.

Q: Is it possible to plagiarize even if you have acknowledged your sources?

A: Yes. It is important to acknowledge not only the ideas that you are using but also the exact wording that you have borrowed from the original source. Quotation marks must be placed around any passages that are being used verbatim from the original source. You must, for instance, put quotation marks around this statement—"The law, in its majestic equality, forbids the rich as well as the poor to sleep under bridges, to beg in the streets, and to steal bread"—even if you have acknowledged that you borrowed the idea from Anatole France. Without quotation marks, this would be a plagiarized statement.

Q: Can I change or alter a quotation in any way?

A: Any insertion of your own words within a quotation should be indicated by brackets. Any internal deletion should be marked with an ellipsis. Both of these marks are explained in *A Writer's Reference*. These marks should be used sparingly and only to clarify a statement or to make a quotation fit into the flow of your own writing. You should never make changes that alter or distort the original meaning of the quotation.

Q: Are there other unethical practices related to academic integrity?

A: Anytime you misrepresent someone else's work as your own, you are violating the principle of academic integrity. Anytime you alter or distort the meaning of another person's ideas, whether it is tampering with the data, omitting key facts or ideas, or deliberately misinterpreting the meaning of their words, you are behaving unethically.

Q: Why is it so important to acknowledge sources in academic writing?

A: The quality of information is dependent on its accuracy and reliability. Misinformation can have many damaging consequences. Only by knowing the exact source of information is it possible to ensure that facts are accurately and reliably reported and that quotations are faithful to the author's intention.

Q: Does plagiarism matter outside the academic world?

A: Yes. Politicians, preachers, and other public figures have seen their careers falter and their reputations ruined when it became public knowledge that they had borrowed their ideas from others without giving credit where credit was due.

1. What is plagiarism?

    _____

    _____

2. Does plagiarism require an intent to deceive the reader? Explain.

    _____

    _____

3. What is the penalty for plagiarizing another writer's work?

    _____

    _____

4. If you paraphrase another writer's ideas, can you still be guilty of plagiarism? Explain.

    _____

    _____

5. How do you properly acknowledge the source of the words and ideas you use in an essay?

    _____

    _____

6. How do you know the exact information that is required in your bibliography and in-text citations?

    _____

    _____

7. Why is it important to follow the exact form for a bibliographic citation?

    _____

    _____

8. How can you cite information from the Internet since many websites don't have an author or publisher in the traditional sense?

    _____

    _____

9. Why doesn't Samford agree on one style manual to be used in all classes?

    _____

    _____

10. Where do you get information about the different forms of manuscript style?

    _____

    _____

11. What is common knowledge?

    _____

    _____

12. If you have to acknowledge every source you use, won't you have to provide an in-text citation after every sentence? Explain.

    _____

    _____

13. Is it permissible to borrow ideas and expressions without acknowledgement if the sources are unpublished or uncopyrighted?

    _____

    _____

14. Is it a violation of academic integrity for students to loan documents they have written to other students? Explain.

    _____

    _____

15. Is it possible to plagiarize even if you have acknowledged your sources? How?

_____

_____

16. How do you legitimately alter quoted material to fit into the flow of your own writing?

_____

_____

17. Which other unethical practices are related to academic integrity?

_____

_____

18. Why is it so important to acknowledge sources in academic writing?

_____

_____

19. Does plagiarism matter outside the academic world? Explain.

_____

_____

Chapter

VII

Essay Format and Grading Standards

Preparation of Manuscripts

Though your instructor may vary this format, in general you should use the following format in preparing final drafts of all your essays:

1. You must produce your essays on a word processor, using only one side of a sheet of paper.

2. Double-space everything, including quotations and the works cited page.

3. Leave one-inch margins on all sides, and use a readable font and reasonable font size such as Times New Roman, 10-12.

Standards

Your essays will be graded to reflect the effectiveness of your writing, which in turn is the result of a complex writing process. Many student writers have to make a conscious effort to put together all they have learned about the written language and how it can be made to work effectively for them. Fortunately, with practice this process becomes less conscious, which is another way of saying that you can learn to write better by getting practice in writing.

Grading of your essays in Communication Arts is not an arbitrary process. You should not assume it is all a question of your instructor's personal opinion. But neither is grading a mechanical matter of adding up points. Grading is based upon standards, and these reflect a general agreement among educated readers and writers as to what constitutes effective prose. You will find these standards described in most rhetoric or grammar books such as *Reading Critically, Writing Well* and *A Writer's Reference*, and these standards are the ones exemplified by most competent writers of non-fiction prose, whether professional or not. In general, there is little argument about the basic principles underlying effective expository writing.

Rather than simply listing these standards here, we have given you a checklist of questions you should ask yourself about any essay you write, whether in Communication Arts or another course. Asking these questions is an important part of learning to think critically about your own writing. Your instructors and textbooks will go into more detail about how to apply these questions to your own work and how the conventions of different essays are related to them.

Becoming an ethical writer and speaker means remembering that you are responsible for your own language, written or spoken. Instructors do not give grades on essays and speeches; you earn them.

How Grades For Your Essays Are Decided

In order to both understand the grades you earn and to improve on them where you can, it will help if you remember that your instructor is using a set of standards when he or she reads your essays. In fact, any reader is going to expect emphasis in content, coherence in argument, and clarity and conciseness in diction and style. Readers also want to be able to take for granted that they will not be disturbed by grammatical errors. Written English is more precise and demanding than spoken English.

Superior (A)

In an "A" essay, there is a significant central idea or thesis, which is clearly expressed and which is supported with substantial, concrete, and consistently relevant detail. This central idea, if not unique, is at least the product of your independent thought, not merely one discussed in class, not merely an elaboration of a cliché. Your essay is clear, logical, organized, and systematic. Your paragraphs are focused, coherent, unified, and adequately developed. Each paragraph has a purposeful relationship to thematic development or argument. The transitions between paragraphs are smooth and fitting. Your sentences are interesting and varied, and your language is clear and economical. Grammar, punctuation, and spelling are in accord with conventional usage.

Good (B)

A "B" essay will do a competent job of developing all the above elements, but without managing to reach a high level of thought and analysis. A "B" essay typically lacks the penetrating and original analysis of superior work. Or, a "B" essay does well in most of the areas above but is slightly flawed in one or two. A "B" grade indicates, then, that you have a generally substantial control over your material.

Inconsistent/Average (C)

The main idea is clear enough but more superficially or less convincingly developed. The organization basically suffices, but it is too mechanical, too general, or just underdeveloped. The ideas have some support, but with insufficient examples or unrelated detail. Paragraphs have some problems with their focus, unity, development, or connection to the topic. Transitions are lacking or inappropriate. The essay has occasional mechanical errors, but few major ones (i.e., lack of subject-verb agreement or incomplete sentences).

Inadequate (D or F)

The thesis is non-existent or muddled, and the argument is unclear or inconsistent. The essay shows little or no development of ideas. Paragraphs lack topics, focus, unity, adequate development, or connection to the topic and purpose of the essay. Transitions are lacking or misdirected. Sentences lack clarity, or they are too often awkward and ineffective. Improper grammar, punctuation, and spelling mar the presentation of the essay's ideas and perhaps even make the writing incomprehensible. The difference between a "D" and an "F" essay is a matter of degree. An "F" essay simply presents problems such as these in an especially blatant way, but in either case such essays demonstrate the writer's failure to control or make adequate use of the material. Even consistent "D" writing can cause you to fail Communication Arts.

1. If your teachers don't base their grading on arbitrary preferences, what do they base their grading on?

    _____

    _____

2. What are some qualities of an "A" essay?

    _____

    _____

3. A "B" essay?

    _____

    _____

4. A "C" essay?

    _____

    _____

5. A "D or F" essay?

    _____

    _____

Essay and Speech Contests/ Coffee House Readings

Communication Arts offers several opportunities for students to showcase excellent essays and speeches. The Samford University Excellent Essay and Excellent Speech Contests and Coffee House Readings are open to all students enrolled in Communication Arts.

Coffee House

In the fall semester, Communication Arts instructors host a night of student and faculty readings in a relaxed coffee house like environment. The event offers students an opportunity to hear the work of their classmates and instructors.

Excellent Essay Contest

The Samford University Excellent Essay contest is open to all students in Communication Arts. The spring semester contest is offered for UCCA 102 students only. Students may be asked by their instructors to submit an especially good essay, or else on their own initiative students may pick up application forms and release statements from the Core Curriculum office in Divinity North 320. The winners will be announced near the end of the Spring semester, and the essays may be published in *A Student's Guide to Communication Arts*. At the end of this section you will find application forms for both the essay and speech contests.

Excellent Speech Contest

The Samford University Excellent Speech contest is open to all students in UCCA 102, and is held in the spring semester. If you take UCCA 102 in the fall semester, you will still be eligible for the contest in the spring. Each instructor is asked to choose one student to compete in the contest, and the student will be officially entered by the instructor.

Other Samford Writing and Speaking Opportunities

Sojourn

Sojourn is a literary and visual arts magazine published twice yearly by the department of journalism and mass communication and the department of English. Students edit and compile each issue with assistance from outside professionals and faculty advisors.

The Samford Crimson

The Samford Crimson is a student-run, campus-wide newspaper. Published weekly, *The Samford Crimson* offers excellent opportunities to all undergraduates, regardless of major or experience, who are interested in writing, reporting, photography, editing, and layout and design in the areas of news, sports, arts and entertainment, and commentary.

Debate Team

The Samford University Debate Team sponsors on-campus debates, high school workshops, and tournaments, sponsoring the Birmingham Area Debate League, and fielding consistently competitive NDT-style intercollegiate teams. Samford teams have won three DSR-TKA national championships and have qualified for the National Tournament 19 of the last 23 years, making this program one of the most successful programs in the nation.

Excellent Essay Contest Application

Student's Name   _____

Instructor's Name   _____

Assignment   _____

Date Submitted   _____

Excellent Speech Contest Application

Student's Name _____

Instructor's Name _____

Assignment _____

Date Submitted _____

Section Review

1. What writing and speaking opportunities do you have available to you outside of class?

   _____

   _____

   _____

   _____

2. How many students are eligible from each section for the speech contest?

   _____

   _____

3. How do you prepare an essay for submission to the Excellent Essay Contest?

   _____

   _____

Chapter

IX

General Course Policies

Attendance

Students in Communication Arts courses who miss more than two weeks of classes—four class meetings for TTH classes, six for MWF—will receive the grade of "FA," failure for excessive absences. This grade carries the same penalty as the "F." Any university absences must be cleared in advance.

Late Assignments

Writing assignments will be penalized one letter grade for each class day they are overdue. All major assignments must be completed to get credit for Communication Arts.

Incompletes/Withdrawals

Incomplete Grades

An "INC" grade indicates "An unavoidable absence from a final examination or an excusable failure to complete laboratory or parallel assignments." Incompletes are allowed in Communication Arts only if a student misses the final assignment in 101 or final examination in 102. An "INC" automatically becomes an "F" if not removed within one calendar year from the date the grade is given. You must fill out the standard form for incompletes and have it signed by your instructor.

Class Withdrawals—Dropping a Course

A student may withdraw from a course without a "W" (withdrawn) grade or academic penalty before the last day to withdraw from course(s) without financial penalty (See the Academic Calendar section of the *Samford Catalog* for the exact date).

A student may withdraw from a course after the last day to withdraw from a course without financial penalty but prior to the date to "withdraw from a course without academic penalty" and will receive a grade of "W." If the course is dropped after the date to "withdraw from a course without academic penalty," the student will receive a grade of "WF."

If a student quits attending a course after the "last day to drop a course" without notifying the Student Records Office in writing or exceeds the maximum absences allowed in a course, a grade of "FA" will be entered on the student's record with the same penalty as a grade of "F."

Grade Appeals

When a student feels that a *final* semester grade is unfair or inaccurate, *the student must first meet with the faculty member* to learn how the final grade was determined. If the student continues to feel that the grade was unfairly assigned, a written appeal form may be completed and submitted to the associate dean of the Howard College of Arts and Sciences. Students appealing grades assume the burden of proof. The appeal shall state and support with available evidence the reasons why the student believes the grade should be changed. Any appeal must be based on a specific problem which the student and the instructor cannot resolve.

Legitimate reasons for appeals are:

- an improper *final* grade has been assigned as a result of prejudice, caprice, mechanical error, or
- the student has received a *final* grade that was determined by means inconsistent with those of other *final* grades in the course section.

Appeals based on the following are not likely to be successful:

- failure to submit work on time,
- a dispute about a grade lowered because of excessive absences,
- a general disagreement with the grade received.

Class Behavior

It is important in a university classroom setting that all students feel free to contribute to class and to be taken seriously. In a class such as Communication Arts, where participation is crucial, it is even more important that students respect their instructors and classmates and value the integrity of the course. Consequently, it is important for you to observe the following rules:

- Come to class on time. Being late is disruptive to everyone and harmful to discussion.
- Do not speak, read, sleep, or be disruptive in any way when someone else is speaking.
- Do not harass or badger other students in or out of class because you disagree with their ideas. You are not entitled to chase someone out of a university because you do not like how or what he or she thinks.
- It is very important for a useful discussion that your remarks actually follow up on those of any speaker (either to disagree, agree, expand the point, etc.). No one should raise his or her hand DURING another person's speech. You may only do so after the first speaker has stopped. This will show that you have actually listened to all she or he has had to say.

- Be careful not to dominate class. You are not graded for the amount of speaking, but the quality and appropriateness of your comments.

- Please use gender-inclusive language (this goes as well for written work). See your *Student Handbook* and Part Two of *A Student's Guide to Communication Arts.*

- Food and drink are not allowed in all classrooms. Your instructor will determine a policy on this issue.

These rules merely elaborate on Samford's Mission to develop social and civic responsibility and academic civility and tolerance.

Diagnostic Writing Sample and Final Examination

Diagnostic Essay

During the first week of the semester you will be assigned a diagnostic writing assignment. All Samford freshmen will write on a uniform essay topic. In addition to giving your instructor a sense of your writing capabilities, the diagnostic essay is often a useful way for you to see how much improvement you need to make over the course of the semester.

Final Examination

All students in UCCA102 will take a uniform final exam at a uniform exam time. This exam will count as 5% of your total grade. Early in the semester you will be told where you will take the final exam. You may only take the exam early in extreme circumstances, and permission to do so is entirely at your instructor's discretion. Students are not allowed to take an early exam until the first day of exam week.

Sample Diagnostic/Final Exam Topic

Read the passage below taken from a book about the influence of technology on civilization. In a previous paragraph, Freud argues the benefits of technology. According to Freud, how has technology influenced civilization in a negative way? Discuss another technological breakthrough which, on the surface, appears to be positive, yet has significant negative consequences for civilization.

> If there had been no railway to conquer distances, my child would never have left his native town and I should need no telephone to hear his voice; if traveling across the ocean by ship had not been introduced, my friend would not have embarked on his sea-voyage and I should not need a cable to relieve my anxiety about him. What is the use of reducing infantile mortality when it is precisely that reduction which imposes the greatest restraint on us in the begetting of children, so that, taken all round, we nevertheless rear no more children than in the days before the reign of hygiene. . . ? And, finally, what good to us is a long life if it is difficult and barren of joys, and if it is so full of misery that we can only welcome death as a deliverer?

(Freud, *Civilization and Its Discontents*)

Students With Disabilities

Samford University is required by law to provide reasonable accommodations to students with disabilities. The types of disabilities covered include low vision, hearing loss, learning disabilities, impaired mobility, health conditions, and attention deficit disorder. In order to meet the needs of disabled students, Samford provides an Advisor for Students with Disabilities within the department of Counseling Services. The Advisor serves as a liaison for students with disabilities in academic and campus life activities and provides information, guidance, and support services.

Every student with a disability must forward recent documentation of the disability from an appropriate professional to Counseling Services. After receiving the documentation, the Advisor meets individually with each student and determines what types of reasonable accommodations are needed to facilitate the student's success. Typical accommodations might include: extended time on tests and assignments, permission to tape lectures, note taking assistance, and other accommodations designed to meet each student's learning needs.

After the accommodations have been determined, it is the student's responsibility to provide the Advisor for Students with Disabilities a list of the courses they are enrolled in and the names of their professors each semester. The Advisor will then contact each professor via letter indicating the accommodations provided for the student. The letter will indicate all of the accommodations available for the student, and the student and professor should meet and work out which accommodations are necessary for that particular course and how best to implement the accommodations.

The Advisor can only send letters after documentation and a semester list of courses and professors have been received. If a student has any concerns or questions regarding disabilities, he or she should contact the Advisor for Students with Disabilities at 726-2105 or Counseling Services at 726-2065.

Students with any of the following are entitled by law to reasonable accommodations:

Low Vision

Current documentation from ophthalmologist or optometrist required; may range from low vision to total blindness.

Hearing Loss

Documentation by an audiologist required; may range from mild to severe/profound loss.

Learning Disabilities

Documentation by a clinical psychologist is preferred; however, documentation from the student's high school is acceptable provided the test results and information are current.

Impaired Mobility

Current letter from physician required; may be due to an accident, but also includes cerebral palsy, severe arthritis, or any other condition which interferes with mobility.

Health Condition

Current letter from physician required; may include diabetes, tumors, lupus, arthritis, seizure disorder, asthma, head injury, or any condition which chronically and significantly interferes with daily living.

Attention Deficit Disorder

Current documentation by qualified medical and/or psychological professional required.

Accommodations and/or assistance may include, but are not limited to:

- extended time on tests
- permission to tape record lectures
- enlarged print or Braille materials
- peer note taker
- use of word processor, spellchecker
- extra time on assignments
- assistance with study skills, time management and organizational skills
- assistance to faculty in implementing classroom accommodations
- information about community resources
- counseling and guidance

Accommodations are individually determined and must be supported by disability documentation. It is the student's responsibility to request accommodations and to provide appropriate documentation. If you have any questions, please contact Marcia Hamby, Director of Counseling Services at 726-2065.

Name: _____

Section: _____

Date: _____

Section Review

1. How many absences are you allowed in Communication Arts?

    _____

    _____

2. What is the penalty for late writing assignments in Communication Arts?

    _____

    _____

3. Under what circumstances are incompletes allowed in Communication Arts?

    _____

    _____

4. When is the last day to drop a course this semester without academic penalty?

    _____

    _____

5. What is a legitimate reason for appealing your Communication Arts grade?

    _____

    _____

6. What should you do if you disagree with another student's ideas in class?

    _____

    _____

7. When is your final exam?

    _____

    _____

A WRITER'S GUIDE

Use of Sources

Annotation Exercise

Instructions: This choral ode appears early in Sophocles' Antigone. *Just before the ode is delivered, Creon has learned of the attempt to bury the disgraced Polyneices. Annotate the text, using the various forms of response that are recommended in* Reading Critically, Writing Well.

~ ODE I

CHORUS: [STROPHE 1
Numberless are the world's wonders, but none
More wonderful than man; the stormgray sea
Yields to his prows, the huge crests bear him high;
Earth, holy and inexhaustible, is graven
With shining furrows where his plows have gone
Year after year, the timeless labor of stallions.

                [ANTISTROPHE 1
The lightboned birds and beasts that cling to cover,
The lithe fish lighting their reaches of dim water,
All are taken, tamed in the net of his mind;
The lion on the hill, the wild horse windy-maned,
Resign to him; and his blunt yoke has broken
The sultry shoulders of the mountain bull.

                [STROPHE 2
Words also, and thought as rapid as air,
He fashions to his good use; statecraft is his,
And his the skill that deflects the arrows of snow,
The spears of winter rain: from every wind
He has made himself secure from all but one:
In the late wind of death he cannot stand.

[ANTISTROPHE 2

O clear intelligence, force beyond all measure!
O fate of man, working both good and evil!
When the laws are kept, how proudly his city stands!
When the laws are broken, what of his city then?
Never may the anarchic man find rest at my hearth,
Never be it said that my thoughts are his thoughts.

(Translated by Dudley Fitts and Robert Fitzgerald)

Paraphrasing Guide

1. Provide an appropriate lead-in for your paraphrase; mention the author of the original (and the work if you are citing more than one work by the same author).

2. Use parenthetical documentation at the end of your paraphrase. Example: (Smith 250) Please Note: *No* commas and *No* "p."

3. Make sure that your restatement of the author's thesis is accurate in letter and spirit. Do not put your own opinion into the paraphrase. The appropriate place for your opinion is *after* you have finished the paraphrase and documented your source.

4. Quote only if the author's word or phrase is exceptionally apt or original. Do not quote large amounts of the original which could just as effectively be put in your own words.

5. Include all topics discussed in the original. Do not add topics to the paraphrase to make it sound better.

6. Remember that grammatical rules apply to paraphrasing.

7. Do not repeat yourself in an attempt to pad your word count.

8. Be specific. Avoid vague, meaningless language.

9. Recognize the difference between asserting, arguing, speculating, suggesting, asking, implying, saying.

10. Use your own writing style.

11. Do not use a thesaurus to find a synonym for every major word in the original. Some so-called synonyms have different connotations than the original word, and some words have more than one meaning. You could accidentally pick a synonym for the wrong meaning. Example: underweight ≠ anemic.

Remember that a paraphrase is the original author's ideas in your own words, not your ideas or your opinion of the author's ideas.

Paraphrasing Exercise

Instructions: Making sure you use the guidelines from the previous page, paraphrase the following passages.

1. "I woke up the next morning, thinking about those words—immensely proud to realize that not only had I written so much at one time, but I'd written words that I never knew were in the world. Moreover, with a little effort, I also could remember what many of these words meant. I reviewed the words whose meanings I didn't remember. Funny thing, from the dictionary first page right now, that 'aardvark' springs to my mind. The dictionary had a picture of it, a long-tailed, long eared, burrowing African mammal, which lives off termites caught by sticking out its tongue as an anteater does for ants."—Malcolm X, *The Autobiography of Malcolm X*

2. "In colleges and universities around the country, students are following Socrates, questioning their views to discover how far they survive the test of argument. Although Socratic procedures have been familiar for a long time in basic philosophy courses, philosophy is now reaching a far larger number of students than it did fifty years ago, students of all classes and backgrounds and religious origins. And philosophy, which at one time was taught as a remote and abstract discipline, is increasingly being linked to the analysis and criticism of current events and ideas. Instead of learning logical analysis in a vacuum, students now learn to dissect the arguments they find in newspapers, to argue about current controversies in medicine and law and sports, to think critically about the foundations of their political and even religious views."—Martha Nussbaum, *Cultivating Humanity: A Classical Defense of Reform in Liberal Education*

3. "It saddened my mother to learn about Mexican-American parents who wanted their children to start working after finishing high school. In schooling she recognized the key to job advancement. And she remembered her past. As a girl, new to America, she had been awarded a diploma by high school teachers too busy or careless to notice that she hardly spoke English. On her own she determined to type. That skill got her clean office jobs and encouraged an optimism about the possibility of advancement. (Each morning when her sisters put on uniforms for work, she chose a bright-colored dress.) And she became an excellent speller—of words she mispronounced. ("And I've never been to college," she would say smiling when her children asked about a word they didn't want to look up in a dictionary.)"—Richard Rodriguez, "The Achievement of Desire: Personal Reflections on Learning 'Basics'"

4. "As photographs give people an imaginary possession of a past that is unreal, they also help people to take possession of space in which they are insecure. Thus, photography develops in tandem with one of the most characteristic of modern activities: tourism. For the first time in history, large numbers of people regularly travel out of their habitual environments for short periods of time. It seems positively unnatural to travel for pleasure without taking a camera along. Photographs will offer indisputable evidence that the trip was made, that the program was carried out, that fun was had. Photographs document sequences of consumption carried on outside the view of family, friends, neighbors. But dependence on the camera, as the device that makes real what one is experiencing, doesn't fade when people travel more. Taking photographs fills the same need for the cosmopolitans accumulating photographies of their boat trip up the Albert Nile or their fourteen days in China as it does for lower-middle-class vacationers taking snapshots of the Eiffel Tower or Niagara Falls."—Susan Sontag, "On Photography"

Paraphrasing Exercise Continued

Documentation

If you achieve a balance between your ideas, arguments, conclusions, and material borrowed from sources, your essay will not be a stream of parenthetical references. On the other hand, the honest researcher gives full credit to the sources used. What might be considered excessive dependence on sources is far less serious an offense than a failure to acknowledge indebtedness to the work of others.

What Must You Document?

You must document (with precise page references) not only all direct quotations but also all paraphrased information, ideas, and opinions taken from sources—except what is considered common knowledge. See the statement on plagiarism in Part One, Section VI for a detailed explanation of what constitutes common knowledge.

How Do You Document?

There are many different ways to document sources in a piece of research. It is important for you to remember that your instructors don't merely choose documentation styles based on personal preference; different fields of study use different methods of documentation. You are responsible for learning the documentation style your field of study requires.

Most documentation will be in the form of parenthetical references to author and page number or just to page numbers if the author has been mentioned. Since parenthetical documentation is a shortened form of citation, whatever is cited in parentheses must clearly refer to a specific source in a list of works cited that follows the text of the essay. Remember, the purpose of documentation is to make clear to your reader exactly what material has been borrowed and from what source. Also, remember that parenthetical documentation is required for both quoted and paraphrased material. A parenthetical reference provides as brief a citation as possible consistent with accuracy and clarity.

The simplest parenthetical reference can be prepared in several ways:

1. Place the author's last name and relevant page number(s) in parentheses immediately following the borrowed material.

   Cinematography is "the one achievement of science, art and craft without which motion pictures could never have progressed beyond such parlour amusements as the zoetrope and praxinoscope" (Turner 24).

2. Give the author's name in the text of your essay and place the relevant page number(s) in parentheses following the borrowed material.

   Kim Newman, a film theorist, observes that cameras increasingly function like additional characters (6).

3. On the rare occasion that you cite an entire work rather than borrowing a specific passage, give the author's last name in the text and omit any page numbers.

   Palladino argues that contemporary poetry is significantly dependent on language theory.

4. If the borrowed material is early in the sentence, place the parenthetical reference after the material and before any subsequent punctuation. This placement will more accurately show what is borrowed and what is your work.

   Language poetry, Mattingly notes, is the dominant mode of poetry in the late twentieth century (66), a movement as widespread as the nineteenth-century Romantic Movement.

5.   Citing two authors mentioned in the text:

Romney and James argue that Almodovar "was the only director at Cannes who made film-making look like a natural talent" (72–74).

6.   Two authors, not mentioned in the text:

The Straight Story is "a gentle sentimental journey with impressionistic landscape photography" (Romney and James 23).

7.   If you cite a book or article whose author is anonymous, cite a key word in the title that refers directly to the works cited page.

The Federico Fellini film Nights of Cabiria "has one of the most startling opening scenes in cinema" ("Night" 4).

8.   If you cite two or more works by the same author, then you must clearly distinguish the specific source in the parenthetical reference.

In the late twentieth century, "American poetry became decentralized, and this decentralization appears to be permanent . . ." (Holden, The Fate of American Poetry 21).

Jonathan Holden explains that it is "voicelessness, together with the countless past echoes that make up the lyric tradition. . ." (Style and Authenticity in Postmodern Poetry 23).

9.   Often one writer will quote another. You must clearly distinguish whom you are quoting from. When you quote or paraphrase one's quotation of someone else, your citation must indicate this.

According to William Carlos Williams, "The poem is a capsule where we wrap up our punishable secrets" (qtd. in Hirsch 13).

According to Hirsch, Auden maintains that "'A poem might be called a pseudo-person. Like a person it is unique and addresses the reader personally'" (13).

Instructions: Write a paragraph on tyranny, drawing from the sources below. You may choose to paraphrase as well to quote these sources.

1. "The *polis* [self-governing Greek city-state], one concludes was a brilliant conception, but one which required so rare a combination of material and institutional circumstances that it could never be realized; that it could be approximated only for a very brief period of time; that it had a past, a fleeting present and no future. In that fleeting moment its members succeeded in capturing and recording, as man has not often done in history, the greatness of which the human mind and spirit are capable."
   (M.I. Finley, *The Ancient Greeks*, 93)

2. "When such men [i.e., those led by selfish desires] with their followers, become numerous in a city, and when they perceive their own numbers, then with the help of the people's folly these produce a tyrant; and he is just the man among them who has the tyrant in his own soul most mighty and prevailing."
   (Plato, *The Republic*, 374)

3. "I'll have no dealings with law-breakers, critics of the government:
   Whoever is chosen to govern should be obeyed—
   Must be obeyed, in all things, great and small,
   Just and unjust!"
   (Sophocles, *Antigone*, Scene III, 212)

4. "I deem it best to stick to the practical truth of things rather than to fancies. Many men have imagined republics and principalities that never really existed at all. Yet the way men live is so far removed from the way they ought to live that anyone who abandons what is for what should be pursues his own downfall rather than his preservation; for a man who strives after goodness in all his acts is sure to come to ruin, since there are so many men who are not good. Hence it is necessary that a prince who is interested in his survival learn to be other than good, making use of this capacity or refraining from it according to need."
   (Machiavelli, *The Prince*, 56)

_____

_____

_____

_____

_____

Citing Sources Exercise Continued

2. 1

Using Sources Exercise

Instructions: Write a paragraph agreeing or disagreeing with Ehrenreich's contention that the United States is a warrior culture. Use at least one separated and one integrated quotation in writing your paragraph.

In what we like to think of as "primitive" warrior cultures, the passage to manhood requires the blooding of a spear, the taking of a scalp or head. Among the Masai of eastern Africa, the North American Plains Indians and dozens of other pretechnological peoples, a man could not marry until he had demonstrated his capacity to kill in battle. Leadership too in a warrior culture is typically contingent on military prowess and wrapped in the mystique of death. . . .

All warrior peoples have fought for the same high-sounding reasons: honor, glory or revenge. The nature of their real and perhaps not conscious motivations is a subject of much debate. Some anthropologists postulate a murderous instinct, almost unique among living species, in human males. Others discern a materialistic motive behind every fray: a need for slaves, grazing land or even human flesh to eat. Still others point to the similarities between war and other male pastimes—the hunt and outdoor sports—and suggest that it is boredom, ultimately, that stirs men to fight.

But in a warrior culture it hardly matters which motive is most basic. Aggressive behavior is rewarded whether or not it is innate to the human psyche. . . . And war, to a warrior people, is of course the highest adventure, the surest antidote to malaise, the endlessly repeated theme of legend, song, religious myth and personal quest for meaning. It is how men die and what they find to live for. . . .

More tellingly, we are unnerved by peace and seem to find it boring. When the cold war ended, we found no reason to celebrate. Instead we heated up the "war on drugs." What should have been a public-health campaign, focused on the persistent shame of poverty, became a new occasion for martial rhetoric and muscle flexing. . . .

Now, with Operation Desert Shield, our leaders are reduced to begging foreign powers for the means to support our warrior class. It does not seem to occur to us that the other great northern powers—Japan, Germany, the Soviet Union—might not have found the stakes so high or the crisis quite so threatening. It has not penetrated our imagination that in a world where the powerful, industrialized nation-states are at last at peace, there might be other ways to face down a pint-size Third World warrior state than with massive force of arms. Nor have we begun to see what an anachronism we are in danger of becoming: a warrior nation in a world that pines for peace, a high-tech state with the values of a warrior band. (Ehrenreich, Barbara. "The Warrior Culture." *Time* 15 Oct. 1990: 22.)

_____

_____

_____

_____

_____

Using Sources Exercise Continued

2. 1

Work Cited Page
Exercise I

Instructions: The list of works cited is precisely what it is a called, a list of the works you cited in your essay. It is not a bibliography, a list of sources on a related subject. If you cite a source, it should appear in your works cited; if a work appears on your works cited page, it should be cited somewhere in your essay. In other words, you should be careful that they match up evenly. Even if you only cite one source, you must still have a works cited page. Your works cited list should appear at the end of the essay and should be on a separate though paginated page. The title Works Cited should be centered on the page, one inch from the top of the page. You should double space within each entry and double space between each entry. If an entry continues past one line, you indent the second and all subsequent lines one-half inch. Correct the mistakes in the following Works Cited page. You may have to invent some information to complete the entries correctly.

MLA Guidelines can be found in the recommended text, A Writer's Reference, *or in the* MLA Handbook, *which is available in the library or in the Communication Resource Center. Tutors in the Communication Resource Center will be glad to assist you with documentation skills.*

1. You read an article called Hot Dogs, Apple Pie, and Mountain Bikes in a magazine called Bicycling. The article was written by Fred Zahradnik and published in Volume XXXI, Number 9 in November of 1990 on pages 86 through 88.

2. You think you may want to refer to an article written by Jim W. Corder that appeared in Rhetoric Review. You notice that the first page of this periodical is page 201. Corder's article, entitled "Academic Jargon and Soul-Searching Drivel," is on pages 314–326 of Vol. 9, Number 2, the Spring 1991 issue.

3. You have a paperback copy of C.S. Lewis's book called Surprised by Joy. The book is published by Harcourt Brace Jovanovich, Publishers. The title page lists offices in San Diego, New York, and London (in that order). The copyright date is 1955.

4. You are quoting from an essay by Caryl Rivers called Rock Lyrics and Violence Against Women that originally appeared in the Boston Globe. You find the essay in a collection called Essays From Contemporary Culture. Katherine Anne Ackley is the editor. The book is published in New York by Harcourt Brace College Publishers, 1998. Rivers's essay appears on pages 395–397.

5. You've found an article called "Gate Crashers" in The Chronicle of Higher Education. This is a weekly newspaper for academics. The article was published in the October 20, 1993 edition and appears on pp. A22 and A23. The author was David L. Wilson.

Name: _____

Section: _____

Date: _____

Work Cited Page
Exercise II

Instructions: Use the information given below to prepare a correct list of works cited in MLA style. Punctuation has been omitted from titles. In some cases, you will be given more information than needed for a complete entry and some entries have typographical errors. Alphabetize your entries.

Works Cited

1. Altieri, Charles. Slef and Sensibility in Contemporary Am. Poetry. NY: Cambridge Univers. 1984: 357-76

2. Breslin, Paul. "How to read the contemporary poem." American Scholar 47. Chapel Hill: 211-213.

3. Wendell Berry. "The Specialization of Poetry." Hudson Review: 11-27.

4. Thucydides. http://www.wsu.edu: 8080 /~dee/GREECE/PREICLes/research/iep/text/thucydides/rep-8/274873901347~23887783457398457.htm

5. Tarnas, Richard. *The Passion of the Westen Mind*. Ballantine: NY, 1991.

6. Irving, John, *The World According to Garp*. Toronto, Canada: First Ballantine Books Edition, 1976, 1977, 1978, 1979, 1990, 1996.

Scholarly (Journals) vs. Popular (Magazines)

Scholarly Journals	Popular Magazines
Peer Reviewed; Refereed; Articles evaluated for quality.	Feature writers; columns, some paid or invited authors.
Bibliographies or references included.	No bibliographies or references, sources difficult to trace at all.
Authors are experts in field.	Authors are often generalists.
Articles are signed by authors	Articles are often unsigned.
Audience is the scholarly reader: Professors, Researchers, Students.	Audience is the general public.
Standardized formats: APA, MLA, etc.	Various formats; often unstructured.
Written in jargon of field.	Popular, written for anyone to understand.
Illustrations support text: maps, tables, . photographs	Often profusely illustrated for marketing appeal.
Examples: *Journal of the American Medical Association (JAMA)* *Social Work Quarterly* *IEEE Transactions on Biomedical Engineering* *American Literature*	Examples: *Time* *Newsweek,* *Redbook* *Psychology Today* *Popular Science* *PC Magazine* *Omni*

1. Where do you include parenthetical documentation when you paraphrase?

   _____

   _____

2. Under what circumstances do you paraphrase or quote directly?

   _____

   _____

3. What is the problem with simply writing Mary Oliver *says* . . . as an introduction to a paraphrase?

   _____

   _____

4. What must you document in academic writing?

   _____

   _____

5. What is wrong with this quote: Mary Oliver argues that "poetry is a unique expression of the soul" (Oliver 32).

   _____

   _____

6. What are at least three differences between a scholarly journal and a popular magazine?

   _____

   _____

Thesis and Paragraph Writing

Thesis Statement

A good thesis statement is a concise and accurate reflection of the subject you hope to illuminate or prove in your essay. In the personal essays you will write in UCCA 101 it may be difficult to limit your main idea to a specific sentence comfortably deposited at the end of your introductory paragraph. Nevertheless, having read your essay a reader should be able to identify a central idea or main point even if the idea is implied rather than stated.

In persuasive writing, however, it is important to state your thesis in a declarative sentence somewhere early in your essay. Your thesis statement doesn't necessarily have to come at the end of your introductory paragraph. Many writing instructors suggest this, however, because it is important to make your central claim before you launch into your supporting points and evidence. You might also think of your thesis as a promise to your readers. If readers can identify a clearly written thesis, they can reasonably expect a unified argument to follow.

Statements of intent ("In this essay I will discuss the use of the death penalty.") and questions ("Is the death penalty a reasonable form of crime prevention?") are not thesis statements. They raise issues; they don't attempt to persuade.

It is important for you to remember that your opinion, your main point, your central idea, may change as the essay is written. You should see your thesis as a working hypothesis or a tentative idea in order to help you better organize your ideas. You might see the development of a thesis idea as part of the invention and research process. If you aren't certain of a particular argument, then let your research help you develop one.

Four Steps to a Thesis:

1. State your initial impression in the form of a debating resolution:

   Resolved: In "The Ache of Marriage" Denise Levertov emphasizes the idea of how spouses often fail to communicate verbally or spiritually with one another.

2. Add because to the preceding sentence:

   because she stresses their isolation and their lack of—their search for—"communion."

3. Acknowledge your opposition or provide a concession:

   Although in "The Ache of Marriage" Denise Levertov seems simply to describe a married couple's physical desire . . .

4. Polish your prose:

   Although in "The Ache of Marriage" Denise Levertov seems simply to describe a married couple's intense physical desire for one another, she in fact, by stressing their isolation and their lack of—their search for—"communion," emphasizes the idea of how spouses often fail to communicate verbally or spiritually.

Instructions: Assess the strengths and weaknesses of the following as thesis statements. Note which ones would most effectively establish the direction of an essay:

1. Photography as a Form of Fine Art.

    _____

    _____

2. Since the invention of the camera, photographs have become one of our more respected art forms.

    _____

    _____

3. Photographs, unlike paintings, have the capacity to actually capture experience and communicate more precisely what it is like to be human. Because the camera doesn't lie, we can always trust the reality communicated through the still photograph.

    _____

    _____

4. More and more people rely on e-mail as an essential form of communication.

    _____

    _____

5. I have always hated technology; it is doubtful that e-mail will be a lasting influence on our culture.

    _____

    _____

6. Parents are important in a child's upbringing.

    _____

    _____

7. Aerobics can teach you flexibility, hard work, and good breathing.

_____

_____

8. Talk radio gives you the opportunity to hear what others think.

_____

_____

Thesis Exercise II

Instructions: Construct an introduction and thesis statement out of the following information. Not all of the information will be useful, and you will have to add some information of your own.

1. *News by the Minute* reports that the national grade point average for college students has dropped from a "B" to a "B-" over the last twenty years.

2. An article in the *American Daily News* reports that four out of five college students list salary as their primary evidence of life success.

3. In 1967 the most popular majors at American universities were philosophy, English, humanities, and ecology. (*Chronicle for U.S. Education*)

4. "What is driving this headlong rush to implement new technology with so little regard for deliberation of the pedagogical and economic costs and at the risk of student and faculty alienation and opposition? A short answer might be the fear of getting left behind, the incessant pressures of 'progress.' But there is more to it. For the universities are not simply undergoing a technological transformation. Beneath that change, and camouflaged by it, lies another: the commercialization of higher education. For here as elsewhere technology is but a vehicle and a disarming disguise." (David F. Noble, *The Automation of Higher Education*)

5. Under the G.I. Bill—officially the Serviceman's Readjustment Act of 1944—veterans were allotted forty-eight months of free education at the college or university of their choice. Although the administrator of Veterans Affairs predicted that only 700,000 of them would do so, under the provisions of the bill 2,232,000 veterans crowded into American universities and colleges after [World War II], with more than a million of them enrolled during the single academic year 1947–1948. . . . 'The uncritical acceptance of largeness became a major legacy of the G.I. Bill,' says the historian Keith W. Olson. 'This legacy, in turn, served as perhaps the most important intellectual foundation for bigness that characterized higher education during the 1960s and 1970s.'" (D.G. Myers, *The Elephants Teach*)

6. In 1998 24.4 percent of all adults in the U.S. ages 25 and over had completed a Bachelor's degree or more. (*U.S. Department of Commerce Current Population Reports*)

7. In 1940 4.6 percent of all adults in the U.S. ages 25 and over had completed a Bachelor's degree or more. (*U.S. Department of Commerce Current Population Reports*)

Thesis Exercise II Continued

Paragraph Writing

An often overlooked aspect of student writing is the need to construct purposeful and well-developed paragraphs. Many writers simply begin new paragraphs when it *sounds* like they need one or whenever it *looks* like they have been writing for too long. Like the construction of the sentence, though, paragraphs have a distinct organizational purpose in an essay. Paragraphs need to meet three standards: unity, coherence, and development.

Paragraph Unity

A paragraph is unified when it has a distinct main idea and every element of the paragraph is committed to that main idea. The main idea is often referred to as a topic sentence, and many writing instructors advise that you make it the first sentence in your paragraph. You will learn, however, that in many writing situations it can seem forced to construct a paragraph developed around the first sentence. In your autobiography essay, for example, the natural flow of your narrative would require that your paragraphs have an implied topic idea rather than a specific sentence. Part of becoming a better writer is learning how to negotiate ideas in your paragraphs so they are clear but not forced. The topic sentence can be particularly useful in the formal arguments you will write in Communication Arts 102. They can make clear the organizing principle at work in your essay and they can help you spot weaknesses in your own argument.

Paragraph Coherence

A paragraph has coherence if its sentences are appropriately connected in logical ways. Transitional words and phrases and the use of pronouns as referents to specific antecedents are merely two ways of making sure a paragraph's sentences coherently follow each other. If you are concerned about coherence, you should proofread closely, asking yourself if each sentence is logically connected to the sentences that surround it.

Paragraph Development

A paragraph is well developed if you have actually fulfilled your promise of discussing your topic idea. You should include sufficient examples so that your readers understand the idea you are promoting. What constitutes sufficient is a matter of audience and purpose. If you are writing an autobiography and you are discussing a particularly harsh winter, you will not need as many examples as you would if you are attempting to prove the dangers of binge drinking.

Look at the following example and notice how the first sentence provides a clear sense of purpose for the examples to follow, how each sentence develops out of the next, and how the writer is generous enough to give several examples as proof of his initial assertion:

> The Mercedes symbol, for example, has nothing to do with automobiles; yet it is a great symbol, not because its design is great, but because it stands for a great product. The same can be said about apples and computers. Few people realize that a *bat* is the symbol of authenticity for Bacardi Rum; yet Bacardi is still being imbibed. Lacoste sportswear, for example, has nothing to do with alligators (or crocodiles), and yet the little green reptile is a memorable and profitable symbol. What makes the Rolls Royce emblem so distinguished is *not* its design (which is commonplace), but the *quality* of the automobile for which it stands. Similarly, the signature of George Washington is distinguished not only for its calligraphy, but because Washington was Washington. Who cares how badly the signature is scribbled on a check, if the check doesn't bounce? Likes or dislikes should play no part in the problem of identification; nor should they have anything to do with approval or disapproval. Utopia! (Paul Rand, "Logos, Flags, and Escutcheons")

1. What makes a good thesis statement?

   _____

   _____

2. What determines whether you have a thesis idea or a specific thesis statement?

   _____

   _____

3. What keeps the following sentences from functioning as a thesis statement: 1. "In this essay I will tell you about what happens if you drink and drive." 2. "Isn't it obvious that children need some form of pre-school?"

   _____

   _____

4. What is meant by "paragraph unity"?

   _____

   _____

5. What is meant by "paragraph coherence"?

   _____

   _____

6. What determines how much you need to develop a paragraph?

   _____

   _____

Persuasion and Argumentation

Arguable and Unarguable Claims

Arguable claims have two characteristics: *definition* and *uncertainty*.

What do we mean by definition? The claim is not broad; it has focus. The claim is not vague; it has words that lack ambiguity.

Uncertainty? Once the claim is clearly definable, it may still be certain. If something is certain, then there is no argument.

Which of the following claims are arguable?

1. Some people oppose abortion.

2. Any law that limits the rights of citizens to own firearms is a step away from democracy and toward a totalitarian government.

3. Since it is a common practice in both commercial and scholarly publishing for editors to correct and revise the work submitted to them by authors, it should also be acceptable for college students to get editorial help with their papers before submitting them to a teacher.

4. Because pollution increasingly threatens life on earth, funds should be devoted to cleaning up and preserving the environment.

5. The language of the United States has been and is English; therefore, the information on official documents, such as ballots, should be printed only in English.

6. Every college student should be required either (a) to demonstrate proficiency with computers or (b) to take a course in basic computer science.

7. No college student should be required to take courses in a foreign language.

8. Government officials should have no sources of income that might create a conflict of interests.

9.   A film is pornographic if it offends the average viewer in a community.

10.   Changes in the lifestyles of Americans would improve their health.

Persuasion and Argumentation

Persuasion and argumentation are two very different terms you might hear used interchangeably. Persuasion is a methodology, the means by which you accomplish an argument. Persuasion typically refers to the ways you try to convince your audience to accept your point of view or follow a particular course of action. Aristotle claimed that we attempt to persuade using three appeals: the appeal to reason (logos), the appeal to character (ethos), and the appeal to emotions (pathos). Argumentation, on the other hand, is the specific appeal to reason, the attempt to convince an audience to accept a point of view by a close look at evidence. A television commercial, for example, will not even begin to refute opposition or analyze evidence. That puts commercials in the realm of persuasion, not argumentation. A formal argument even has a specific structure. The more complex your argument, the more you will vary this structure. Essentially, though, a formal argument will perform in such a manner:

- Assertion or Claim

- Evidence

- Analysis of Evidence

- Refutation of Opposition

Certain conditions must exist before you are actually engaged in formal argument.

1.   An argument must make a point. Before anything else, you must have a clearly focused point of debate that you pursue throughout the essay.

2.   An argument must concern an arguable issue. Make sure you test your thesis against the standards on the previous page. "Convocation meets at 10:00 a.m." is not arguable. It's either true or false.

3.   An argument must have relevant evidence. This will depend on your evaluation of sources and your ethical credibility as a reliable researcher. Is *National Inquirer*, for instance, relevant evidence in determining someone's guilt or innocence?

4.   An argument should incorporate values. We do not seek meaning in a vacuum. In a reasoned and sensible debate we want to make clear the values that we consider relevant to the argument. "We should not want to live in a society in which deliberate brutality is legally authorized and publicly applauded" (*Washington Post*).

5.   An argument requires awareness of the topic's complexity.

6.   An argument has an audience. What terms need defining? How much background needs to be supplied? What kinds of evidence will be most effective? What counterarguments would come from those opposed to your stand? You will also want to consider audience so that you can find whatever common ground exists between you and those prepared to disagree with you.

Aristotle's Three Means of Persuasion:

1. appeal to reason (logos)

2. appeal to character (ethos)

3. appeal to emotions (pathos)

Thesis, audience, and situation will determine which of these appeals you emphasize.

The Appeal to Reason

An appeal to reason is essentially an argument or a proposition supported by evidence to prove that proposition. There are several ways you may argue logically:

Induction

Induction: the process by which we reach inferences—opinions or conclusions based on facts, or on a combination of facts and less debatable inferences. The inductive process moves from particular to general, from evidence to a conclusion that is either a generalization or a hypothesis. To reach the conclusion, we perform an inductive leap: We infer something to be so based on our collection and analysis of evidence. Clearly, then, the more evidence the more convincing the argument. No one wants to debate tomorrow's sunrise; the evidence for it is too convincing.

Generalizations: Assertions about all (or most or many) members of the same group or class. The basic pattern of an inductive argument leading to a generalization looks like this:

> Fish 1 has gills. Fish 2 has gills. Fish 3 has gills. Fish 3,652 has gills.
> Therefore: All fish have gills.

or

> American society has become increasingly violent in the last twenty-five years, in that people of many ages and backgrounds seem more ready to use violence to solve problems. According to figures quoted in a 1986 article by Adam Smith, each year in America now about 10,000 people die from gun deaths, in contrast to 4 in Great Britain and 17 in West Germany. An increasing number of victims are teenagers and children who are settling quarrels over drug territories or girlfriends by shooting. Sometimes the victims are parents, the murderers their children who are ending arguments over money or the use of the car. And sometimes the victims are children, the abusers their parents. In the first three months of 1989 in Washington, D.C., over 100 people were murdered, many teenagers, many deaths drug-related. A youngster in a Maryland community shot both parents in a quarrel over money. A Virginia teenager shot his stepmother and left her body in a truck by the roadside. The trial of a Manhattan man who beat his daughter to death is only one recent celebrated case of child beating. Further, in 1989 CBS reported that suicides have increased since 1986. Added to that are the Los Angeles area freeway shootings by frustrated drivers. The causes for this increase in violence are certainly numerous and complex, but the conclusion that "average" citizens, not crooks, are increasingly resorting to violence seems inescapable.

Hypothesis: a conclusion reached to explain a group of related facts. A hypothesis is an explanation of one incident or situation, but it is still an inference, as the generalization is. The doctor infers that you have a virus after gathering the following facts: You have a fever of 101 degrees; you are complaining of muscle aches; you have trouble keeping food in your stomach. A hypothesis is also what a jury reaches at the end of a trial.

Deduction

Unlike induction, with deduction you are not trying to support a hypothesis or generalization. In an inductive argument you are saying to your audience, "Look at the evidence and you will reach this particular conclusion." In a deductive argument you are saying, "This is what I think and here is why." A deductive argument, if valid, is more definitive. An inductive argument hopes that the audience will reach the same conclusions. Deduction is the reasoning process that draws a conclusion from the relationship of a broad judgment and a more specific assertion.

The Rogerian Argument

In his book *On Becoming a Person*, psychologist Carl R. Rogers explains that much of the time people, when talking, do not exchange information but rather evaluate one another's opinions, agree or disagree, and then seek to defend their own position. Because most of us connect our opinions closely to our sense of self, Rogers says we feel threatened when those opinions are challenged and become more concerned to defend ourselves than to listen to and learn from an opposing viewpoint.

According to Rogers:

1. If we want an audience to examine our views and evidence, we must find ways to reduce their sense of being threatened when we take a position they do not share.

2. Strongly worded, forcefully expressed statements and statements containing slanted, emotional language are the most threatening.

3. Arguments containing statements that show understanding of opposing viewpoints and a desire to communicate rather than attack are the least threatening.

When writing a Rogerian or conciliatory argument, then, you want to follow these guidelines:

1. State your position in objective language.

2. Express the opposing view in equally objective, unbiased language.

3. Explain the positions or views shared by both sides.

4. When presenting solutions to a problem, accommodate desires of the opposing side as much as possible.

In other words, find common ground.

Argument From Cause

1. Make sure that you focus on only one of the many causes and that you understand the effect is the result of more than the one cause you are discussing. If there is only one cause, then there is no argument.

2. Make clear that you are explaining a sequence or chain of causes.

3. Make clear if you are asserting the existence of conditions or influences and not causes. You would not want to try to support the assertion that your high-school government teacher *caused* you to attend college when what you mean is that she *influenced* your decision in certain ways.

4. Make clear the precise, limited effect of the cause. Don't ruin your argument by suggesting or implying a greater effect than the cause is likely to produce. If you do this, you will fall into the slippery slope fallacy.

Argument for Solutions

1. Demonstrate that a situation exists.

2. Reveal that the situation is a problem. Not everyone sees the same situations as problems, so you have to demonstrate either that the situation you are examining is indeed a problem or that the problem is more serious than most people realize.

3. Pinpoint the causes of the problem.

4. Explain your solution.

5. Explain the process for achieving your solution.

The Appeal to Character

Often an argument will be based on the persuasive value of the writer's character. If you are not well known, you have to go a long way toward establishing your authority. For instance, if you are not an expert on chemical warfare, you must rely on the ethos or expertise or character of experts. Advertisers use this technique all the time, but falsely and manipulatively: You should buy Hanes underwear because Michael Jordan wears it.

The Appeal to Emotions

One of the strongest and most common methods of persuasion is the appeal to emotions. You can watch just about any television commercial or political speech and hear the appeal to emotion. The child car seat manufacturer wants you to see images of children playing to persuade you that use of a car seat will insure that your kids live through a car accident. President Clinton invites cancer survivors to his State of the Union Address to encourage Congress to increase funding for cancer research. Any time someone tries to attach a human face to a persuasive message, the emotional appeal is being used.

Though the appeal to emotion can be valuable, it needs to be used with caution. As an academic writer you need to first depend on proving your arguments. You should see the appeal to emotion as an aid to your evidence, not as a substitute. If you only use the emotional appeal, your audience might think you have no evidence. The appeal to emotion can sometimes be used to distract the audience from looking at rational evidence. Since cigarette manufacturers cannot appeal to our sense of reason or character, they are left with deceptively appealing to our emotions. Advertisers typically use the appeals of sex, status, wealth, ego, belonging, security, fears, curiosity, and self-fulfillment to persuade us to buy their products.

Appeals Exercise

Instructions: Identify the appeals in the following passages. Some passages have more than one appeal.

1. Moreover, a cursory glance at ancient history shows clearly how in different parts of the world, with their different cultures, there arise at the same time the fundamental questions which pervade human life: Who am I? Where have I come from and where am I going? Why is there evil? What is there after this life? These are the questions which we find in the sacred writings of Israel, as also in the Veda and the Avesta; we find them in the writings of Confucius and LaoTze, and in the preaching of Tirthankara and Buddha; they appear in the poetry of Homer and in the tragedies of Euripides and Sophocles, as they do in the philosophical writings of Plato and Aristotle. They are questions which have their common source in the quest for meaning which has always compelled the human heart. In fact, the answer given to these questions decides the direction which people seek to give to their lives. (Pope John Paul II, *Encyclical Letter on the Relationship Between Reason and Faith*)

    _____

    _____

2. Poor Hetty, my fellow slave, was very kind to me, and I used to call her my Aunt; but she led a most miserable life, and her death was hastened (at least the slaves all believed and said so) by the dreadful chastisement she received from my master during her pregnancy. It happened as follows. One of the cows had dragged the rope away from the stake to which Hetty had fastened it, and got loose. My master flew into a terrible passion, and ordered the poor creature to be stripped quite naked, notwithstanding her pregnancy, and to be tied up to a tree in the yard. He then flogged her as hard as he could lick, both with the whip and cow-skin, till she was all over streaming with blood. He rested, and then beat her again and again. Her shrieks were terrible. The consequence was that poor Hetty was brought to bed before her time, and was delivered after severe labour of a dead child. She appeared to recover after her confinement, so far that she was repeatedly flogged by both master and mistress afterwards; but her former strength never returned to her. Ere long her body and limbs swelled to a great size; and she lay on a mat in the kitchen, till the water burst out of her body and she died. (Mary Prince, *The History of Mary Prince: A West Indian Slave*)

    _____

    _____

3. When your child suffers from diarrhea, dehydration can happen quickly. Unlike juice and sports drinks, Pedialyte is formulated with the right balance of carbohydrates and electrolytes to restore fluid and minerals lost as a result of diarrhea. That's why, at the first sign of diarrhea, pediatricians often recommend great-tasting Pedialyte to help prevent dehydration. Pedialyte comes in kid-

pleasing grape, bubblegum and fruit flavors, and is also available unflavored. For your toddlers and older children, try Pedialyte Freezer Pops. (www.pedialyte.com)

_____

_____

4. The effects of aspirin-like substances have been known since the ancient Romans recorded the use of the willow bark as a fever fighter. The leaves and bark of the willow tree contain a substance called salicin, a naturally occurring compound similar to acetylsalicylic acid, the chemical name for aspirin. In 1897, a German chemist with Friedrich Bayer and Company was searching for a treatment for his father's arthritic pain and began to research acetylsalicylic acid, which worked well. As a result, he developed a product introduced as Aspirin. By 1899, The Bayer Company was providing aspirin to physicians to give to their patients. (www.bayeraspirin.com)

_____

_____

5. Pete Rose should definitely be in the baseball Hall of Fame. He had more hits (4,256) than anyone else, he had a 44 game hitting streak, and he played in more games (3,563) than anyone else.

_____

_____

6. Recently two of the largest icebergs in existence broke off from Antarctica. One is 80 miles by 12 miles (130 km by 20 km). The other iceberg is 183 miles by 23 miles (295 km by 37 km), roughly the size of Jamaica. This evidence would suggest that global warming is having catastrophic effects on our environment.

_____

_____

7. According to the _London Sunday Times_, "After examining brain scans of a number of soldiers who served in the 1991 [Gulf] war, James Fleckenstein, a Professor of Radiology at the University of Texas Southwestern Medical Centre in Dallas, said he had found that veterans who were ill had up to 25 percent lower levels of a certain brain chemical than healthy ones. 'This is the first time ever we have proof of brain damage in sick Gulf War veterans.'" The conclusion, then, is indisputable. We cannot continue to neglect those brave Americans who served courageously under the stars and stripes. Washington and Lincoln would be ashamed that we so carelessly treat those who give the ultimate sacrifice for their country.

_____

_____

Evaluating Information

1. FACT—a statement of how something exists. Irrefutably verifiable.

   The Constitution of the United States requires that you be at least 35 years old to be President of the United States.

2. ALLEGED FACT—needs verification for people to accept it.

   The English poets Robert Southey and Samuel Taylor Coleridge once planned to build a utopian commune in Pennsylvania.

3. OPINION—a judgment based on facts, a conclusion that needs factual evidence to support.

   The death penalty should be banned in the United States because, more than anything else, it perpetuates a culture of death.

4. BELIEF—a conviction based on cultural or personal faith, morality or values, not on facts.

   I believe that getting angry in traffic is a fundamental denial of God's love.

5. PREFERENCE—expression of taste, what a person likes or dislikes.

   The Bruce Springsteen concert was the best this year. He truly is the Boss.

7. INFERENCE—a conclusion derived from a fact or set of facts. It forms an assumption from the evidence.

   Seasonal temperatures continue to be erratic, the polar caps are melting, and dangerous tornadoes plague the United States in record numbers. This evidence suggests that global warming is radically altering our climate.

8. INTERPRETATION—an opinion on the significance or meaning of something.

   Oprah Winfrey's Book Club has had amazing success. Americans must really have a hunger for reading.

9. PREJUDICE—an opinion based on insufficient or unexamined evidence.

   It doesn't surprise me that Allison doesn't have an active social life. She's an accountant after all.

Evaluating Information Exercise

Instructions: Identify the following types of information.

1. Whenever I visit Colorado, I love the way the mountains loom over the horizon.

   _____

2. Isn't it interesting that Sarah suddenly became interested in bug collecting at the same time she became interested in Herbert?

   _____

3. Tornados have struck Shades Mountain every year for the past four years. It appears that residents of Shades Mountain can expect more destruction.

   _____

4. You will damage your eyes if you stare into the sun.

   _____

5. Cigarette smoking is largely responsible for the increase in lung cancer.

   _____

6. I love the taste of dark chocolate.

   _____

7. Because the Internet is so dangerous, parents should keep it out of their homes.

   _____

8. A decrease in lung cancer diagnoses indicates a reduction in smoking among young people.

   _____

9. There is no question that Mark Rothko paintings are beautiful works of art.

   _____

10. Denver is a great place to live if you don't mind being around a bunch of liberals.

   _____

Logical Fallacies

Fallacies Resulting From Oversimplifying

1. Overstatement—an unqualified generalization. It refers to all members of a category or class. Signaled by words such as all, every, always, never, none. Needs only one exception to disprove them.

2. Hasty or Faulty Generalizations—assertions that oversimplify by arguing from an insufficient number of examples or by arguing from only part of the available evidence.

3. Non Sequitur—means literally "it does not follow." Applies whenever conclusions are not logically connected to the reasons, suggests that a given fact will lead to a particular consequence.

4. The Slippery Slope—we should not agree with an assertion because terrible consequences will follow.

5. The False Dilemma Fallacy—only two alternatives.

6. False Analogy—a comparison of two things known to be alike in one or more features and a suggestion that they will be alike in other features as well.

7. Post Hoc Fallacy—connects cause and effect solely on the basis of time sequence.

Fallacies Resulting From Ignoring the Issue

1. Begging the Question—making an undemonstrated claim. Assuming something without proving it.

2. Circular Reasoning—a restatement of an assertion as a reason for accepting it.

3. Red Herring—a foul smelling argument, one that introduces a side point that is irrelevant to the debate.

4. Straw Man—attributes to opponents erroneous and usually ridiculous views they do not hold so that their position can easily be attacked.

5. Ad Hominem—attacks the person rather than the argument.

6. Bandwagon—everyone does it.

7. False Appeal to Authority—use of a name outside the person's area of expertise.

8. Extension—an extension of the question until a different issue altogether arises.

9. Ad Populum—"to the people." Appeals to an audience's shared values.

10. Fallacy of Definition—shifting the meaning of terms to avoid the actual argument.

Name: _____

Section: _____

Date: _____

Identify the Fallacy

1. Okay, if you think psychokinesis isn't possible, explain to me how Uri Geller can bend keys just by looking at them.

   _____

2. Of course you oppose no-fault insurance. You're a lawyer.

   _____

3. "I'm tired of being called a racist. I'm not a racist. The racists today are Jesse Jackson and the NAACP."—Rush Limbaugh

   _____

4. I don't like the idea of abortion either, but I think it's better than having some poor woman kill herself trying to raise 11 or 12 children.

   _____

5. "Just two days after Liz Taylor announced plans to wed Larry Fortensky, her ex-husband Eddie Fisher took an overdose of painkillers and was rushed to a hospital in a life-and-death crisis." —*National Enquirer*

   _____

6. Jim and Tammy Bakker are suffering right now, just like Job and his wife. And like Job, they will rise to new prosperity and happiness.

   _____

7. Creationism in public schools? Pretty soon we'll have to give time to the stork theory.

   _____

8. "You'll love the meat lovers pizza if you like meat and you like pizza."—Pizza Hut Ad.

   _____

9. It's not right to end the life of a terminally ill loved-one. St. Paul wrote, "If we are to live like Christ, we must die like Christ."

   _____

10. "Millions of people are misnamed at birth, causing them problems and unhappiness throughout their lives."—Krishna Ram-Davi

    _____

1. What are the two characteristics of an arguable claim?

   _____

   _____

2. What are at least three of the conditions that must exist before you are engaged in formal argument?

   _____

   _____

3. What is the difference between persuasion and argumentation?

   _____

   _____

4. What is the difference between induction and deduction?

   _____

   _____

5. Explain the Rogerian argument.

   _____

   _____

6. What is a danger of the appeal to character?

   _____

   _____

7. What is a danger of the appeal to emotions?

   _____

   _____

8. What is an opinion? Give an example.

    _____

    _____

9. What is an inference? Give an example.

    _____

    _____

10. Identify the following and give an example for each: Non Sequitur, False Dilemma, Post Hoc Fallacy, Straw Man, Ad Hominem.

    _____

    _____

PART **2**

Chapter

IV

Revision and Editing

Revision

According to Maxine C. Hairston, "When (professional) writers revise, they make changes in four ways: they delete, they add, they substitute, or they rearrange, and they do it on all levels—word, phrase, clause, sentence, paragraph, or larger units of discourse."

Cutting:

1. Most student writers "pad" their writing by adding useless filler phrases. Search for these and eliminate them.

    It is the case that . . .
    There exists a need for . . .
    The reason that the . . .
    I will attempt to show . . .
    I will strive for a way . . .

2. Try to use a single word that can replace a phrase:

    Original: "I try to present a tone that will reveal that I know what I am talking about, but assume such a manner that the audience will not be offended by my argument."

    Revision: "I will strive for an authoritative but not offensive tone."

3. Cut doubling words:

    The group will *control* and *regulate* the industry.

    You should *check* and *verify* the results.

Adding:

1.   Add examples or illustrations.

2.   Improve the visual/descriptive presentation.

3.   Divide paragraphs at logical points and fully develop.

Changing:

1.   Change prepositional phrases to stronger modifiers. Prepositional phrases overload and drag down sentences.

2.   Reduce the number of derived nouns to their parent forms: cancellation to cancel, admiration to admire, visitation to visit, production to produce.

3.   Move from the abstract to the concrete, or use downshifting. Downshifting, a term coined by grammarian Francis Christensen, is the process that a writer uses to explain an abstract term for which there is no concrete equivalent. There are four levels to downshifting:

     1.   The abstract statement.
     2.   Illustration of statement.
     3.   Specific interpretation of statement in level 3.
     4.   A more specific illustration of statement in level 3.

     Example:

     > Existentialism is a philosophy of personal responsibility. It holds, as Sartre puts it, that "man is condemned to be free." That statement means that no one can claim that he is a victim; he alone is responsible for his behavior. If other people exploit him, it is because he allows himself to be exploited.

     Downshifting also applies to moving from the general to the specific:

     Example:

     > Although the court had forced Cullen to cough up nearly $4,000 for her current medical expenses, Priscilla was strapped. The mansion's electric bill alone was $4,150. The country club bills averaged $500. Priscilla had been forced to borrow a considerable sum of money from a bank, using her jewelry and a $23,000 Ching dynasty jade carving as collateral. The jade and the jewelry (including a 16.31 carat diamond and platinum bracelet) were still in hock, and the money was almost gone. ("Solitary Confinement," *Texas Monthly*)

Peer Editing

1.   *Listen carefully to what is being said*

     One way to indicate your respect for another person's writing is to listen to it carefully. If the essay is being read aloud, you may want to take notes as you listen so that your mind doesn't wander. If you have time, you may want to hear the essay read twice—the first time for general meaning and the second time to take notes about your specific concerns. Even if you have a copy of the essay to read, you will still want to make notes that will guide your discussion of the essay.

2. *Respond as if you were the intended audience*

When possible, try to imagine how the intended reader would respond to the essay. You may want to begin your comments by saying, "If I were your boss . . ." or "If I had never read this book before. . ." to indicate the basis for your response.

3. *Make observations rather than evaluations*

Perhaps the most common response after someone has finished reading an essay is "I thought it was good" or "I didn't like it." Instead of making evaluative comments, begin by simply making observations about what the writer did in the essay. Before judging how well someone has communicated, it is good to agree upon what has been communicated. Here are some sample remarks of this kind:

> "So there were three main parts to the essay: how to choose a daycare based on price, location, and quality of care."

> "I thought the waiter always kept the whole tip, but you said that where you worked everybody shared the tips equally. I had never heard that before."

> "You were so funny when you described living in a small town. I grew up in a small town, but I can see how it would have been strange for you when you saw the cars parked at an angle on Main Street."

4. *Ask questions if you don't understand*

One of the ways you can be most helpful to a writer is by simply noting that something has confused you. We often write about subjects that are very familiar to us, and we forget that other people might not know what a "scone" is or when to use a "shim." Of course, it's possible that the intended audience for the essay may know these terms, but it doesn't hurt to raise the question.

> "In the beginning you said that most people spend too much for a car. Did you ever explain why they do?"

> "I was confused when you said 'blue eyes are really colorless.' What makes them blue?"

> "At one point in the essay you said that Mike was the meanest person at Westmont High. Later you said he was always helping people out. I don't understand how the same person could be so different."

5. *Test the writer's observations against your own experience*

All of us can easily fall into the trap of thinking that everyone else shares our feelings about people and places. Suppose you are listening to an essay in which the writer claims that most people would rather eat simply in a casual atmosphere rather than go to an elegant restaurant. If you love going to fine restaurants, you might want to question this statement. However, you should simply offer your experience as an alternative view rather than accusing the writer of being wrong.

6. *Encourage the writer by your comments*

Writing is not easy, and all of us appreciate some encouragement when we are struggling to express an idea. Don't go on a "fault-finding expedition" with another person's essay. When you have finished responding to the essay, the writer should be thinking about ways to improve the essay—not ways to dispose of it. If you think many of your comments are being interpreted as "attacks" upon the writer, you should make an extra effort to show your approval for the writer's accomplishments.

On the other hand, simply telling the writer that the essay is "good" or "splendid" isn't necessarily an encouragement. The writer may think you are just trying to be polite. If the essay really is splendid, you should explain what made it so good. By observing these marks of excellence, you will be reinforcing the writer's good habits and rewarding the effort that went into preparing the essay.

If you are the writer whose work is being evaluated, you can help this process go smoothly. If your essay is being presented orally, be sure that you read your work loudly and clearly. After you finish reading, give your group an adequate amount of time to review their notes and collect their thoughts. As comments are being made, don't be defensive about your work. You may not necessarily agree with what others have to say, but if you seem angry or argumentative, you may miss out on valuable commentary that could help you improve your writing (and your grade). Finally, you can encourage response by asking questions about your work. If you think your writing may be confusing at some point, ask your group if it is. If you think you've given too much detail on some minor point, ask the group's opinion. When a group works together well, the writer of an essay should hear comments the way a hungry diner hears a waiter explaining the house specialties. When a group works poorly, the writer hears comments the way a sullen defendant hears charges read against him or her by a prosecuting attorney. Your response to the comments being made can dramatically affect the atmosphere in the group.

Section Review

Using the questions on the previous page, edit one of the student essays in Part Four. In addition, identify at least ten parts (word, phrase, sentence, paragraph) of the essay that could be cut, five parts that need development, and five parts that should be changed for clarity. Take one of the writer's main points and go through the process of downshifting.

_____

_____

_____

_____

_____

_____

_____

_____

_____

_____

_____

_____

_____

_____

_____

_____

_____

_____

_____

Stylistics

Elements of Style

Style—"the arrangement of words in a manner which at once best expresses the individuality of the author and the ideas and intent in the author's mind. . . . Style is a combination of two elements: the idea to be expressed, and the individuality of the author." Holman's *Handbook of Literature*

"What then, can oratorical imagery effect?" Longinus asks. "Well," he answers, "it is able in many ways to infuse vehemence and passion into spoken words, while more particularly when it is combined with the argumentative passages it not only persuades the hearer but actually makes him its slave." *On The Sublime*, XV

It was Quintilian who most explicitly related the figures to the logos, pathos, and ethos of an argument. Quintilian looked upon the figures as another means of lending "credibility to our arguments," of "exciting the emotions," and of winning "approval for our characters as pleaders." *Institutio Oratoria*

I. WORD CHOICE—Diction: choice and use of language

   1. Denotation—dictionary definition

      Connotation—association called up by a word

   2. General and abstract vs. specific and concrete

II. SHOWING v. TELLING

   In much of the writing you will learn how to do in Communication Arts, you are much better off showing your audience what you are talking about than merely telling them. Showing your audience lets them begin to draw some conclusions about your subject matter, and it improves the authority of your writing. For example, notice the difference between the two passages below:

   Telling: My roommate has never really shown much respect for me, so I am moving out.

   Showing: My roommate is always leaving his dirty plate on my desk and his dirty clothes on my bed. There hasn't been a time when he hasn't had friends over until late at night. I've come back from weekends at home to the smell of cigarette smoke and stale beer, my bed tussled as if someone had slept in it. The final injustice was when he used a picture of my parents as a coaster. I have to move out.

III.   SENTENCE STRUCTURE

   1.   Simple sentences expanded by many modifiers create formal style. Overly simplistic sentence structure is sometimes used to show the writer thinks the subject is silly or childish or insulting.

   2.   Long compound sentences do not increase formality.

   3.   The virtual sentence can be used for emphasis.

   4.   Parallelism signals readers that items are equally important.

   5.   Antithesis creates tension, highlighting by contrast and juxtaposition of contrasting ideas.

   6.   Climax—items arranged in order of increasing importance.

IV.   FIGURATIVE LANGUAGE can reveal much about a writer's perception of subject matter.

   1.   Simile

   2.   Metaphor

   3.   Hyperbole

   4.   Allusion

   5.   Understatement

V.   REPETITION OF KEY WORDS AND PHRASES

   1.   Clarify meaning

   2.   Enhance coherence

   3.   Produce an effective cadence

   4.   Add weight and seriousness to the work

   5.   Add emphasis to ideas

BAD REPETITION: 1. Filler phrases

   2. Unnecessary repetition

   3. Redundant phrases

KINDS OF REPETITION SCHEMES USED TO CREATE PLANNED EFFECT

   1.   Anaphora—Repetition at the beginning of clauses.

   2.   Epistrophe—Repetition at the ends of clauses.

   3.   Polyptoton—Repetition of words derived from the same root.

   4.   Alliteration—Repetition of consonants for emphasis and force.

   5.   Epanalepsis—Repetition at the end of a clause that occurred at the beginning.

   6.   Anadiplosis—Repetition of the last word of one clause at the beginning of following clause.

   7.   Antimetabole—Repetition of words in successive clauses in reverse grammatical order.

V. VISUAL TECHNIQUES

    1. Quotation—writer usually questioning word's validity or meaning in that context.

    2. Italicizing—writer gives certain words emphasis.

    3. Capitalization of words not normally capitalized—same as italicizing.

VI. OTHER STYLISTIC CONSTRUCTIONS

    1. Asyndeton—deliberate omission of conjunctions between a series of related clauses.

    2. Polysyndeton—deliberate use of many conjunctions between a series of related clauses.

Examples of Style

1. Parallelism

    " . . . for the support of this declaration, with a firm reliance on the protection of Divine Protection, we mutually pledge to each other our Lives, our Fortunes, and our sacred Honor."
    —*The Declaration of Independence*.

2. Antithesis

    "Those who have been left out, we will try to bring in. Those left behind, we will help to catch up."—Richard M. Nixon, "Inaugural Address," January 20, 1969

3. Asyndeton & Polysyndeton

    Note the difference in style:

    This semester I am taking English, history, biology, mathematics, sociology, and physical education.

    This semester I am taking English and history and biology and mathematics and sociology and physical education.

4. Alliteration

    "Already American vessels had been searched, seized, and sunk."—John F. Kennedy

5. Anaphora

    "Why should white people be running all the stores in our community? Why should white people be running all the banks of our community? Why should the economy of our community be in the hands of the white man? Why?"—Malcolm X

6. Epistrophe

    "To the good American many subjects are sacred: sex is sacred, women are sacred, children are sacred, business is sacred, America is sacred, Mason lodges and colleges are sacred."
    —George Santayana, *Character and Opinion in the United States*

7. Epanalepsis

    "Year chases year, decay pursues decay."—Samuel Johnson, "The Vanity of Human Wishes."

8. Anadiplosis

    "The laughter had to be gross or it would turn to sobs, and to sob would be to realize, and to realize would be to despair."—John Howard Griffin, *Black Like Me*

9. Antimetabole

    "Ask not what your country can do for you; ask what you can do for your country."
    —John F. Kennedy, "Inaugural Address"

10. Polyptoton

    "Not as a call to battle, though embattled we are."—John F. Kennedy, "Inaugural Address"

Style Exercise

Instructions: Identify the stylistic devices used in the following sentences, and put the numbers on the appropriate lines below.

1. "Perfect evenings begin with sunsets and end with Godiva Chocolates."

2. "It will be seen, heard, and loved for generations." Ridgeway Clocks

3. "Past Glories, gloriously updated." Wedgewood China

4. "You don't have to make space for a Spacemaker Oven."

5. "When the going gets tough, the tough get going."

6. "He was dead before we realized he was dying." James Baldwin

7. "No two people are alike, and no two colds are alike." Triaminic Cold Syrup

8. "Dry dusting scatters dust, Pledge dusting gathers dust."

9. "Sparkling clean glasses for less money; that's the Smarter Sparkle."

10. "You won't taste the diet in Diet 7UP."

11. "Treat yourself to buttery taste without butter's calories." Orville Redenbacher

12. "After all the treats, treat them to Crest."

13. "No smoke. No odor. No hood." Modern Maid Indoor Grill

14. "Flowers and Flowers. Flowers and Borders. Borders and Borders. A Border and a Flower." Dansk Dinnerware

15. "For Major celebrations and Minor victories." Bailey's Irish Cream (the ad has a piano player in it.)

16. "It's long. It's slim. It's elegant. It's more you." More Cigarettes

17. "Today Eastern can take you to yesterday and tomorrow."

18 "Give them the Gift that keeps on Giving." Southern Living

19. "When things get hot, Saran Wrap beats the others cold."

20. "Different ages have answered the question differently." Virginia Woolf

Antithesis	_____	Anaphora	_____
Epistrophe	_____	Epanalepsis	_____
Anadiplosis	_____	Climax	_____
Antimetabole	_____	Polyptoton	_____

1. What is the difference between connotation and denotation?

    _____

    _____

2. What is style when it comes to writing or speaking?

    _____

    _____

3. Give an example of a word that is general and abstract. Give an example of a specific and concrete word.

    _____

    _____

4. How do most readers respond to overly simplistic sentence structure?

    _____

    _____

5. Identify the following terms: 1. hyperbole, 2. allusion, 3. understatement, 4. simile, 5. metaphor. Create an example for each.

    _____

    _____

    _____

    _____

    _____

    _____

    _____

6. What does repetition of key words and phrases do for your writing?

_____

_____

7. What happens to your prose when you deliberately omit conjunctions between related clauses?

_____

_____

8. What happens to your prose when you deliberately add conjunctions between related clauses?

_____

_____

Chapter

VI

Discriminatory Language

In all of your writing, in Communication Arts and in your other courses, you should avoid stereotypes and sexist or racist language. You will discover that in most walks of life and in most professions, sexist, racist, and other types of discriminatory language are unacceptable. Only one example will disprove a stereotype. You would need to find only one male who doesn't mind asking for directions or one female with a stellar driving record to dispel those stereotypes. You should ask yourself if it is worth losing a job, suffering a bad grade, or, more importantly, damaging someone's self-esteem over terms that you could easily avoid using. More important than career or grades, avoiding discriminatory language is a fundamental part of Samford's mission as a Christian university. You should make yourself aware of Samford's policy on inclusive language and work toward establishing a writing style that avoids offensive language of all types.

Samford's Advisory Council on Women drafted the following statement which the University has adopted and supports fully.

> Language—how it is used and what it implies—plays a crucial role in Samford University's mission to nurture persons. Because verbal constructions create realities, inclusive language can uphold or affirm those whom we seek to nurture, while exclusive language can damage or defeat them. We therefore actively seek a discourse in our university community that supports the equal dignity and participation of men and women; we seek to avoid verbal constructions that diminish the equal dignity of all persons. It is an affirmative—and affirming—part of our mission to educate students, staff, and faculty in the creation of a community of equality and respect through language.

Though some ways are more awkward than others, there are many ways you can avoid sexist language. You need to decide on a prose style that is suitable for your writing purpose. Cluttered prose is a less serious offense than discriminatory language.

Many writers simply double the pronouns:

- A doctor should always consult his or her PDR during every office visit and certainly before he or she prescribes medicine.

- A doctor should always consult his or her PDR during every office visit and certainly before s/he prescribes medicine.

- A doctor should always consult his/her PDR during every office visit and certainly before he/she prescribes medicine.

As you might imagine, all of these possibilities can become awkward, especially in a sentence or paragraph where you need a lot of pronouns. Likewise, it can become distracting or inaccurate if you simply alternate pronouns:

- When a student comes to orientation, he must always first see his advisor. Then, she should visit the registrar's office to pay tuition.

A more suitable way of handling the issue is to avoid pronouns if you can:

- A student coming to orientation should first see an advisor, then visit the registrar's office to pay tuition.

When you can't avoid the pronouns, try recasting the sentence so you don't have to alternate "his or her" more times than you need. The goal you should have in mind is writing an efficient and smooth-sounding prose that doesn't imply discriminatory attitudes.

Section Review

Instructions: Identify what is at issue in each of the following sentences.

1. Women who send their children to daycare don't really care about having someone else raise their children.

_____

_____

_____

_____

2. Henry Louis Gates, Jr., a black professor from Harvard, has written a lot about slavery.

_____

_____

_____

_____

3. Though my friend Mark is blind, he does quite well for himself.

_____

_____

_____

_____

4. You should meet the new quarterback, Henry. He's very articulate.

_____

_____

_____

_____

5. An engineer in today's society understands that he will probably need graduate work to separate himself from the pack.

   _____

   _____

   _____

   _____

6. For the life of me, I can't understand why blacks are always complaining. My friend James is black, and he's never experienced racism.

   _____

   _____

   _____

   _____

7. There are a lot of women writers on this syllabus. I guess I'm stuck with another feminist professor.

   _____

   _____

   _____

   _____

8. During my visit to the emergency room, I had the misfortune of being attended to by a male nurse. But what are you going to do? I guess they have to find jobs somewhere.

   _____

   _____

   _____

   _____

Chapter

VII

Computing Skills

Simeon E-mail Activity

Instructions: Every Samford student should know how to operate the campus e-mail system. The Simeon system is designed to make it easy to send, retrieve, and save e-mail messages. You must know your user name and your password in order to use the e-mail system. Call User Support at 726-2662 if you have problems with your password or need help in completing this exercise.

STEP 1

Open Simeon and enter your user name and password.

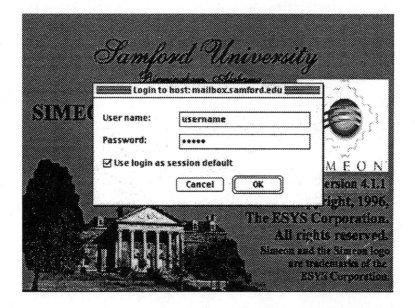

STEP 2

Click on the "Compose" button on toolbar.

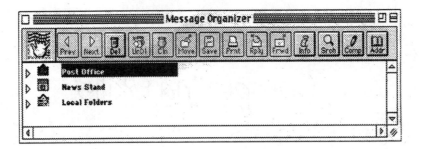

STEP 3

Type *[your instructor's ID]@samford.edu* in the "TO:" area. Enter your user name in the "CC:" area to get a copy of the message you send.

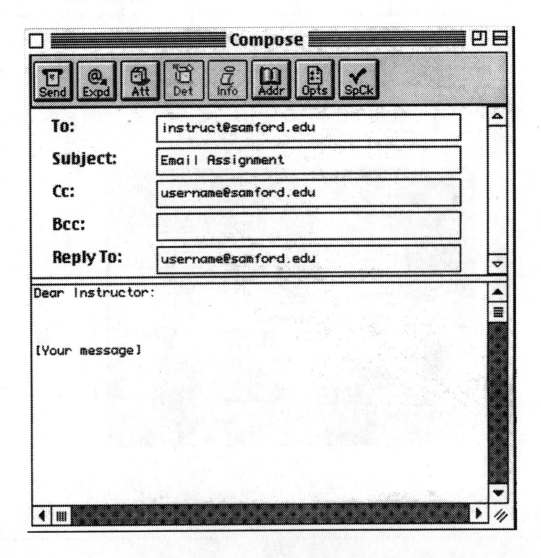

STEP 4

Your message should contain the following information:

- Your name

- Campus phone

- Hometown

- Name and occupation of your parents

- Names and ages of your siblings

- Publication information for a book related to Cultural Perspectives that you found in the Davis Library

- A quotation taken from this book and the page number where it was found

- The reason you selected this quotation

- Any mistake in writing down the quotation will cause you to get a *zero* for this assignment.

Word Processing Activity

1. Open Microsoft Word.

2. Write a paragraph describing your experience in Cultural Perspectives (or another course you are taking). The paragraph should be 5–7 sentences.

3. Center a title above your paragraph.

4. Use the Footer command to make sure that today's date will appear in the lower right hand corner.

5. Italicize a phrase within the paragraph.

6. Use the Header command to insert your name and the course in the upper right hand corner.

7. Double space the paragraph.

8. Use the spellchecker.

9. Select a word and use the Thesaurus to find a substitute for it.

10. Change the top margin to 1.5 inches.

11. Select two sentences of your paragraph and set them up as a block quotation.

12. Save your file to a disk.

13. Give your file another name and save it again.

14. Print the file.

1. Open Microsoft PowerPoint. Create a new presentation by selecting "Design Template" in the presentation options.

2. You will be given a choice of several presentation designs. Preview these until you find one that you like. Select it.

3. Create a Title Slide for your presentation. This is usually the first choice in the AutoLayout menu.

4. Click in the appropriate box on your Title Slide and type in your title. The subtitle is optional.

5. Create a New Slide from the Insert menu. Choose "Bulleted List" from the AutoLayout menu.

6. Write a main idea and three subheadings on this slide.

7. Use "Preset Animation" from the Slide Show menu to add movement to your subheadings. You must select the text with your cursor before you can add animation.

8. Insert another slide. Choose "Text & Clip Art" for the layout.

9. Add clip art to the slide by double clicking on the clip art box on this slide.

10. Design three more slides.

11. Change the layout of one of your slides. Choose "Slide Layout" from the Format menu.

12. Look at your presentation in Slide Sorter View (from the View menu or the buttons at the bottom of slide window).

13. Change the order of your slides by clicking and dragging one to a new place.

14. Look at your presentation in Outline View.

15. Change some of the text on one of your slides. Return to the normal Slide View.

16. Go through your slides in the Slide Show View.

17. Print your slides. When the print window opens, you will see a box near the bottom of the window that says, "Print what." Click the arrow and select "Handouts (6 slides per page)."

18. Turn in your final product to your instructor.

Using Table and Graph Functions in Microsoft Word

Create the following table using the Table command in Microsoft Word.

Student	A	B	C
Mid-Term	86	64	95
Final	77	82	97

1. Open the Microsoft Office Suite.

2. Open Microsoft Word.

3. Use the Insert Table command from the toolbar.

4. Create a 3 x 4 table by dragging your cursor down and to the right until you see the correct setting.

5. Enter the information from the table above. You must use the TAB command to move from cell to cell (or you can use the mouse to select the cell).

6. If you are feeling confident, you might try the following effects. Select the top row and make all the headings bold. Use the "Borders and Shading" command (Format Menu) to put a double line under the first row. Select a 5% shade for the first row.

Create the following chart using Microsoft Graph.

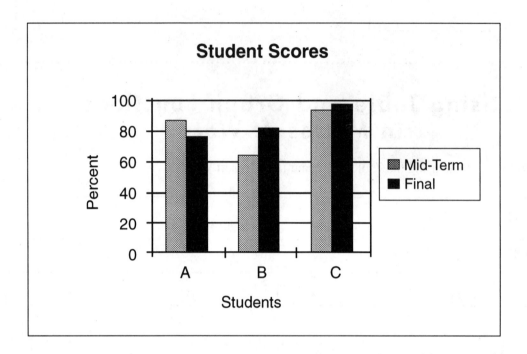

1. Select the table you created above (by clicking and dragging across it).

2. Select "Object" from the Insert menu. Scroll down and select MS Word 97 Graph.

3. Click on the window that has your main document to see the completed graph.

Try making the following changes in your graph. Begin by double-clicking on the graph while you are in MS Word. This will open the graph editor. Change the chart type to a two-dimensional column chart. Select the plot area and use the fill command to change the background to white. Select the left columns and change the color to black and the pattern to dotted. Select the right columns and change the color to black. Use the "Titles" command on the Insert menu to add the title "Student Scores." Add an X-axis title of "Students" and a Y-axis title of "Percent." Change the Y-axis title to be aligned vertically, if necessary. Use the "Borders" command in MS Word to put a border around the chart.

Name: _____

Section: _____

Date: _____

Introduction to the Internet Exercise

Key terms:

Internet	World Wide Web	Web Site	server
browser	address	URL	http://
home page	hypertext	links	image map
bookmark	search engine	FTP	FAQ
download	listserv	newsgroup	post
thread	spam	virus	emoticon
.com	.org	.edu	.gov
.uk	HTML	cross posting	cookie

1. Visit one or more of the following sites. Describe what kind of information you find.

   www.nasa.gov   promo.net/pg/lists/list.html   www.usatoday.com

   www.stat-usa.gov   www.discovery.com   www.nytimes.com

   www.whitehouse.gov   www.vtourist.com   www.nea.gov/

   www.nationalgeographic.com/   www.nsf.gov/   www.neh.gov/

   _____

   _____

   _____

   _____

   _____

   _____

2. Conduct a search to answer one or more of the following questions:

   a. Where is Karl Marx buried (city, country, cemetery)?

   b. What is the name of the Greek astronomer who calculated the circumference of the earth 1,500 years before Columbus sailed?

   c. According to Grant himself, what does the middle initial "S" stand for in "Ulysses S. Grant?" (Note: It's not "Simpson.")

   d. How many blue whales are left on planet Earth?

e. How many hours a day does the average American child watch television?

f. What woman led the fight to clean up Love Canal in the 1970s?

g. Who coined the term "rock and roll?"

h. In what year did it become illegal for employers to discriminate against people with physical disabilities?

i. How many times did Robert Frost win the Pulitzer Prize?

_____

_____

_____

_____

_____

_____

_____

_____

3. Conduct a search on a defined topic (e.g., "Pulitzer Prize winners" not "journalism" or "awards.") using AltaVista and Yahoo search engines. For each of those, record the topic, the search engine, the number of hits, and the URL of the first hit.

_____

_____

_____

_____

_____

4. Visit www.liszt.com. Select two listserv discussion groups that sound interesting to you. (You will have to go through one or more subdirectories before you actually find the name of the list) Write down the name of the group (i.e., ENVIRONMENT-L) and the name of the listserv where you would subscribe (i.e., listproc@cornell.edu).

_____

_____

Section Review

1. How do you change the order of your slides in a PowerPoint presentation?

    _____

    _____

2. What would you expect to find on an FAQ page?

    _____

    _____

3. What is a listserv?

    _____

    _____

4. Name a couple of useful search engines.

    _____

    _____

5. What is Samford's e-mail system called?

    _____

    _____

Resumes

Resumes

The resume is the primary document used in the employment search. Although most students think of the resume as a document they will need at graduation, many find that a resume is required when applying for part-time and summer employment, when applying for scholarships and fellowships, and when seeking internships.

The resume is also used for promotional and marketing purposes. For instance, when soliciting new business, companies frequently provide biographical information about the team that will be doing the work. The resume shows the experience and capability of the various team members.

There are many types of resumes and many places to find examples. You can visit Samford's Career Development Center for examples or consult www.jobweb.org/catapult/jsguides.htm. There are also many reputable books that include sample resumes for different professions. There is no single appropriate resume style, but there are some general guiding principles you should follow. Resumes are usually organized in reverse chronological order. Begin each section with your latest responsibility and work backwards to earlier positions.

You should proofread your resume carefully. A single misspelling can undermine your chances for an important position. You will discover that employers are much less forgiving than your teachers. Avoid the temptation to be cute or clever in your resume. However, you do need to think strategically. For instance, "Managed accounts for Kimel, Walbach, and Dunbar" sounds much more professional than "Worked for daddy last summer."

Remember, in a resume you are trying to sell your education, your experience, your very best qualities.

There are four standard approaches to resume organization: 1) chronological, 2) functional, 3) skills, and 4) imaginative. Because the approach you choose will highlight your experience in a particular way, you should select the approach which best represents your qualifications to a prospective employer.

1. CHRONOLOGICAL—Work experience is organized in inverse chronological order. from most to least recent. Dates may be displayed in a separate column or may be included after the employer's name. This approach emphasizes your current activity as the most important and is appropriate if your work experience is closely related to the job you are seeking. There are three inherent dangers in this approach: a) The resume may become only a fact sheet without

highlighting significant features. b) This kind of layout is often dominated by dates. Remember: dates do not sell your ability. c) In keeping with strict chronological order, important facts are sometimes buried.

2.   FUNCTIONAL—In this format, work experience is arranged in order of importance with the most significant first, regardless of chronological order. Each job is categorized by function (e.g., program designer, research consultant, case worker); then each function is briefly described by detailing responsibilities held, action taken, and results achieved. Employers' names are subordinated and dates are made inconspicuous. This approach is useful if you have impressive job titles, duties to feature, work experience which cannot be listed in chronological order without large gaps, or a number of jobs from which only some pertain to the position being sought.

3.   SKILLS—This format stresses skills and abilities, regardless of where they were developed. One section lists your three or four strongest skills related to the job you are seeking and then describes what you have done to demonstrate these skills and abilities. You may include a list of your employers, job titles, and dates employed at the end of qualifications described. This approach is especially useful when the actual skills developed are more impressive than the job titles or length of experience and when your skills have been developed through unpaid activities.

4.   IMAGINATIVE—This type includes the same information as the other formats but structures it individually. Most suited for people seeking creative or artistic positions, this approach presents qualifications while showing the applicant's artistic skills.

Resume Assignment

1. Prepare a current resume that reflects your actual experience. You may include honors you received and organizations you joined in high school.

2. Locate an actual job announcement in a field which you would like to pursue as a career after graduation. If you haven't decided on your life's vocation, you should simply find a job that represents a potential career. On the Internet you can begin your search at www.jobweb.org.

3. Create an ideal resume that you would like to submit in applying for this job. The experiences and activities you include must be legitimate. You might want to inquire about possible internships with Career Development, leadership positions with SGA, or honorary organizations with your major advisor.

4. Write a cover letter to send with your ideal resume. Consult www.jobweb.org/catapult/jsguides.htm for advice on writing the cover letter.

Instructions: Evaluate the following resumes and identify potential problem area.

412 Scottish Way
Tartan, AL 35777
Phone: 205.555.5555
E-mail: sjwilling@samford.edu

Samuel J. Willingham

Objective	An entry level position as a financial officer
Education	1996-2000 Samford University Birmingham, AL B.A. Banking and Finance (3.85/4.00)
Honors	Summa Cum Laude Phi Beta Kappa
Activities	Student Association Government Vice President Sigma Nu Fraternity Associate Editor, The Crimson (student newspaper)
Language	French (fluent)
Work Experience	1997 Bank of London London, England Intern for European Banking Branch • Intern of the Year (Selected from 74 Interns) • Helped mediate transfer of funds arrangements with emerging bank industry in Balkans
Service	Habitat for Humanity YWCA Afterschool Tutoring Program Meals on Wheels
References	Available on Request

Anthony Girardello

8986 Ridgepoint Boulevard
Baltimore, Maryland 22442
Home Phone: 256-5555

Job Objective: To find fulfilling job in company in which I can attain my goals and
further my skills

Education

Sapulpa Junior High   Principle: Harold Peck
Melanta, Vermont   Graduated: 1985
(802) 313-4763   Studied English, Math, etc.
Received Best Center Award on Sapulpa Fightin' Ice Warriors in 1985

Rosemont High School   Principle: Roberta Wright
Seneca, MA   Graduated: 1989
(413) 847-0827   Took college-track courses
Honored for athletic and academic honors as sophomore in 1987.

Acalde Community College   President: Dr. Owen
Laner, NH   Graduated: 1991
(603) 897-9765   Associate of Biology
Took the following: HIS 312, HIS 313, NUR 346, BUS 219, BIO 101, BIO 210,
BIO 312,
ACC 113, MAT 222, MAT 311, REA 266, NUR 117

New Hampshire State   President: Dr. Gorgias
Hanford, New Hampshire   Currently enrolled
(603) 263-4529   Attending 5 courses/week
Completed many courses for a degree in general science. Completed many
intramural activities

Employment

Belford Herald Times   Superviser: Jody Massey
Belford Vermont   Began: June 1, 1982
(802) 417-0927   Terminated: August 19, 1983
Delivered newspaper on bicycle. Route covered approximately 6 miles.

Sammy's Auto Part's and Repair   Owner: Big Sammy Stallings
Seneca, MA   Began: Sept. 1, 1988
(413) 847-9274   Terminated: Decem. 16, 1988
Stocked parts for GM, Ford, and Chrysler vehicles, inspected cars and trucks for
emission standards, changed batteries and alternators, assisted in minor
automotive engine repairs.

Hotshot Pizza House   Superviser: Tommy Denman
Laner, NH   Worked Seminers, 1991 & 1992
(603) 927-8763   Terminated: Went out of business
Delivered pizzas hot to residential customers throughout surrounding Laner area, business cutomers, and students at my college. I also prepared ingredients, cooked pizzas, calzones, and bread sticks, and served food within the rest. Operated cash register and credit card machine. Cleaned rest. at night after closing.

Currently unemployed while finishing school.

Personal

Am of presentable appearance. 5' 9", 163 lbs., dishwater blond hair, hazel eyes. Enjoy (1) Workout at Gold's gym, (2) time with friends renting movies, (3) dating. Marriage in imminent future.

p.s. I am a hard worker who has experience in many areas of business as indicated by the above resume. Please call me at number above. Will travel.

Cover Letter

You cover letter is essentially an introduction to your resume. Functionally, it isn't very different than walking into an interview and having to discuss your background. You would want to give an interviewer a general overview of your experience and qualifications rather than delve into all of the specifics. You would want to emphasize two or three of your accomplishments that might distinguish you from other applicants. Your cover letter is an opportunity for employers to see that you know how to address what is most important in your background as well as an opportunity to show some of your professional qualities. Other than poor writing, the most dangerous mistake you can make in a cover letter is summarizing your entire background.

The cover letter is also an appropriate place to show that you know something about the company you are applying to and are aware of its needs. You don't want an employer to think you are blindly applying to every job you see advertised. And in general, it is wise for you to avoid applying for jobs when you don't meet the advertised requirements. You should consider the following questions before you write your cover letter:

Q: Do I have to write a cover letter?

A: Yes, you should write a cover letter for every position. If the job ad doesn't ask for a cover letter or says "Send resume only," that means the employer doesn't want you to send ancillary materials like transcripts. It doesn't mean you shouldn't send a cover letter.

Q: Should I take into consideration the aesthetic qualities of the cover letter?

A: Yes, your cover letter should be visually appealing and professional. That means you should use standard 8-1/2 by 11 inch white, ivory, or gray paper. You can find this paper in office supply stores under "Resume Paper." You should avoid using the standard white paper you find in copy machines and printers. Times New Roman 11 or 12 pt. font is an appropriate choice of font style. Clever graphics on a cover letter tell a potential employer that you are either unable to make even the simplest of professional decisions or that you are insecure about your qualifications. You might own some cute stationery covered with images of Scottish Terriers but it is inappropriate for job application materials.

Q: Is it okay to simply write a form letter and change the address?

A: No, you should personalize each cover letter. This is time consuming, but you are trying to present yourself as a professional who cares about your career. One of the dangers of simply changing the address on a cover letter is the possibility of forgetting to also change the salutation.

Q: What is the appropriate tone and writing style for a cover letter?

A: A cover letter should be written in a plain but formal style, much like what you are reading right now. Avoid using a lot of multisyllabic words unless they are technical terms. You should avoid trying to impress someone with your vocabulary or skill with a thesaurus. Your letter should be as active as possible, using verbs like "coordinated," "managed," and "designed." Most employers would find third person obtrusive and arrogant. It is best to use first person in a cover letter.

Q: Is it really a big deal if I have a typo in my cover letter or resume?

A: Yes, it is extremely important that you proofread your cover letter and resume. You will be merely one of the lucky if an employer doesn't immediately reject application materials with careless mistakes.

Q: Is it okay to use correction fluid if I make a mistake?

A: No, you should fix any errors on your word processor and reprint the letter.

Q: What should I say about the position I am applying for?

A: You should show an interest in the position and avoid suggesting you simply want to apply for general employment. Employers want to know that you are interested in a specific position.

Q: Can I include other interesting information that might catch an employer's attention, even if it has nothing to do with the position?

A: No, even if you are trained in CPR, the employer is only interested in your qualifications most applicable to the job in question. You shouldn't see the cover letter or resume as an opportunity to show off.

Q: Isn't it a good idea to catch someone's attention with a joke or amusing story?

A: While it might be appropriate in a speech, it isn't in a cover letter. Typically you haven't met the potential employer, so you should remain polite and professional.

Q: How long should my cover letter be?

A: Your cover letter should be no more than a page. This means you should limit the letter to three or four paragraphs.

Q: How should I conclude the letter?

A: You should conclude the letter by thanking the employer for his or her time and by requesting an interview. It is generally a good idea to tell the employer that you are available at his or her convenience, and you should never demand an interview or imply that you expect one. It is also wise to make sure you have given appropriate ways to contact you: telephone numbers and e-mail addresses.

Q: If I have some weaknesses, isn't it a good idea to show I'm not perfect?

A: No, you want to avoid emphasizing flaws; they only give an employer an excuse to dismiss your application. The employer already knows you aren't perfect, and will probably ask you about weaknesses in an interview.

Q: How much should I try to sell myself?

A: You want to emphasize your strengths, but you should avoid making bold demands like: "You really should hire me; you won't regret it." Allow your strengths to argue on your behalf.

Q: How much personal information should I include?

A: In general, it is best to avoid giving any personal information (age, race, height and weight, marital status, religion) unless it is relevant to the position you are seeking.

Instructions: Evaluate the following cover letters and identify potential problem areas. Revise the cover letters to solve these problems.

Box 0000
Samford University
Birmingham, AL 35229

Elizabeth O'Bryan
Controller
A Horse is a Horse, Inc.
1140 Quarterhorse Way
Lexington, KY 40588

Dear Ms. O'Bryan:

I would like to apply for the position as cost accounting manager you recently advertised in the *Lexington Herald*.

I will graduate in May with a 3.25 grade point average, and my college record demonstrates I have a long record of success in a variety of leadership positions. I have also been fortunate to gain experience in a variety of internships in the accounting profession. I believe I am very qualified for this position.

My course work at Samford encompassed not only my required accounting courses, but elective courses in Business Writing, Web Design, and Business Management. I have taken a variety of courses for my English minor in order to better develop my communication skills. My experience working for the Bank of London during a semester overseas has, no doubt, broadened my understanding of international business relations.

I have enclosed my resume, which includes a good summary of my experiences at Samford. I am available at your convenience should you want to schedule an interview. Please contact me at the above address or (205) 555-5555 or sspector@samford.edu. Thank you for your consideration.

Sincerely,

Stanley Spector
Enc. resume

Cindy Partidge
Owner
Travel Express, Enc.
1140 Main Street
New London, CT 06320

Dear Mrs. Appleby:

I am applying for your position as travel agent.

On my resume, you will notice I have lots of experience in SGA, Crimson, Band, Chorale, intermural sports, and BSU. I have also taken many courses that could help me in this job. I have taken all the business course in my major. I took Communication Arts I and II were I learned communication skills valuable for the position in which you are advertising. Additionally, I have a lot of experience in the travel industry. I recently spent six weeks at a Christian camp in Colorado. I have also been to Antigua, Barbados, Guyana, Jamaica, Trinidad, Tobago, Barbuda, Dominica, Grenada, Montserrat, Saint Kitts, Saint Lucia, and Saint Vincent as part of a cruise which helped me to see first hand some important parts of the tourism trade. I was fortunate to interview some of the crew to gain valuable insights into tourism. I like to travel and would like the chance to travel more as a travel agent..

Additionally, I have worked three summers for the Pelham Chamber of Commerce on increasing tourism to the greater Pelham area, I have benifited greatly from this experience.

Please call me at 555-5555 for an interview.

Sincerely,
Dixon Solomon

Section Review

1. Describe each of the different types of resumes.

   _____

   _____

2. Do you have to write a cover letter? Why?

   _____

   _____

3. What are some important considerations about the appearance of your cover letter?

   _____

   _____

4. What are the dangers of writing a form letter?

   _____

   _____

5. What is the appropriate tone and writing style for a cover letter?

   _____

   _____

6. Why is it so important to proofread your cover letter and resume?

   _____

   _____

7. What should you do if you make a mistake in your cover letter or resume?

   _____

   _____

8. What should you say about the position you are applying for?

_____

_____

9. What do you do if you have some interesting personal information you'd like to include in the cover letter?

_____

_____

10. How long should a cover letter be?

_____

_____

11. What is a good way to conclude a cover letter?

_____

_____

Chapter

IX

Media Literacy

Media Journal

To provide an opportunity to:

- Identify your own media-usage patterns;
- React to and evaluate various media messages, practices, and effects.

1. For several days, log and analyze your own media usage. Assume a broad definition of media. Include your clock radio in the morning, bumper stickers, posters, T-shirts, etc. What kind of media consumer are you?

2. Interview three people who fit in a common demographic group (peers, faculty, staff, etc.) and determine their media usage. Do group members have similar media habits and/or tastes? Be specific.

3. Using one medium, determine its demographic audience. In TV and radio, study one specific daypart. For magazines and newspapers, study several consecutive issues. Why did you choose a particular medium?

4. Compare a common news story in two different publications. Look for differences in language, photographs/graphics, style, bias, placement, etc.

5. Compare a common news story in your local paper with one on a local newscast. Again, look for commonalities and differences.

6. Compare a common advertisement in a print publication with one on TV. Who is the target audience? Demographics?

7. Write a letter to the editor of the *Crimson* about some aspect of its coverage—or lack—of an issue/event. Focus on the paper's coverage, rather than the issue/event itself.

8. Write a letter to the editor of the *Crimson* about some aspect of the media. For example, express your concern regarding TV violence, questionable advertising, censorship, etc.

TV News Analysis

In *Amusing Ourselves to Death: Public Discourse in the Age of Show Business*, Neil Postman makes a brief list of the attributes that he feels make the format of televised newscasts serve the purpose of entertainment rather than delivering coherent, serious information, including the "exciting music that opens and closes the show, the vivid film footage, the attractive commercials." How much of the following is oriented to delivering news and how much to entertain?

1. The hosts: Do they fit the appearance of "sincerity, authenticity, vulnerability, attractiveness"? Do they influence the viewer's attitude about the serious news they report?

2. Music: When is it used? What emotions does it try to evoke? What is the purpose of theme music?

3. The stories: What is the length of each story? Do trivial stories get as much or more time than serious ones? How much time is spent on the relevant part of a story versus the drama/sensational aspect of the events (i.e., recreating/retelling the actions that might have taken place in a crime? Do the stories deal with complex social issues, or do they focus on dramatic ones? Is there any context or background information given with a story? What would the average viewer not know about a particular subject that the story leaves out?

4. The film footage: Is the footage necessary for the viewer to understand a story? Is the drama of the footage the main reason the story was aired?

5. Juxtaposition: Back-to-back placement of serious and trivial news stories. What effect does this have?

6. "Teasers": Upcoming stories, either in the current broadcast or in future news shows; Station "promos"—ads for the station, news show, or stories in upcoming broadcasts.

7. Weather/Medical/Stock Market news: Of what use or interest to the average viewer?

8. Sports/Entertainment/Celebrity/Shopping/Fashion "news": What is being promoted in reports on these? Of what interest to the average viewer? Call-in opinion polls: Do they have any news value?

9. "Human interest" stories ("puff pieces"): heroic deeds, bloopers, animals. These are almost always at the end of the broadcast—why?

TV Advertising Analysis

1. Provide a short description of the ad—colors, layout, text, etc.

2. What is the purpose of the ad? Does it try to create a market for a new product? Build brand loyalty? Create positive associations with an organization or company? Prompt immediate action? You are not limited to those choices.

3. Who is the target audience? Local? National? Age? Gender? Income? Lifestyle?

4. What techniques are used to capture the audience's attention? Images? Music? Slogans? Jingles? Trademarks or logos? Clever twists on audience expectations? Humor? Drama? Voice-over narration? Celebrity endorsements? Associations with famous or historic places, people, or events?

5. What appeals are made to the audience? Status? Better health? Physical pleasure? Altruism? Friendship? Safety?

6. What mood does the ad create? The "good life?" Adventurous? Domestic? Outrage? Nostalgic? Public spiritedness? Comic? Serious? Trendy? Old fashioned?

7. What evidence does the ad use to support the claims being made? Is the evidence implied (someone dressed like a physician advocating the use of a particular analgesic) or direct (percentage of doctors advocating the analgesic)? Is the evidence suspect in any way? Does the evidence support the claim?

8. How successful will this ad be in reaching its target audience? Rate the ad on the following items with five being the highest:

5 4 3 2 1 Creating a memorable impression (need not be pleasant)

5 4 3 2 1 Establishing product identity

5 4 3 2 1 Having a strong aesthetic appeal

5 4 3 2 1 Achieving its overall purpose

Magazine Advertisement Analysis

Write a paragraph in which you analyze an ad from a magazine. Address the following issues:

1. Identify the name and nature of the product. Indicate what kind of argument the ad makes (logical, illogical, both). Does the ad attempt logic and then slip into logical fallacies?

2. What kinds of appeals does the ad make? What basic drive or desire does it try to tap: sex, status, wealth, ego, belonging, security, fears, curiosity, self-fulfillment?

3. What is the target audience for this ad? Consider the magazine it appeared in, the price range, the level of the appeal (i.e., sex, security, fears, are more basic than status).

4. Are there logical fallacies in the ad? How does the advertiser use this fallacious reasoning? Is it deliberate, an attempt to manipulate? Do arrangement, color, typeset, or other factors help get these meanings across?

TURN IN THE AD OR A PHOTOCOPY WITH YOUR PARAGRAPH.

Name: _____

Section: _____

Date: _____

Advertising Analysis

....

Examine the following techniques in a magazine advertisement:

A.   Emotional Appeals/Psychological Tricks
1.   Promises
2.   Identification
3.   Flattery

B.   Deception
1.   False Implications
2.   Ambiguity
3.   Fineprint Takeback
4.   Inconsistency
5.   Bait and Switch

C.   Jargon
1.   Meaningless Slogans
2.   Scientific/Technical/Statistical Jargon
3.   Evaluative Words

D.   Suggestive and Emphatic Imagery
1.   Color
2.   Texture
3.   Sex

E.   Fallacious Reasoning

F.   Manipulation of Statistics

G.   Figurative Language and Style

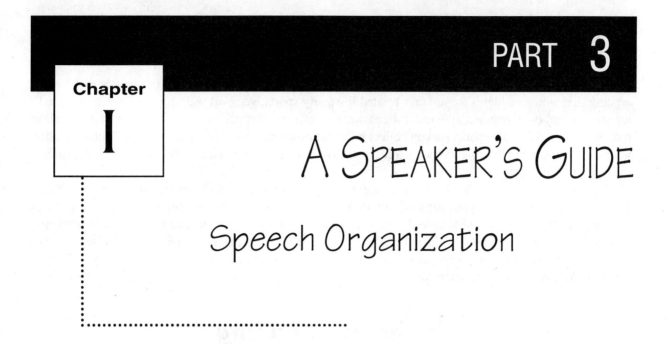

Chapter

1

A SPEAKER'S GUIDE

Speech Organization

Writing and speaking are both integrated within Communication Art 101 and 102 because they incorporate many of the same broad communication skills. However, there are accommodations which must be made in transforming a piece of written communication to a speaking/listening situation. This section focuses on these special considerations and touches on listening skills, speech delivery, interviewing, small group communication, and special occasion speaking as well.

Oral communication shares many common features with written communication. Indeed, the study of rhetoric, the principles that underly effective communications, has traditionally made little distinction between written and spoken discourse. This is one of the reasons that Communication Arts has combined the study of these two areas. In most cases, both writing and speaking are involved in any successful communication activity. We typically discuss our ideas with each other orally before producing a written document. After it is written, the document will often be reviewed by others in an open discussion. This is not to say that there are not important differences in oral and written communication, but it is important to understand the similarities as well as the differences in these two modes of communication.

One of the ideas that is important to both oral and written discourse is the rhetorical triangle. We typically think of discourse (the spoken word or the written text) being shaped by three major influences: the self, the subject, and the audience.

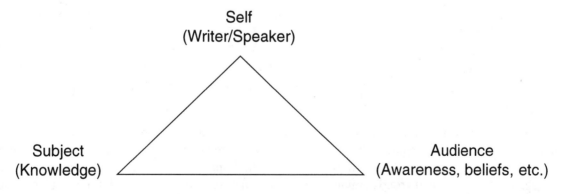

For instance, if you are asked to give a speech for your class, your choice of topic would be influenced by your background and interests. If you are an athlete, you will be more likely to speak on issues related to the athletic program than someone who has no interest in sports—this is the "self" dimension of the rhetorical triangle.

You will also be influenced by the subject matter you have chosen to discuss. For instance, if you are arguing that women athletes are unfairly treated in varsity sports, you will want to do research on Title IX legislation, interview women athletes and coaches on campus, and perhaps survey fellow students about their interest in women's sports. As you collect information about your subject, this will undoubtedly affect your own ideas about the role women's athletics plays in campus life. This is the "subject" dimension of the rhetorical triangle.

The third dimension of the rhetorical triangle that helps shape your discourse is the audience. What do people already know about your subject? You don't want to bore your audience with the repetition of well known ideas. Furthermore, what attitude does your audience have toward the subject? Are they supportive of women's athletics or hostile toward them? If your audience has a negative opinion of your subject, you will probably need more evidence and more persuasive arguments to bring them around to your way of thinking. You will find more information about audience analysis in a later section of this handbook.

Types of Speaking

The rhetorical situation (who is speaking to whom and for what purpose) varies widely depending on how many people are involved. One-to-one communication (called *dyadic*) is usually short, spontaneous, and interactive. Dyadic communication would include casual conversation in the cafeteria, a job interview with a prospective employer, or a meeting of the President with a visiting Prime Minister. Another important area of rhetorical studies is group communication. You will frequently find yourself assigned to groups in your Communication Arts classes for various purposes: to discuss each others' papers, to engage in problem solving, to make presentations. Like dyadic communication, group discussion tends to be spontaneous and interactive. However, having several members in a group makes the communication flow more complex and the role to be fulfilled by each member more demanding than informal dyads. Studying the section "Working in Small Groups" can make you more effective in your role as a group participant.

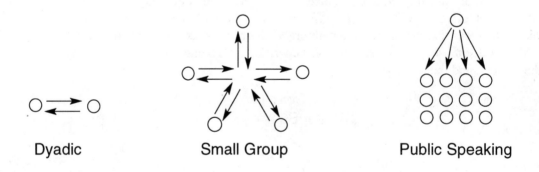

Dyadic   Small Group   Public Speaking

One of the most visible forms of oral communication is public address. Unlike the more formal and interactive forms of communication, a public speech tends to be an occasion that requires careful planning and rehearsed performance. You will probably be called upon less often to give a public speech than to engage in dyadic or small group communication, but when you do give a speech for a large audience, there are generally much higher expectations for your performance. This is only natural since many people have given up their time to hear your speech. In your Communication Arts class you'll have the opportunity to refine your speaking skills in a supportive environment of your own peers. If you excel at public speaking, you may have an opportunity to speak before a larger audience in the Communication Arts Speech Contest.

These three forms of communication—dyadic, small group, and public speaking—will all be practiced in your Communication Arts classes. As you continue to refine your skills you will be come more confident and more accomplished in different communication settings.

Speech Organization

Most of the speaking assignments in Communication Arts are tied to an essay assignment. While issues such as topic choice, purpose, and audience have usually been dealt with in writing the essay, you might wonder, "How do I now turn my essay into a speech?" While many considerations of speech organization are the same as for essay organization—like essays, speeches need an introduction, a body, and a conclusion—there are some differences that must be addressed in transforming even a good essay into a successful speech. Making memorable introductions and conclusions, clearly signposting points within the speech and transitioning between those points, and clarifying syntax and diction are of particular importance to making a good speech. Though audience was dealt with in writing the essay and might have been different from the class audience, the real world audience for the speech is the class. No matter how far the speaker asks the class audience to role play, accommodations have to be made if that real time, classroom presentation is to be a successful one.

The Body
Because the body comprises the bulk of the speech, it is a good place to begin discussing organization. With a specific speech purpose and thesis in mind, you should break the material into two to five main points. Realistically, with the length of speeches assigned in Communication Arts, you should limit your speech to no more than two to three points. This raises an immediate challenge if you are changing a written essay to a speech format, as the typical speech length in Communication Arts is three-to-six minutes while the average essay length is three-to-six pages. When double-spaced, a typed page of text is read at normal speaking rate in approximately two to two-and-a-half minutes. Therefore, a three-page essay would take roughly six to nine minutes to read. Not only is it impossible to read your speech, it is undesirable to do so. Reading a speech tends to make the material dull and lifeless. More information about methods of delivery is in the next section of this guide.

The most common speech organizational patterns or orders are **chronological, spatial, logical,** and **motivational** (organizational patterns also used in writing). Typically, the body of the speech predominantly follows one of these orders though other orders may be incorporated to some degree within portions of the speech.

Chronological
Chronological order is simply time order. Any time you relate an event—as in the autobiography assignment—or share an anecdote, you are using chronological order. Journalism, personal letters, e-mails, and journals are typically written in chronological order. For the concept assignment, you might choose a topic that requires dealing with a historical period or some explanation of a process, which, of course, involves chronological order. There are specific words and phrases you need to remember—in writing or speaking—that signal chronological order: then, later, next, afterwards, meanwhile, before, immediately, first, second, at the same time, all of a sudden, now, and finally, etc.

Spatial
Spatial order organizes based on physical space or geography. In a speech on changing climate patterns, you might divide your essay geographically into world hemispheres or continents. Spatial order is often appropriate for topics that are descriptive. Spatial organization enables the listening audience to "see" the information and fix it in space.

Logical

Logical organization is a broader category that includes several patterns: illustration, definition, comparing and contrasting, dividing and classifying, analyzing causes and effects, and considering problems and solutions. The first three of these should be the most familiar. To illustrate is to use example. Defining is saying what something is and often what something is not. Comparing is finding similarities while contrasting is showing differences. Dividing is simply breaking a single topic or point into parts and then using definition to label those parts before discussing them. Classifying is grouping similar items together; essentially you are setting up "files" for the listening audience and categorizing information by points within the speech. Dividing and classifying are sometimes referred to as topical organization.

The last of these two logical patterns—analyzing causes and effects and considering problems and solutions, are more common in the persuasive essays and speeches of Communication Arts 102 than in the more autobiographical and informative essays you will write in Communication Arts 101 though you might incorporate them to some degree in writing the autobiography, observation, reflection, and concept assignments. Causal analysis is an organizational pattern that moves either from cause to effect or effect to cause. A speaker seeks to deal with some known activity or condition and convince the audience that it will produce a certain effect or prove that it has a certain cause. The problem-solution pattern seeks to address an ongoing problem and to present a solution to that problem. In this organizational pattern you will typically define the problem first and then persuade the audience that your solution is best.

Motivational

Motivational organization—a specific type of problem solving pattern—involves addressing some need of the listening audience, presenting a solution to that need, helping the audience visualize that need, and defining what actions the audience must take to fulfill the need.

Introductions and Conclusions

Audiences tend to remember the beginning and end of a speech. Given that, you will want to take full advantage in creating memorable, well-developed, purposeful introductions and conclusions that enhance the body of the speech. Your introduction needs to get the audience's attention, clearly present the topic you are covering, build your credibility, show a reason or need to listen, establish the significance of the topic, and lead smoothly into the body by previewing the points to be covered. Just as you want to include a "hook" in the opening paragraph of an essay, you must grab the listening audience's attention in the opening seconds of a speech. Very often the introduction is a place of adjustment in moving an essay to a speech. What works on the written page isn't quite energizing enough for a speaking situation.

Ways to Catch the Audience's Attention

1.   Ask a direct or rhetorical question.

2.   Stimulate the audience's curiosity or imagination. This is often done through the use of anecdotes or snapshots. Anecdotes are brief stories, usually about a particular event; snapshots are brief descriptions. This technique is especially applicable in the observation assignment. Startling statements also serve to pique the audience's curiosity.

3.   Address a need of the audience or promise them something beneficial.

4.   Use humor. It must be tied to the content of the speech, and it must not be ethnic, sexist, or off-color in nature. Review the section on Discriminatory Language. With these cautions in mind, humor can be a highly effective way to open a speech.

5. Use a quotation. This can enhance the speaker's credibility if the quote is from someone highly regarded as a sage or expert.

6. Refer to the audience, occasion, or current events. This helps the audience to see that the speaker has taken them into account in preparing the speech.

Other Functions of a Speech Introduction

1. Clearly state the topic. It only takes a few seconds, but it is vitally important.

2. Establish your credibility. If you have expertise on a topic, mention it.

3. Give a reason to listen. This is more applicable to the Communication Arts 102 assignments because of their persuasive nature, but if your topic taps into some need of the audience, present it up front.

4. Preview your key ideas. Like the thesis of an essay, previewing the key ideas of a speech "tells us what you're going to tell us" in the introduction. A listening audience cannot control the rate of information a speaker gives them, and they cannot go back and reread a sentence or paragraph as they can in an essay. Therefore, it is imperative that you forecast your main points so your audience knows what to listen for.

Conclusions

Speech conclusions serve many of the same purposes of essay conclusions. They should:

1. Leave the audience satisfied that a full discussion has taken place.

2. They should tie the speech together and provide a strong note of finality or closure. Often summary is used. Because nonverbal communication is so important to a message's content, you should mark the end of the speech by slowing your speaking rate, maintaining direct eye contact, and pausing briefly before and after the final sentence uttered.

3. Conclusions provide the last opportunity for you to impress your message upon the audience's minds and to create desired effects.

A common way to provide closure is to return to something said in the introduction. Many of the techniques mentioned above for grabbing the audience's attention can be used in speech conclusions, though you augment the techniques through nonverbal behavior so that instead of grabbing attention, you impress the message upon the audience, leaving them something to think about after the speech is finished.

Signposting and Transitioning

Signposts indicate the main divisions of a speech. The simplest way to signpost your speech is to enumerate your main points ("The first phase of American democracy was . . ."). Sometimes speakers use catchy phrases to signpost their speeches:

> In order to understand the importance of cancer research, you need to know the *causes* of cancer, the *cost* of research, and the potential for a *cure*.

Whenever you move from one idea to another in the speech, you will need to supply a transitional statement. For instance:

> As we better understand the causes of cancer, it becomes apparent why cancer research is so costly. These costs include basic research funding, experimental studies, and medical technology.

Transitional statements are vital for a listening audience to understand where you have been in the speech and where you are going. The most common conjunction or transition in spoken American English is "and," which is often used to string sentences together. In talking we sometimes use vocal qualities such as tone of voice, pitch, rate, and volume, as well as nonverbal behaviors like facial expression, eye contact, posture, and gestures as a substitute for precision in language. But just as in essay writing, "and" is usually not the best transitional device in giving a speech. As a speaker you want to use every tool you can to successfully communicate. Why use "and," which sets up a parallel construction, when what you really want to do is show comparison, contrast, or a logical relationship? *A Writer's Reference* has a list of common transitions on page 35, which are as invaluable in speaking as in writing. It is crucial that you clearly transition with word choice from point to point within the body of a speech, but also from the introduction to the body and from the body to the conclusion. You should also signal changes in direction through vocal inflection, through physically moving (even if it is simply a matter of shifting weight from one foot to the other), and holding up fingers to indicate points within the body of the speech. Visual aids can also help with signposting. Turning to a new page on a flip chart or changing slides in a PowerPoint presentation clearly signals progression to a new point.

Outlining

Many Communication Arts instructors require formal or informal outlines for speeches and essays. See *A Writer's Reference*, pages 11–13, for outlining guidelines. The sample outline below is meant to show you a potential way of organizing a speech outline. Remember though, that different speeches require different organizational patterns.

A Sentence Outline for a Concept Speech

Speech Title: Understanding Abstract Expressionism

Specific purpose: To inform the audience of the concept of abstract expressionism.

Thesis statement: Abstract expressionism has changed how artists express themselves and how viewers examine art.

Introduction:
An American art movement that expressed the feelings and frustrations of artists through gestures and motion occurred during the 1940s and 50s. Abstract expressionism began to change how artists expressed themselves and how viewers examined art. A new way of painting and thinking hit America head on.

Discussing this type of work with other students usually results in comments such as, "That's art? Looks like a two-year-old did it!" Students must be exposed to this art movement and understand that abstract expressionism has been the fastest growing art in history and is continuing to spread today. Therefore, even if one does not enjoy abstract art, one needs to be educated about it because it is becoming a part of everyday culture.

Body:

I. The description of abstract expressionism varies.
    A. Different styles are brought out in abstract art.
    B. Abstract art emphasizes spontaneous personal expression; not representational or narrative.

II. There have been important influences on abstract art and expressionists.
    A. The base of abstract art is color.
    B. Expressive tendencies in painting came from well-known artists.
        1. Van Gogh led inspiration for other artists.
        2. Gauguin focused on creativity with color.

(Present 1st Visual Aid to Class)

III. Society often has a negative outlook on abstract art.
    A. Abstraction has been proven to be a problematic concept.
    B. Abstract art has been described as offensive and as a joke.
    C. Abstraction is a nonobjective art.

IV. Skill is evident in abstract art.
    A. Abstract art is a challenge.
    B. Artists use creative imagination.
    C. Latest trends in today's society display abstract expressionism.

(Present 2nd Visual Aid to Class)

Conclusion:

Abstract expressionism has influenced and inspired greater artistic activity and achievement. Without abstract art, one would not be able to express his or her emotional condition to the fullest because he or she would be tied down with tradition. This form of art has and will bring joy to both the artist and viewer of the past, present, and future.

Bibliography:
Landau, Ellen G. *Jackson Pollack*. New York: Abrams, 1989.
Lynton, Norbert. *The Modern World*. New York: McGraw-Hill, 1965.

Chapter

II

Audience Analysis

Audience Analysis

Audience analysis is a fundamental and basic step in preparation for any rhetorical act. Even as you begin to select a topic for your speech, you must be aware of the audience you will address. Audience should determine much about your topic and the types of supporting materials you use. Knowledge of the audience should influence what you communicate and how that information is communicated. Initially, we must examine what makes up an audience.

Karlin Kohrs Campbell outlines four types of audiences in her book *The Rhetorical Act*:

Empirical Audience
The empirical audience is comprised of people exposed directly to the speech or performance. For example, if a politician speaks to journalists in a press conference, those members of the press make up the empirical audience.

Target Audience
Each time you stand up to speak you choose a target audience. This is the audience you seek to persuade, inform, or entertain. For example, a politician speaking at a press conference might address the American public, even if the politician is speaking directly to members of the press.

Agents of Change
Additionally, you should consider how you communicate with agents of change. Agents of change may or may not be the empirical or target audience, but they are the individuals who can accomplish the desired action. For example, an activist calling for reform might speak to the public and call for his or her audience to seek action from Congress. In this case, Congress is the agent of action the activist seeks to influence.

Particular Roles
Finally, you might cast your audience in particular roles. For example, lawyers and judges ask twelve normal citizens to play the role of jurors in order to decide an issue of the law. While there might be carpenters, plumbers, or teachers in the jury box, all twelve are asked to adjudicate the trial as fair and impartial jurors.

An understanding of the different types of audiences is important when you begin to analyze an audience. A few questions necessarily arise. What is the goal of my speech or essay? Who are the specific people I want to persuade, inform, or entertain? What actions do I want the audience to take? What audiences will I be addressing? In other words, you look for the desired end to be achieved in the act of communication and those who will be addressed during that act. For example, when President Clinton speaks in front of Congress and others in his State of the Union address, he carefully considers the audience gathered in Washington, D.C. He also analyzes the way his other target audience, the public, will perceive the words he speaks. This affects the manner in which Clinton gives his speech and the types of proposals he makes.

After analyzing the goals of the speech, you should begin with a few fundamental observations of the audience. The purpose of the audience's gathering is central. Is the audience a voluntary meeting of a group or is it a captive audience? Is the audience happy about the occasion or filled with dread? Understanding the reason for gathering will indicate how much justification of the rhetorical act you must do. For example, teachers must often explain the relevancy of a topic to their classes, but an explanation of relevancy would be unnecessary in an infant CPR class for young parents. Generally speaking, a voluntary, happy audience will require less of the speaker or writer than a captive, worried, or disgruntled audience will (Zarefsky, 1996).

You should further examine your audience in at least two ways. Every speaker should attempt a demographic analysis and a psychological analysis. Initially, you need to understand the demographic nature of your audience. This includes age, gender, education, occupation, and ethnic background, etc. You should look for groups the audience members feel allegiance to and ways in which the audience identifies itself. As you read in the section on discriminatory language, it is important that you avoid offending the audience. This doesn't mean that they should always agree with you, but you don't want to drive them away before they've even had a chance to listen. For example, if you find yourself speaking to an audience that views itself as a distinct ethnic group in the United States, you could avoid offending the audience by avoiding patriotic, jingoistic, or nationalistic remarks. Additionally, you could create a common understanding by demonstrating awareness of any unique concerns of the audience.

You should also analyze the psychology of your audience. How large will the audience be? Where will the speech be given? What are the attitudes of the audience towards the speaker? This should allow you to regulate the time spent establishing credibility, help you make decisions concerning speaking style, and provide clues about necessary types of proof. For example, if you know you will be addressing a capacity crowd in a large auditorium, you should use a more formal style.

Putting audience analysis into practice requires effort before, during, and after a performance. You must gather information through observation, interviews, or more formal methods. You must analyze the data and look for trends in the audience. Additionally, you must use that information to prepare the speech. While time-consuming and at times laborious, this work should allow you to make decisions about evidence, choose a style, choose a specific topic, make connections with the audience, and avoid offensive practices.

Here is an example of a basic speech analysis:

Speech Topic: My Trip to Egypt
Audience Analysis: Maple Hills Retirement Center
Age: 65 and older
Gender: primarily female
Education: mostly high school and above
Occupation: varied, but more professional, clerical, and service occupations than skilled trades
Ethnicity: primarily white
Religion: primarily Methodist, but includes other Protestant denominations and Catholics.
Income: middle class to affluent

Audience Knowledge: probably some familiarity with pyramids, Nile River, etc.
Audience Interest: general interest in exotic sights
Audience Attitude: no strongly held beliefs for or against

How will this analysis affect my speech?
I will probably need to build audience interest through visuals. Because I am discussing a culture my audience probably has never experienced, I will want to give them a broad sense of the culture—food, language, architecture, religion, art, literature, etc. The audience would probably respond to biblical connections (Moses and the Pharaoh, Joseph and Mary, etc.) Most of the audience would be more interested in history and culture than in tourist information (transportation, hotels, etc.)

Audience Analysis Exercise

Name: _____

Section: _____

Date: _____

Instructions: Using the following speech topics and audience, create the appropriate demographics and analyze the audience.

Speech Topic: The Internet in Public Schools
Audience Analysis: The Pittsfield PTA
Age:
Gender:
Education:
Occupation:
Ethnicity:
Religion:
Income:
Audience Knowledge:
Audience Interest:
Audience Attitude:

How will you tailor your speech for this audience?

_____

_____

_____

_____

_____

_____

_____

_____

_____

_____

_____

Speech Topic: Proposal for a Faculty/Student Colloquium
Audience Analysis: Committee on Academic Awareness, St. Ignatius University
Age:
Gender:
Education:
Occupation:
Religion:
Income:
Audience Knowledge:
Audience Interest:
Audience Attitude:

How will you tailor your speech for this audience?

_____

_____

_____

_____

_____

_____

_____

_____

_____

_____

_____

_____

_____

_____

_____

_____

Speech Topic: The Importance of Public Service
Audience Analysis: COMM102: Communication and Culture
Age:
Gender:
Education:
Occupation:
Ethnicity:
Religion:
Income:
Audience Knowledge:
Audience Interest:
Audience Attitude:

How will you tailor your speech for this audience?

_____

_____

_____

_____

_____

_____

_____

_____

_____

_____

_____

_____

_____

_____

_____

1. Describe the four types of audiences.

_____

_____

_____

_____

_____

_____

_____

_____

_____

_____

2. Why is it important to know the audience's purpose in gathering?

_____

_____

3. What are some demographics concerns you should take into consideration?

_____

_____

4. In general, what type of speaking style should you use for a large audience?

_____

_____

Chapter

III

Delivery

Modes of Delivery

When you deliver a speech, you will most often use one of three different methods:

1. Speaking off-the-cuff with little or no preparation (impromptu).
2. Reading from a prepared text.
3. Delivering a memorized speech.
4. Speaking extemporaneously (with notes).

   The first mode of delivery, impromptu speaking, is used sparingly in Communication Arts—most often in self or peer introductions, a quick report regarding progress on an assignment, or as an exercise to help you gain confidence in public speaking. Although the next two modes of delivery, reading from a manuscript and delivering memorized speeches, certainly have their appropriate uses, speaking extemporaneously is usually the most effective type of public speaking and will certainly be the best for your speeches in Communication Arts and other classes. The extemporaneous mode is the mode that seems the most sincere and relaxed. It allows more audience awareness because you are free to maintain more eye contact with the audience if you are not buried in your notes or searching your memory for a word, phrase, or point. You want to establish a relationship with your audience, and delivering from a script inhibits such a possibility. In public speaking you want to achieve a well-planned speech that sounds very natural—spontaneous. In extemporaneous speaking—though you have prepared beforehand—you select your words as your speak so your audience feels you are connected to them as if you are having a conversation.

Characteristics of Effective Extemporaneous Speaking

Delivered Using Notes

You should avoid writing your entire speech on your note cards. Many students try to fit an entire speech, word for word, on one note card. This is dangerous because you will tend to read anything you have written on your note cards. Every time you look at your notes, you break contact with your audience. Consequently, you will want to avoid writing on the back of your note cards. When you flip note cards you destroy the illusion that you are speaking spontaneously. If you have multiple note cards, you should slide them rather than flip them.

Effective Introductions and Conclusions

Earlier you learned how to write effective introductions and conclusions. Rehearse these more than the rest of the speech. The introduction will begin the process of engaging your audience's attention, and the conclusion will leave them remembering your message.

Natural Sound

Avoid over rehearsing or you will tend to memorize your speech. The best speakers sound very spontaneous, and if you know your main points, you should not have to practice the wording of the speech repeatedly.

Characteristics of Effective Vocal Delivery

Moderate in Speed

Many people speak very quickly, especially when they are nervous. When you speak in front of an audience your adrenaline increases, and this often manifests itself in speaking too quickly. You should make a conscious effort to speak slowly, even if you need to write a reminder on a note card.

Spoken Clearly

Sometimes this is directly related to the rate in which you speak, but often speakers tend to slur their words. They do not *articulate* precisely. *Articulation* is the shaping of speech sounds within words and phrases so that they are recognizable to the listening audience. *Articulation* is often confused with *pronunciation*, the form and accent of various syllables within a word. The most common articulation errors are adding a sound where none should appear (ath*a*lete for athlete), omitting a syllable or letter (li*b*ary for library), transposing sounds (re*v*alent for relevant, mo*dren* for mo*dern*), or distorting sounds (tru*f* for tru*th*). While spoken English will always have some running together of sounds, check to make sure you are not guilty of excessive slurring of words and phrases or of dropping the endings (particular consonants) of words and phrases. Also, if you are using an unfamiliar vocabulary, you may need to check a dictionary for the precise pronunciation of words.

Free of Interjections

Pauses are effective ways to move from one idea to another or to give the audience time to reflect on something you have said. Spend some time working on pausing in your speech and try not to fill in the pauses with interjections such as "um" or "uh" or "like" or "you know."

Avoids Monotony

Be aware of your vocal inflection. Some people speak in a monotone, a voice which contains very little inflection. It is very difficult for an audience to listen to a monotonous voice, and if yours is naturally so, you can work on bringing the pitch of your voice higher and lower, giving it more variety.

Strong Voiced

If the audience can't hear you, your message will be lost. If you have a naturally soft voice, then you may need to work on your volume. One way to make your voice much stronger is to learn to breathe from your diaphragm. Correct breathing will also help with a shaky voice.

Characteristics of Effective Physical Delivery

Appropriately Dressed

For any formal speaking occasion you should carefully consider what you wear. Your clothing will be part of communicating your message, and there are several factors to think about. You should be comfortable in your clothing, and you should wear clothing that is flattering to you. For the types of speeches you will deliver in Communication Arts, you should typically dress casually but professionally. That typically means dress pants and a nice shirt for men and a dress or dress pants and a nice shirt for women. Your instructor will be more specific about what to wear, but you should consider what is appropriate to wear for every speaking situation. You should also be careful about hair style and accessory selections. Hair falling in your face and noisy jewelry can be very distracting to an audience.

Purposeful Gesturing

Your hands and arms are, of course, your gesturing tools. Some people gesture very naturally in their everyday speaking, and others tend not to gesture much. If you can learn to gesture gracefully and naturally, this will enhance your speaking tremendously. When you use gestures, keep two principles in mind: Keep them above the waist and keep them wide. Gestures that are below the waist or too close to the body tend to make a speaker look nervous. If you are not using gestures, keeping your hands loosely by your side is probably best. Never clasp your hands in front of or behind your body, never stick them in your pockets, and never rest them continuously on the podium. Again, these gestures will make you appear nervous.

You should also be careful about fidgeting with your feet, so you should decide to either move deliberately or not at all. If you want to move, don't be afraid to walk away from the podium a bit or even in front of it. The closer you get to your audience, the more self assured you will feel. You should avoid, however, nervous movement with your feet such as swaying or tapping your feet.

Natural and Relaxed Facial Expression

A natural and relaxed facial expression will help communicate your message, but people who are nervous often have a blank expression on their faces. Try to make a conscious effort to smile even if it doesn't come naturally. If you are speaking extemporaneously, your facial expression will tend to be more natural.

Eye Contact

Eye contact is one of the most important elements in effective communication. When you don't look at your audience, you will appear nervous or unprepared or too dependent on your notes. Even if you don't feel confident, making eye contact throughout the room is one way to appear confident. Try to make eye contact with everyone in the room rather than focusing on one or two people.

Name: _____

Section: _____

Date: _____

Pronunciation Exercise

Instructions: What is the correct pronunciation of these words? Write the diacritical markings as they appear in your dictionary. If alternate pronunciations are given, list these as well.

1. epitome

2. vociferous

3. xenophobic

4. pusillanimous

5. diatribe

6. hegemony

7. facile

8. New Orleans

9. insidious

10. loquacious

11. pontificate

12. perspicacious

13. noxious

14. interest

15. anguent

16. legerdemain

17. caesura

18. occidental

19. preternatural

20. clandestine

21. renaissance

22. incorrigible

23. specious

24. voluminous

25. importune

Speech Ethics

Speech Ethics

Ethics can be defined as a system of principles of right and wrong which govern our behavior. At this point, you should have read the section on Plagiarism and Academic Integrity in Part II of *A Student's Guide to Communication Arts*. While the guidelines concerning writing and the use of sources hold true for speeches also, there are some special considerations of ethics in speaking. Four of these areas include attributing credit to sources, building trust and goodwill, revealing true intentions, and discussing both sides of a controversial issue.

A speaking situation varies from a writing one in that credibility is immediately personal. As the writer of an essay, you may be unknown to your reading audience. As a speaker you are directly and immediately connected to the words you use. Many communication experts (including Aristotle in his *Rhetoric*) cite credibility (or character) as perhaps the most important factor in communication, especially in persuasion. Plagiarism—intentionally or unintentionally stealing the ideas of others and presenting them as your own—is not only highly unethical but risks perhaps your most valuable asset as a speaker—your credibility. Plagiarism ranges from outright theft of an outline or entire speech, to borrowing from another student, to splicing together material from several sources without properly attributing credit, to failing to cite sources while presenting the speech. Remember that even though you may have given a bibliography to your instructor, you still must give credit where credit is due when you are delivering the speech. You may be tempted to use ideas or words that are not your own without attributing credit, assuming that no one will be the wiser. However, the consequences can be dire, including the loss of credibility with classmates and the instructor, failure of the course, and even suspension or expulsion from the university.

Using another student's speech outline or speech notes to deliver a speech is tantamount to cheating on an exam or handing in someone else's essay. If an outline or speech notes are willingly given to another student, the original author can face the same penalties as the plagiarist.

In the case of splicing together material from a variety of sources without properly giving credit, you may have actually done a lot of work. Consequently, you may believe that in revealing the material comes from others you will diminish your credibility by showing that others know more than you. In reality, citing sources builds credibility because it shows you have done your homework and that you take into account the ideas of others. In addition to fulfilling an ethical obligation, properly giving credit is one of the best ways to build a sense of good will.

You might also commit plagiarism if you fail to cite sources even though you have turned in a bibliography to your instructor. Plagiarism has occurred because the listening audience cannot distinguish between your ideas and those of others if you have failed to use lead-in or tag phrases to acknowledge sources. If you use a direct quote, you are also obligated to make that clear by either stating that you are using a direct quote or by changing your tone of voice to signal you are using someone else's words: "To quote John F. Kennedy . . ." or "As Ronald Reagan said . . . ," etc.

Building trust and good will does not generally happen in just one speech. In an academic situation you build good will and a reputation for honesty over the course of a semester or entire academic year. Good will is the perception of the audience that you have their needs and best interests at heart. If you are audience-oriented and clearly communicate a desire to serve the audience, you are much more likely to avoid risky ethical situations. Trust refers to the audience's perception that your words are honest and can be believed. You obviously risk your credibility if even one audience member catches you in a lie. Even distorting evidence through omission or changes in context also put you in a position of risking credibility. It is your responsibility to check the validity of your evidence and to represent it truthfully. It is permissible for you to simplify statistics (rounding off complicated numbers, for example), though the integrity of the fact, example, or statistic must be maintained. In light of this discussion, you should reread the sections of *A Student's Guide to Communication Arts* on logical fallacies and evaluating information. An ethical student speaker strives for trust and good will by avoiding these fallacies in speaking and writing.

Along the same lines as truthfulness in speaking is the importance of revealing your true intentions. Failing to reveal intentions or misrepresenting your true intentions is unethical. However, in the case of trying to persuade a hostile audience of a controversial point of view, establishing common ground with the audience may be an effective strategy before moving to areas of disagreement. Establishing what you have in common with the audience before attempting to persuade them to accept your point of view is no guarantee that they will adopt your view, but establishing common ground does create more possibility that you will be given the opportunity to be heard. Again, if you have your audience's needs and best interests at heart, you will be better able to evaluate the best approach to take in order to persuade the audience and, at the same time, maintain trust and good will.

Besides revealing true intentions, you should present both (or in some cases, several) sides of a controversial issue. Many of the same strategies for building an argument in an essay work well within a speech. One of these strategies discussed in *Reading Critically, Writing Well* is counterarguing. You should be informed enough to anticipate your reading or listening audience's potential objections to your argument. At the very least, you should anticipate questions they might ask. You can choose to accommodate your audience's objections or questions by acknowledging them and modifying your argument. Or, you might acknowledge your audience's objections and then refute them. Students sometimes think that bringing up opposing viewpoints will weaken their arguments. However, raising possible audience objections and questions serves to build your credibility and to establish good will with the audience. If you are able to refute opposing viewpoints, then you are more likely to persuade the audience to agree with your point of view.

1. Why is credibility so important in speaking situations?

   _____

   _____

   _____

   _____

2. What are some different ways you can slip into plagiarism in speaking situations?

   _____

   _____

   _____

   _____

3. What are two ways of indicating you are using a direct quote in a speaking situation?

   _____

   _____

4. How do you build trust and good will in speaking situations?

   _____

   _____

5. Why is it important to acknowledge opposing viewpoints in speaking situations?

   _____

   _____

Chapter

V

Special Occasion Speaking

Special Occasion Speaking

Special occasion speaking is a broad category of public speaking which includes speaking-off-the-cuff or impromptu (already covered under methods of delivery), speaking on television, presenting or accepting an award, and speaking to entertain. Eulogies, welcomes, and introductions are also included under the umbrella of special occasion speaking. The types of special occasion speeches you will learn in Communication Arts include imminently practical speaking situations, which even at the undergraduate level, you may be called upon to do outside the classroom. Five types of special occasion speeches commonly covered in Communication Arts are presentation and acceptance of a gift or award, welcome of a speaker or visitor to a ceremony or meeting, toast or speech of tribute, and announcement.

These five examples of special occasion speaking focus not on the speaker, but on someone else, the special occasion itself, or on imparting information to the audience. While extemporaneous speaking is emphasized throughout Communication Arts, in the case of these five examples, speaking from a manuscript is preferable because you don't want to take away from the occasion or diminish the importance of the guest's presence by rambling or stumbling over a name. These five types of special occasion speeches tend to be quite short, ranging from as little as thirty seconds to five minutes, so the "manuscript" may be a single note card. Nevertheless, it is a good idea for you to think through and write out what you wish to say. Over time, socially acceptable "formulas" have developed for each of these types of speaking.

Presentation of a Gift or Award

1. You should state the purpose of the award or recognition.

2. You should focus your speech on the achievements for which the award is being made.

3. You should organize the speech according to whether or not the audience knows the name of the recipient before he or she speaks.

   • If the audience does not know the honoree's name, you should capitalize on their curiosity by withholding the recipient's name until the end, using gender-neutral pronouns so as not to prematurely give away the recipient's identity. Begin with general comments that could apply to anyone, getting more specific as the speech progresses.

- If the audience knows the honoree's name, you should begin the speech with specific comments about the individual and end with general comments that summarize the reasons for the presentation.

4. If you are announcing the winner from a group of nominees, you should briefly compliment the entire group.

Accepting a Gift or Award

1. You should be brief but eloquent.

2. You should be genuine.

3. You should acknowledge the award or honor and, if appropriate, the committee that chose you and the other nominees for the award.

4. You should seek to connect with the audience and engender liking.

Welcome of a Speaker or Visitor

1. You should focus on the visitor or upcoming speaker and not on yourself. The purpose is certainly not to upstage the upcoming speaker or visitor. In fact, you should mention the person's name three times or more in the course of the speech. While this might seem excessive, it is crucial that the audience hear and remember the speaker or visitor's name.

2. You should be brief in your welcome.

3. You should establish the speaker or visitor's credibility. If a visitor is not speaking, you should establish the significance of his or her presence.

4. You should create realistic, not highly inflated expectations for the upcoming speech.

5. You should set the tone for the featured speaker's speech. This will help your audience understand how to react to his or her speech.

Toast or Speech of Tribute

1. You should open and establish the purpose for gathering and paying tribute.

2. You should establish noble themes or grounds for esteem.

3. You should provide vivid examples that explain why the person, group, or event is held in such high esteem.

4. You should try to express what you believe to be the audience's feelings as well as your own.

5. You should seek to create a memorable (but appropriate) image of the person, group, or event.

6. You should be genuine, avoiding excessive sentimentality or emotion.

7. A toast involves a formal call, which is asking for a round of applause or a raising of drinking glasses, etc. It is your responsibility to lead the formal call.

Announcement

1. Your opening should be a succinct statement of the activity.

2. You should state only relevant facts or details.

3. You should appeal for action or support of the activity.

4. You should repeat key facts: what, where, when, who, and cost, slowly and clearly enough for interested listeners to jot these down.

1. In special occasion speaking, why is it acceptable to read from a manuscript?

   _____

   _____

2. When you present a gift or award, what is the first thing you should say to your audience?

   _____

   _____

3. How long is the typical special occasion speech?

   _____

   _____

Chapter

VI

Research Interviewing

Research Interviewing

One often underutilized source of support for your speeches and essays is the research interview. One critical advantage of the interview is that you can get specific and up-to-date information in a timely fashion. For example, if you are giving a persuasive speech on the new campus housing policy, you are unlikely to find much research in the library to support your point of view. And you may find it difficult to find information on the World Wide Web. Some topics are so specific to a time or place that you have to be creative in how you find information. In order to obtain information for a speech on a student housing policy, you will probably need a local source such as a Dean of Students or another official on campus who might have immediate information at hand. You might also e-mail or telephone other universities to further research campus housing policies in general. Such interviews will not only give you the information you need to support your thesis, but your credibility as a knowledgeable speaker and researcher will also be enhanced if you are able to quote or paraphrase reliable experts during the course of the speech. Additionally, interviewing gives you an opportunity to speak with a credible expert who may give you guidance concerning further avenues to research. For example, the Dean of Housing could refer you to a series of articles concerning housing policy in a periodical for college administrators.

Interviewing may sound easy enough, but it actually takes a lot of thought, preparation, and follow-up. There are three phases to a successful interview: the pre-interview phase, the interview, and the post-interview.

Pre-Interview

The success of most research interviews depends on how well you prepare for the interview. Once you have established the purpose of the interview, you must find the most appropriate person to interview in order to accomplish your objectives. In short, you should choose the most knowledgeable and accessible person on a particular issue. You may need to make some preliminary phone calls to find out who you need to talk to. You wouldn't want to make the effort of interviewing a resident assistant about important housing issues when the person you really need to interview is the Dean of Housing.

There are many options of interview formats. Obviously the most optimal format is the face-to-face interview. However, when distance, time, and availability make it difficult for a face-to-face interview, you should consider e-mail or telephone interviews as well. In any case, you should contact the person far in advance and request an interview. You should never demand an interview, and you should always subordinate your convenience to the interviewee's. Some people might be wary of appearing in print, so it is also important that you make your purpose clear.

Before going to the interview, you need to prepare a list of questions. The questions should move from easy to answer, non-threatening questions to probing questions. "Tell me about your job," is a much more appropriate question than "Why do you support such a controversial policy?" Remember that you are doing research, not doing an investigative report for *60 Minutes*. Plan on questions that work toward gathering information, not toward tripping someone up. You should also formulate open-ended questions that allow the interviewee the opportunity expand his or her thoughts. You should prepare more questions than you have time for, making sure your most important questions are asked early.

Interview

If you are meeting the interviewee in person, you should dress professionally and arrive on time. First, remind the expert of the purpose of the interview and then begin asking questions. In order to keep the interview on track, use the prepared list of questions as a basic outline. Sometimes, an answer will give rise to follow-up questions that may be asked for clarification or further research. You should always be aware of such opportunities to gain more information. If you need to tape the interview, you should ask first and respect the wishes of the interviewee if he or she prefers that you don't. You might also ask the interviewee if he or she knows any additional resources. Above all else, remember that the interviewee is doing you a favor. No one is obligated to give you information for your research. Make sure that you thank the interviewee for his or her time.

Post-Interview

After the interview, you should review your notes or recording as soon as possible in order to have reliable information. If something isn't clear from your interview, this would be the time to contact the interviewee to ask for clarification. You can then use notes from the interview to help shape your essay or speech. A thank you note is common courtesy and may open the avenue for future interviews.

Interviewing Exercise

Instructions: Suppose you are researching the feasibility of starting a coffeehouse on the Samford campus. What questions would you address to each of these sources?

1. Dean of Students

   _____

   _____

   _____

2. A freshman in campus housing

   _____

   _____

   _____

3. A senior who lives off campus

   _____

   _____

   _____

4. The manager of a local coffeehouse

   _____

   _____

   _____

Section Review

1. How should you prepare for your interview?

   _____

   _____

2. How can the personal interview help your research?

   _____

   _____

3. What are some important standards of etiquette you should follow when you interview someone for research?

   _____

   _____

   _____

   _____

4. What might be some advantages of tape recording an interview? What might be some disadvantages?

   _____

   _____

   _____

   _____

Chapter

VII

Working in Small Groups

Working in Small Groups

The ability to work collaboratively in groups is essential to the success of almost every organization. People meet in small groups to brainstorm new ideas, to deliberate changes in policy, to review program effectiveness, and for many other purposes. Small groups make it possible to benefit from the shared knowledge of people with different backgrounds and experience. They also create a sense of shared purpose and common identity. Everyone is more inclined to get behind a project when they feel they had input into planning and designing the work. Groups also benefit from a concept called *synergy*. As group members work together to solve a common problem, they stimulate each other's thinking. The result is a more thoughtful and effective solution than any member could have generated working alone. For all of these reasons, groups are a powerful way of getting things done in our world.

Working in groups does have its drawbacks. Groups take longer to resolve an issue than an individual decision maker. Anyone who has sat through a long committee meeting knows how painfully slow some groups can be in making a decision. Furthermore, coming to a consensus can be a difficult process. When there are differences of opinion within the group, relationships can become strained and tempers can flare. Furthermore, some people use the group as an excuse to avoid individual accountability for decisions that have been made. Using a group to solve a problem or formulate a policy is not a guarantee of an efficient solution or a fair policy. The quality of the group's work ultimately rests on individuals who are responsible, well informed, and willing to sacrifice personal gain for the benefit of others.

The dynamics of group interaction are closely connected to the size of the group. Small groups may range in size from three to seven members, but the ideal size is about 4–5 members. As groups grow larger, there is less chance for each member to voice an opinion. Also, some people are less likely to speak up in larger groups. Ideally, a group should be seated in a circle with the chairs in close proximity. If a member of the group has a chair removed from the circle, he or she may be less likely to interact with other members of the group.

Some groups are primarily social in nature. When you and your friends go out to eat or see a movie, you simply want to have a good time and enjoy each other's company. On the other hand, some groups are formed to accomplish a specific task. If you are on a committee to plan a campus event, you will evaluate your success on how well the event comes off. In reality, all groups have a *social function* and a *task function*. Even if you get together with friends to go to dinner, you must decide when and where to eat—the task function. Similarly, every successful task group must maintain a congenial social atmosphere. If the members are constantly bickering, they are unlikely to accomplish their task effectively.

Characteristics of Effective Group Interaction

Because all of us communicate in groups everyday, it is easy to assume that anyone can work effectively in a group. However, effective group interaction requires a special set of skills—just as much as public speaking or interviewing or acting or any other form of communication. Here are some of the characteristics shared by most successful groups:

Purpose

Every group meeting should begin with a clear statement of the goals to be achieved. In many cases, this means that there is a written agenda that specifies the different tasks to be accomplished. At the very least, the group should reach an oral agreement on what should be accomplished.

Preparation

Before the group meets, everyone should review any written instructions for what the group is to accomplish, often referred to as the *charge* of the committee. If individuals have been assigned specific tasks (reading background materials, collecting information, etc.), they should come prepared to make a report to the group.

Punctuality

If one member of a group arrives late, the whole group loses valuable time. Once the scheduled time has arrived, the group leader should move quickly to get business underway even if one or two group members are still missing. The group should also set a time for the meeting to end. Having a defined amount of time to accomplish the goal helps the group to use their time more effectively.

Participation

Ideally, everyone in the group should contribute equally to the discussion. If one person begins to dominate the discussion, it is easy for other members to become withdrawn or complacent. If you are naturally talkative, you may have to consciously limit the amount of time that you speak. Conversely, if you are shy or introverted, you may need to force yourself to speak up and let your ideas be heard.

Process

Good group decisions require thorough consideration of the matter at hand. Some groups come to a premature conclusion before reviewing all of the facts of the case. Sometimes one group member will seize upon a solution early in the decision making process and try to force this idea on everyone else. This problem was brilliantly illustrated in the movie *Twelve Angry Men*, the story of a jury that is saved from rushing to a guilty verdict by one juror who insists that the evidence be carefully reviewed. Slowly, the jury becomes convinced of the innocence of the defendant. It requires courage for one person to speak up and challenge the thinking of others in the group, but it is absolutely essential to successful deliberation.

Group Leadership

One of the first tasks of a group is often to select a leader. The group leader should have strong communication skills and a high level of responsibility. The group leader shouldn't necessarily be the most talkative person in the group. Good group leaders draw out others rather than talking too much themselves. They make sure that the group stays on task, and they serve as a peacemaker when differences of opinion arise. Good leaders have a positive attitude and help encourage the group to do its very best work.

Individual Behaviors in a Group

Listening

Sometimes we are so eager to make our own contribution to the group, we fail to listen carefully to what others are saying. Failing to listen to others means that valuable information is lost, or the group may lose time repeating ideas that were already discussed once. You may also create hard feelings if you make a comment that repeats an idea mentioned earlier by someone else. Group members quickly become alienated when they feel no one is listening to their ideas.

Responding

Good group interaction is a dialogue, not a series of monologues. Respond to others with verbal cues—"I agree with John that we need to take a closer look at the parking problem."—and nonverbal cues (eye contact, head nodding, smiling). Try to connect with what others in your group are saying.

Questioning

A good question indicates that you are listening to what others are saying and that you are responding to their ideas. Asking a question should be based on a genuine desire to learn more, not as a means to belittle or bully someone else. "Whoever heard of such a ridiculous idea?" is not a good question. A good follow up question might be worded like this: "You mentioned that there were a number of factors that had driven up the cost of healthcare. Could you elaborate on some of those factors?"

Clarifying

Sometimes a group member will make a comment or use a term that is not familiar to you. Asking for clarification is a perfectly normal part of the group discussion. In fact, if the idea is not clear to you, it is probably not clear to others in your group. Sometimes a direct question will help clarify the idea: "What do you mean by the FICA deduction?" Sometimes it is helpful to clarify an idea by restating it in your own words: "If I understand you correctly, you're saying that the cost of legal action for a death penalty case actually exceeds the cost of lifetime imprisonment?" This technique, which is sometimes called the *sayback* method, gives the speaker a chance to correct any misunderstandings or to confirm the validity of a controversial statement.

Summarizing

In a lengthy discussion, it is quite possible for the group to lose track of what has been covered and what remains to be discussed. Periodically, the group leader should summarize the progress that has been made. In a discussion about the effects of television on children, the leader might sum up by saying: "So the sources we've found so far have suggested that television may contribute to shortened attention spans, hyperactivity, and violent behavior in children. Has anyone found any sources that found positive effects from watching television?"

Dealing with Group Conflicts

Depending on the topics being discussed and the personality of the group members, it is possible for strong feelings to emerge during group discussion. Unless you want the group to turn into the *Jerry Springer Show*, you need to take immediate steps to deal with conflict when it arises. The group leader usually plays a particularly important role in resolving these conflicts. Here are some strategies for conflict resolution:

Change the Subject

If the conflict is related to a single issue, it may be possible to simply move on to another area with a promise to return to the disputed item later. Such a move often helps to put a small disagreement into perspective.

Establish the Expectations for Civil Behavior

When tempers begin to rise, the group leader may want to reiterate the ground rules for group interaction. Every group should agree that threatening or intimidating behavior is unacceptable. Shouting or abusive language should never be permitted, but neither should sarcasm, ridicule, or personal remarks. Simply repeating this list of expectations may help to eliminate inappropriate behaviors.

Declare a Recess

If two or more members of a group are getting out of hand, the group leader should declare a recess to allow everyone to calm down. The recess will also provide an opportunity to talk individually with the members about the problems that have arisen.

Address the Underlying Problems

In some cases, aggressive or antisocial behavior stems from personal problems unknown to the group. A group member who has lost a family member to a drunk driver may find it difficult to discuss DUI laws in an objective manner. Knowing the personal dimension of the problem can help everyone understand behavior that might otherwise seem irrational. The group leader may want to ask a group member in private to explain why he or she feels so strongly about an issue.

Get Outside Help

If the group feels that the problem has gotten beyond their control, they may want seek a third party to help resolve the conflict. Sometimes an authority figure—whether it is a teacher, a group sponsor, or a counselor—may be able to get the group back on track.

Group Presentations

As well as problem solving, groups are often used for disseminating information publicly. Group presentations generally fall into one of three categories. A *panel discussion* is a public discussion of a topic by a group. Group members are expected to be knowledgeable about the subject, but they don't usually deliver set speeches. The moderator of the panel provides guiding questions and helps control who speaks and for how long. A *symposium* is a set of speeches on a specified topic. Usually each speaker takes a limited area of the topic related to his or her area of expertise. The *forum* allows the audience to ask questions of the group. Controversial decisions about public policy—for instance, building a minimum security prison in a community—are often preceded by a public forum where citizens can express their concerns and get additional information about the proposal. Many events use a combination of these methods. Here are some tips for effective group presentations:

1. Make sure that all the panelists can be seen and heard by the audience.

2. Have the moderator introduce each member of the panel.

3. Prepare a discussion outline—a series of guiding questions—that will provide structure to the discussion.

4. Practice appropriate group and individual behaviors (i.e., responding, questioning, clarifying, etc.)

5. Adhere to the time limits for the discussion.

6. Make sure that audience questions are repeated so that they can be heard by everyone.

Technology and Group Discussion

Most of the advice given in this section has assumed a traditional discussion setting in which audience members are physically present in the same room. Computer technology, however, has enhanced other forms of group interaction. Group interaction over a network is generally categorized as *synchronous* or *asynchronous*. Synchronous discussions (sometimes called "real-time" discussion) occur in a computer chat room where all the participants are able to send and receive messages with almost no delay. Synchronous discussion can also take place through a conference phone call or a video conference. Asynchronous discussions do not require all group members to be present at the same time. A discussion over an e-mail listserv is asynchronous because messages are being read and sent at different times. The benefit of synchronous electronic discussions is that they don't require physical presence for participation. You can engage in a dialogue with someone in Fairbanks, Alaska as easily as you can with someone on the computer down the hall. The advantage of asynchronous discussion is that not all members have to be present at the same time. You can reply to a question at the time that is most convenient for your schedule. All mediated forms of discussion tend to lack some of the dynamism and immediacy of face-to-face group interaction. On the other hand, technology has removed many of the barriers to traditional group forma-tion. Although electronic discussion will never completely replace traditional group interaction, it is a highly effective way of accomplishing some group goals.

Name: _____

Section: _____

Date: _____

| 3. VII |

Discussion Outline Exercise

Instructions: Your group has been asked to make a presentation about the effect of television on our society. Complete the discussion outline below with appropriate questions to guide the group discussions.

I.   Introduction

II. The Effect of Television on Social Behavior

   A. Does television contribute to violence in our society?

      1. How does television affect preschool children?

      2.

      3.

   B.

      1.

      2.

      3.

III. The Effect of Television on Family Interaction

   A. Does television promote meaningful conversation?

      1. How does television programming affect the way families spend their free time?

      2.

      3.

   B. How could television be used to promote family interaction?

      1.

      2.

IV. The Effects of Television Advertising on Consumer Behavior

    A. What makes television advertising effective?

        1. What images are used to promote products?

        2.

        3.

    B. What are some negative effects of television advertising?

        1. Is there a relationship between consumer debt and TV advertising?

        2.

        3.

V. Summary

1. What are three characteristics of effective group interaction?

   _____

   _____

2. What are your responsibilities as an individual in a group?

   _____

   _____

   _____

   _____

3. Explain three effective ways of dealing with group conflict.

   _____

   _____

   _____

   _____

4. What are the three different types of group presentations, and what are their differences?

   _____

   _____

   _____

   _____

   _____

   _____

   _____

5. Clarify the difference between synchronous and asynchronous discussions.

_____

_____

_____

_____

Chapter

VIII

Visual and Audio Aids

Visual and Audio Aids

We live in a visual culture. Newspapers go out of business on a daily basis, replaced by the visual immediacy of television news and the World Wide Web. In our culture it is becoming increasingly difficult to imagine communication without a visual component. If you watch a television news broadcast, you will notice that stories are organized around the image and not the word. No one wants to watch someone read; we want to see the news. We even have television stations completely devoted to presenting image based news in fifteen and thirty second intervals. Increasingly we are getting our information from the World Wide Web, a medium that assumes an audience without the leisure time to read, an audience who can be best informed by image, sound, and movement.

Though not every speaking assignment in Communication Arts will require a visual aid, you should always be thinking of ways you can improve the presentation of your ideas. Vivid and precise words are your best tool for communicating ideas. In fact, many skillful speakers see words alone as visual aids. Visual aids can add both positive and negative dimensions to the communication process. You should not assume that a visual aid is necessarily good. As the communication theorist Neil Postman has noted, it is difficult to imagine someone like William Taft (who weighed 300 pounds) being elected president: "The shape of a man's body is largely irrelevant to the shape of his ideas when he is addressing a public in writing or on the radio or, for that matter, in smoke signals. But it is quite relevant on television." This example should at least demonstrate the importance of presentation when it comes to visual aids.

A purposeful and well-designed visual or audio aid reinforces and clarifies your message. Some speeches absolutely demand an accompanying image or sound. Imagine someone delivering a speech on twentieth-century art without samples of Pablo Picasso and Jackson Pollock or jazz music without Dizzy Gillespie and John Coltrane. As an audience, you would want to feel invited to participate in the experience of learning. If you think back through your education, you will probably best remember those learning experiences where you were able to have some hands-on participation.

There are several types of aids you might consider for your speeches in Communication Arts: handouts, photographs, graphs and charts, posters, compact discs, videotape, transparencies, projection slides, and three-dimensional objects. In particular, you will learn how to present information through PowerPoint software. PowerPoint is a presentation software that essentially replaces the inconvenience of photographing and organizing slides. PowerPoint software lets you design your own presentation slides and then easily project these using an LCD projector. PowerPoint presentations are a way of revolutionizing public speech because they can easily incorporate animation, video, photography, graphs and tables, and art work with the written text to create a uniform presentation.

Keep in the mind the following characteristics of an effective visual aid:

Appropriate to the Occasion

You should make sure that your visual aid actually supports the topic you choose and is appropriate for the audience. If your topic is of a scholarly nature, you will probably want a visual aid that outlines or supports your argument in some manner. In most academic or professional situations, a hand-lettered poster is inappropriate.

Fulfills Audience Expectations

If your topic is on music or television, your audience will probably expect sound or video clips. Your audience will expect that your aid actually supports your material. In a speech on Gershwin, it might be nice to see his photograph, but your audience will really expect to hear some of his music. If you see your visual aids as support for your topic, then you will have your audience in mind. You can also work toward fulfilling audience expectations if you use the visual or audio aid only when you need it. If you keep a PowerPoint slide on the screen after you've moved on to discuss your next point, your audience could easily get distracted. If you reveal your visual aid before you make your point, your audience may wonder what purpose it serves. At the very least they will probably not pay attention to what you are saying.

Visually Appealing

Your visual aid should be readable and indicate to your audience that you have actually devoted some time to your argument. As you read above, part of successful speech making is generating good will with the audience. If they can't read your visual aid, then they will resent anything you have to say. If you are using PowerPoint, make sure you use light colored text on dark backgrounds (or the inverse) and that you haven't cluttered information on the slide. You should also avoid mixing your fonts, and you should concentrate on strong fonts that emphasize your points.

Practiced and Prepared

Your audience will have no difficulty telling if you've practiced using your visual or audio aid. If they can't see the words on the screen or transparency, if the tables or graphs make no sense or have no bearing on your specific points, if your PowerPoint presentation suddenly makes sounds you weren't prepared for, or if your audiotapes are unintelligible, then your audience will immediately see you as incompetent. Being prepared also means having a back-up aid. It is very easy to experience technical problems with PowerPoint or overhead projectors. You will gain the respect of your audience if you are able to provide alternatives to your preferred aid.

Tips for an Effective PowerPoint Presentation

1. Be sure to stand in a position where you don't block someone's view of the screen.

2. Make reference to your slide with gestures or a pointer, but don't read the text word-for-word to your audience.

3. Avoid gimmicks such as animation and sound that detract attention from your message.

4. Limit the number of slides you prepare. Usually 7–10 slides is more than enough for your classroom speeches.

5. Prepare an introductory slide with your name and the speech title and a closing slide that sums up your ideas or makes a clear recommendation.

Using PowerPoint
Effectively

What problems do you detect in the PowerPoint slides below:

Slide 1

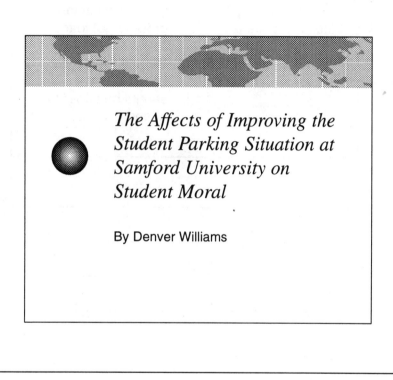

_____

_____

_____

_____

Slide 2

The Current Student Parking Situation

- Faculty Have too much of the parking thereby making it look like there is preferential treatment for faculty over students.

- Often students must walk great distences in harsh weather in order to get to their classes. This makes student morals very low when they should be eager to attend classes.

_____

_____

_____

_____

Slide 3

Problems caused by lack of parking at Samford University

- Low student moral causing deflation in grading and class performance.
- Faculty are given preference of placement of parking putting Samford's customers the students in harm's way.
- Sometimes it can appear to outsiders that Samford really doesn't care much for student moral and attitude, thereby posing a public relations disaster.

_____

_____

_____

_____

Slide 3

Slide 4

_____

_____

_____

_____

Slide 5

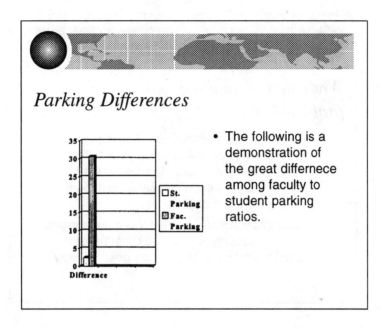

Slide 6

What should be done about this problem???

- Contact faculty members and find those who agree with you on the issues at hand. You can ask faculty members to write letters to administration or even to local newspapers pointing out the problem.

- If students went one semester without bringing cars then security would lose ticket money— (Who knows where that money goes anyway)

_____

_____

_____

_____

Slide 7

What should be done about this problem???

- Write letters to Crimson, Birm. News, et al

- Have a day of refusing to park in student parking. We could all park in faculty's parking to show unity. Security won't give tickets to every student parked there.

Slide 8

Counterarguments

- Students need to walk anyways
- All faculty members have to drive and all students don't. Many students live on campus and don't have to have cars.
- Exercise
- Some students don't need the distractions from school of having a car and parking worries.

Slide 9

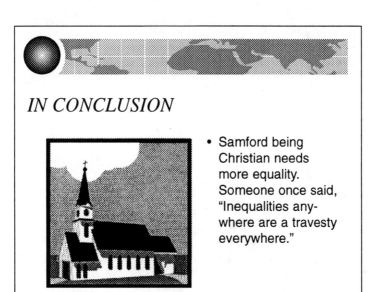

Visual and Audio Aid Activity

Instructions: What would be some appropriate visual or audio aids for the following topics:

1. The Music of George Gershwin

    _____

    _____

2. James Dean: Hollywood's Anti-Hero

    _____

    _____

3. Fire Safety at Home

    _____

    _____

4. A Day at Churchill Downs

    _____

    _____

5. Polyclitus and the High Classical Age of Greek Sculpture

    _____

    _____

6. Fad Diets: Healthy or Hazardous

    _____

    _____

7. The Principle of Synergy in Group Dynamics

_____

_____

1. What can visual or audio aids do to help your speeches?

   _____

   _____

   _____

   _____

2. What should you be careful of in visually arranging PowerPoint slides?

   _____

   _____

3. What are three characteristics of an effective visual or audio aid, and why are they important?

   _____

   _____

   _____

   _____

   _____

   _____

   _____

   _____

   _____

   _____

   _____

PART 3

Chapter

IX

Communication Anxiety

Communication Anxiety

Whatever you call it—stage fright, speech fright, nervousness, shyness, jitters—communication anxiety is perfectly normal. This combination of excitement, fear, and arousal occurs when you face a speaking situation with an unpredictable outcome. Actually communication anxiety can be helpful. You should understand, expect, accept, control, and use communication anxiety to make yourself a better speaker.

Communication anxiety is the speaker's "fight or flight" scenario. Your body goes on auto pilot—you perspire, your muscles tense, and your heart rate and breathing become rapid. This physical reaction results in several symptoms:

1. Butterflies—One of the first symptoms. Energy in your body needs to be pumped to those parts that can get you out of danger, the arms and legs. The stomach and digestive tract shut down, and food just sits until the speaking situation is over. Avoid eating before a presentation, or if you do, make it light, energy food—no grease or meat.

2. Dry Mouth—Digestion begins in the mouth. Saliva production is halted. Drinking water doesn't help much until the body realizes that the "dangerous" situation is over. Avoid soft drinks because of their sodium content, which might make you even thirstier, and because of their carbonation.

3. Rapid Breathing—Muscles run on oxygen carried by blood; they need added super-charged fuel to meet the demands of "danger," so the body responds. Rapid heart rate occurs for the same reason.

4. Trembling Hands, Weak Knees, Unsteady Voice—These symptoms are actually occurring throughout your body. Voice production is produced by skeletal muscles; when they tremble, the voice trembles.

5. Perspiration—The body produces more perspiration in an effort to control temperature. More blood is circulating near the surface of your body, creating more heat. Perspiration glands are your body's radiator; you can't turn them off, or you would pass out from hypothermia.

While these physical reactions are your body's automatic response, there is a three-stage treatment:

Long Term

- Understand your condition. By reminding yourself of what your body is doing, you take away at least part of the fear of the unknown.

- Talk about communication anxiety. Discuss your fear with someone you trust; they can help build your confidence by reminding you of past successes and by putting the experience you are facing into perspective.

- Be realistic about the situation. Work out best and worst case scenarios. No one since ancient Rome has been killed for a bad speech performance. Poke fun at yourself; recognize the absurdity of your worst fears. No matter what happens, life will go on.

- Develop realistic expectations. You invite anxiety when you place unrealistic expectations on yourself.

Short Term

- Be prepared. Know your content inside and out, and rehearse the entire speech.

- Talk about what is happening now. To verbalize nervousness is to objectify it and gain a measure of control.

- Check out the physical space you will be speaking in. Classrooms are often empty during portions of the day. Try to get the feel of the room by yourself when it is empty. Stand at the front of the room and behind the podium if you plan to use it. On the day of your presentation, come early and get comfortable.

- Burn up excess energy in the hours preceding your speech through mild exercise such as walking.

- Get plenty of sleep the night before.

- Before your speech you should avoid stimulants like caffeine or sugar.

- Spend a few minutes before your speech taking deep breaths. This will help relax you and help you concentrate on your breathing.

First Aid On The Spot

- Think about communicating rather than performing. Connecting with the audience is your goal.

- Pause before you speak.

- Channel your excess physical energy into the performance through gestures, physical animation, and vocal variety.

- Look for friendly faces. Maintain eye contact throughout your speech so you register positive feedback from the audience and so you can adjust your message if their feedback indicates that something in your speech is unclear.

1. What are some characteristics of communication anxiety?

    _____

    _____

2. What are at least two long term solutions for communication anxiety?

    _____

    _____

3. What are at least two short term solutions for communication anxiety?

    _____

    _____

4. What can you do at the time of your speech to ease your anxiety?

    _____

    _____

Chapter

X

Listening Skills

Listening

Although we tend to focus on the art of speaking when we think about communication, giving a speech is obviously a pointless activity if no one listens to it. Being a good listener is a valuable skill. In our interpersonal relationships we all want someone who demonstrates their concern for us by listening to our ideas and experiences. Good listening is also a key to success in our academic and professional lives. If we fail to listen to instructions or to understand the task we have been assigned to perform, we know that there will be consequences for our inattentiveness.

Hearing v. Listening

Hearing is the first step in the listening process. You should make it a habit to be in a position where you can easily hear the speaker. You will find it easier to hear and easier to concentrate, for instance, if you take a seat near the front of the room. You should also avoid distractions whenever possible. If you are on a date and you spend most of your time watching a ballgame on the television at the restaurant, you are unlikely to make a favorable impression.

Good listening usually means making eye contact with the speaker. You may be able to read a magazine or write a note to a friend at the same time as you listen, but you won't be able to convince the speaker that you're really interested in what is being said.

As well as making eye contact, you can improve your listening by various forms of feedback. Nodding your head, for instance, is one way of showing the speaker that you are listening carefully and in agreement with what is being said. You can also encourage the speaker by smiling, by sitting up straight, or even by leaning forward to hear an important point.

When appropriate, you should give vocal feedback as well. This is especially important in a telephone conversation since the speaker lacks nonverbal cues. An occasional "yes" or "O.K." lets the speaker know that you are still paying attention. Of course, in a large crowd you don't want to speak out and interrupt the speaker's concentration, but in small groups an occasional comment or question is usually acceptable.

Taking Notes

One important way to improve your listening skills is through effective notetaking. This is especially true when listening to a lecture. It is easy for our minds to wander during a lengthy recitation if we don't write down important ideas. However, remember that your goal is to listen more effectively—not to transcribe the speech.

Begin your notes by placing a heading at the top of the page that indicates the speaker, the subject, and the date. This will help you organize your notes and to locate the information you need at a later date. As the speech begins, look for hints as to the main ideas that will be discussed. If the speech is well organized, this may be a simple matter, but in some cases you may have to listen for recurring themes and other clues to the main idea. Although such listening is more challenging, a complex speech may ultimately be more interesting and provocative than a simple exposition of familiar themes.

Some students like to divide their notebooks into two columns. On the left, they put the substantive points made by the speaker. On the right side, they put their own responses and questions.

Dr. Haddon Hammergood
The Rise of American Democracy
September 11, 2000

Content Notes	*Response Notes*
Jeffersonian democracy a product of Enlightenment thinking	How is Jeffersonian democracy different from classical democracy (pre-Enlightenment)?
Rationalists believe humans must live by reason alone	Can one give a reason for morality? Can you be good without God?
Thomas Paine, Diderow(?) espoused the rationalist cause	*Look up Diderow*
Deists accept divine order, but reject divine intervention in daily existence	
Jefferson accepted deist position; advocated separation of church and state	Division between "state" schools and "religious" schools still exists (UVA v. Samford)

However you organize your notes, strive to make them neat and orderly. When possible, go over your notes after class and look up any information that wasn't clear in your textbook.

Evaluating Speeches

If you hear a controversial speech, you may be tempted to reject the idea out of hand or to accept the speaker's point of view unreservedly. Either of these reactions is a mistake. No matter how much you disagree with an idea, you can benefit from hearing an opposing point of view. If your own position can withstand the counterarguments of an adversary, you will be that much stronger in your beliefs. On the other hand, you may get new information that causes you to modify your former stance.

It is probably even more difficult to listen critically when we are in agreement with the speaker. But a good listener should never listen passively to a speech. How are the arguments being made? What sources are being used? What are the implications of this line of reasoning? How would these principles apply to current situations in the world or in my life? Most speakers will be flattered that you have not accepted everything being said at face value.

Rhetorical Criticism

As well as listening to the content of a speech, there are times when you want to consider the method of delivery as well. We can all learn from observing the technique of effective public speakers. For instance, how does the speaker establish rapport with the audience? How does the speaker use his or her voice to reinforce the message? What are some techniques of nonverbal communication being used? Does the speaker have characteristic mannerisms or a unique vocal style? What is there to emulate in the speech? What could be improved?

Rhetorical criticism also takes into account the effect of the audience and the occasion on the speech. What difficulties did Winston Churchill face in his famous war speeches? How did President Nixon overcome public criticism in his famous "Checkers" speech? A study of great speeches can provide models for the way you can handle difficult situations through your own public speaking.

Effective rhetorical criticism should not be confused with petty fault finding. Some listeners become so distracted by a speaker's hairstyle or manner of dress that they fail to benefit from the important ideas being shared. Although you may recognize the weaknesses of a particular speaker, you should always look for positive features of the speech. A good way to practice your listening and evaluation skills is to attend Samford's Excellent Speech Contest. At the end of this section there are forms for you to evaluate contest speeches.

Audience Behavior

Whenever you listen to speeches in your Communication Arts classes (or anywhere else), you should observe some rules of common courtesy. Avoid any behavior that would be distracting to the speaker: shuffling papers, passing notes, talking with a friend, opening candy wrappers, etc. Even if you disagree with the speaker, you should never interrupt the speech or heckle the speaker. Free speech is the sacred birthright of every American. Many ideas that are now commonly accepted were at some point considered heretical. You should be polite and respectful when listening to those with whom you disagree.

You should always try to arrive early whenever you are coming to hear someone speak. This will allow you time to find your seat and get settled before the speaker begins. Especially in a small classroom, it is very disruptive for people to walk in during a speech. And, unless there is an emergency, you should never walk out during a speech. Observing these rules will serve you well at all public events: a concert, a dramatic production, or a convocation.

Listening to Videotaped Speeches

Some of your speeches in Communication Arts will be videotaped. Watching yourself on tape can be extremely helpful in improving your speaking technique. Although you may feel embarrassed by distracting mannerisms or lapses in your delivery, the videotape gives you an unparalleled opportunity to see and hear yourself as an audience member would. Your instructor may request you to complete an evaluation of your own speaking. Forms for this purpose are enclosed in this chapter.

Speech Contest Response Form

1. Speaker _____   Topic _____

Strong points _____

_____

Weak points _____

_____

2. Speaker _____   Topic _____

Strong points _____

_____

Weak points _____

_____

3. Speaker _____   Topic _____

Strong points _____

_____

Weak points _____

_____

4. Speaker _____   Topic _____

Strong points _____

_____

Weak points _____

_____

5. Speaker _____   Topic _____

Strong points _____

_____

Weak points _____

_____

6. Speaker _____   Topic _____

Strong points _____

_____

Weak points _____

_____

7. Speaker _____   Topic _____

Strong points _____

_____

Weak points _____

_____

8. Speaker _____   Topic _____

Strong points _____

_____

Weak points _____

_____

9. Speaker _____   Topic _____

Strong points _____

_____

Weak points _____

_____

10. Speaker _____   Topic _____

Strong points _____

_____

Weak points _____

_____

Review of Videotaped Speeches

Name _____   Topic _____

Assignment (autobiography, proposal, etc.) _____

Instructor _____   Class/section _____

Date of Review _____

1. Evaluate the organization of your speech. What was your method of introduction? Were your main points clearly identified? Did you leave out anything you intended to say? Was your conclusion rushed?

2. Evaluate your physical delivery. Did you maintain eye contact with the whole audience? Did you look down at your notes frequently? Did you have any distracting mannerisms?

3. Evaluate your vocal delivery. Did your voice seem confident? vibrant? Did you speak too fast or too slow? Did you hesitate over the pronunciation of any words? Did you use interjections, such as "uh" or "um"? Did your voice seem to support the meaning of your words?

4. Based on your review (and your instructor's critique), what elements of your presentation need to be improved for your next speech?

Review of Videotaped Speeches

Name _____   Topic _____

Assignment (autobiography, proposal, etc.) _____

Instructor _____   Class/section _____

Date of Review _____

1. Evaluate the organization of your speech. What was your method of introduction? Were your main points clearly identified? Did you leave out anything you intended to say? Was your conclusion rushed?

2. Evaluate your physical delivery. Did you maintain eye contact with the whole audience? Did you look down at your notes frequently? Did you have any distracting mannerisms?

3. Evaluate your vocal delivery. Did your voice seem confident? vibrant? Did you speak too fast or too slow? Did you hesitate over the pronunciation of any words? Did you use interjections, such as "uh" or "um"? Did your voice seem to support the meaning of your words?

4. Based on your review (and your instructor's critique), what elements of your presentation need to be improved for your next speech?

Review of Videotaped Speeches

Name _____   Topic _____

Assignment (autobiography, proposal, etc.) _____

Instructor _____   Class/section _____

Date of Review _____

1. Evaluate the organization of your speech. What was your method of introduction? Were your main points clearly identified? Did you leave out anything you intended to say? Was your conclusion rushed?

2. Evaluate your physical delivery. Did you maintain eye contact with the whole audience? Did you look down at your notes frequently? Did you have any distracting mannerisms?

3. Evaluate your vocal delivery. Did your voice seem confident? vibrant? Did you speak too fast or too slow? Did you hesitate over the pronunciation of any words? Did you use interjections, such as "uh" or "um"? Did your voice seem to support the meaning of your words?

4. Based on your review (and your instructor's critique), what elements of your presentation need to be improved for your next speech?

Student Evaluation of Speech

Date _____

Speaker _____

Topic _____

Voice (clear, animated, easy to hear)

Gestures (appropriate, good eye contact)

Audience awareness (relevant, interesting)

Organization (well planned, easy to follow)

Content (well informed, useful ideas)

My favorite part of this presentation was:

The speech could be improved by:

Reviewed by _____

Student Evaluation of Speech

Date _____

Speaker _____

Topic _____

Voice (clear, animated, easy to hear)

Gestures (appropriate, good eye contact)

Audience awareness (relevant, interesting)

Organization (well planned, easy to follow)

Content (well informed, useful ideas)

My favorite part of this presentation was:

The speech could be improved by:

Reviewed by _____

Student Evaluation of Speech

Date _____

Speaker _____

Topic _____

Voice (clear, animated, easy to hear)

Gestures (appropriate, good eye contact)

Audience awareness (relevant, interesting)

Organization (well planned, easy to follow)

Content (well informed, useful ideas)

My favorite part of this presentation was:

The speech could be improved by:

Reviewed by _____

1. What are some ways to insure you can hear better during a speech?

    _____

    _____

2. List a few ways you can improve your listening skills.

    _____

    _____

3. Why is it so important to evaluate speeches as an audience member?

    _____

    _____

4. What is appropriate behavior for an audience member?

    _____

    _____

Chapter

1

SAMPLE STUDENT ESSAYS

Autobiography

Mike
by
Kimberly Kornman

1. I have moved twice in my life: from Alabama to Georgia, then back to Alabama. For the most part, the people I encountered in Georgia were replicas of my friends in Alabama. I was still in the South, the Bible Belt. Like me, my friends went to church on Sunday morning, Sunday night and Wednesday night. The hymns were the same, as were the sermons that focused not so much on hell and damnation as they did on the loving nature of Jesus, and how to receive the free gift of salvation.

2. The fact that religion did not change from one state to another was perhaps the most comforting aspect of the moving transition. God was still there, and it was obvious to anyone willing to look out the window of a car. Churches were on every street corner, as were signs advertising fellowships and Vacation Bible School. Denomination was a mere formality, as long as one was a Christian.

3. When I moved back to Alabama, I sought refuge in the closest First Baptist Church I could find. I prayed, read my Bible, and attended services whenever the doors were open. Again, my religion helped me to accept the transition. My fellow classmates in Sunday School became some of my closest friends at school. Religion was a part of us, and we lived underneath the same bubble, the one where people in front of and behind you are like those broken lines on the highway; practically carbon copies of the ones before them. That is, all of us except for Mike.

4. His brown hair was wavy and untamed; his eyes a mosaic of brown, yellow, and green, the kind that seemed to look straight into one's soul and know whether or not the truth was being spoken. His walk was one of confidence, a slow stride that came across as a strut to most of us. Words were spoken only after deep thought and contemplation, and his voice was smooth and persuasive. He was different, idolizing the music of Jerry Lee Lewis and Bruce Springsteen; he even owned a pair of brown boots, which he wore every day, that were replicas of those once modeled by "the Boss"

himself. But, while his dress and behavior differed from the majority of our junior class, what truly made him unique were his religious beliefs, or rather, his lack of them.

5. Until meeting Mike, I had yet to encounter someone who did not believe in God. I had met those who only went to church at Christmas and on Easter Sunday, and even those who had not been in years. However, Mike did not belong in either of these categories; he was an atheist, and a vocal one at that.

6. I became acquainted with him through the two classes we shared out junior year of high school: English and creative writing. One day, we were instructed to describe an imaginary visit from an angel. I wrote about a man being comforted in the midst of the loss of his soon-to-be-bride; Mike refused to do the assignment. He told Mrs. Bearden that he could not write about something if he did not believe in it.

7. "Pretend," she said.

8. "I can't," he answered.

9. His mother was a devout Catholic woman. She believed in God and insisted that Mike and his younger brother attend mass with her while they were children. Over those years, as he listened to the priest and observed communion, he decided that he did not agree with the message presented in the Bible. He was not "filled with the Holy Spirit" and had no desire to be either. Instead, Mike decided that religion was a personal choice, that it was not for everyone, and it certainly was not for him. The last time he set foot inside a church was before he turned thirteen, when it was required of him.

10. Being a simple, Southern Baptist girl, I was astonished that someone could actually reject the idea of God. After all, I could not recall a time when I had not regularly attended church.

11. He once asked me why I worshiped God. I answered, "Because that is why He created people: to praise Him and honor Him in our companionship."

12. Imagine my shock when he responded by saying, "Well, your God seems selfish to me."

13. God was my Comforter; he had provided for me in the midst of moving from state to state. But how much did I really know about my God? I decided to make it my personal goal to make a positive impression on Mike. I began to question my own beliefs in a way that I had not done before. I consulted my youth minister, and even read up on the Bible's credibility. I sought convincing information that I could use in my war against atheism.

14. And even though I made these attempts, my conversations with Mike were basically hopeless. They ended up in the same position as they had begun; talking religion to him was a seemingly never ending cycle of questions and answers that were not effective enough for him to have a sudden change of heart.

15. Oddly enough, he did not push me away or turn me off with his behavior. Instead, I found him to be one of the most intellectual and intriguing people I had ever encountered. True, I was discouraged that my picture of Christianity was not pretty enough for him; nevertheless, I did not give up.

16.   Mike and I became even better friends our senior year. We spent another year together in English class; he sat beside me. We discussed religion at least once a month. I prayed for him.

17.   I wish I could say that our discussions eventually led to his salvation, but they did not. A few weeks after we graduated, Mike and I had our last religious conversation. I had decided that arguing my theory was useless. It was at that point that I decided that my "church-going faith" was not going to be good enough for him. Mike needed convincing answers, not Sunday School lessons. Perhaps the only way to make an impression was to tell my story, my living testimony. I explained to him a more personal side of religion: what it meant to me.

18.   He listened. He did not interrupt. His eyes never left mine.

19.   And when I was finished, I took a deep breath, and waited.

20.   He thought for a moment, the way he always did before saying anything, and then responded, "Kimberly, I can tell that your religion means more to you than what is written in the Bible. It is personal, and it makes you happy. That is what is important, the happiness. I think that is the true reason behind a Supreme Being, to find contentment in this life. But it doesn't do that for me, and therefore, I cannot accept it."

21.   Many disagreed with my friendship with Mike; I heard the whispers of my church friends when my name was mentioned with his. But I did not care what they or anyone else thought. Mike, being an atheist, taught me more about Christianity than any Christian ever had. He made me realize the true joy I found in my relationship with God by forcing me to question the reason I believed.

A Rag Doll Lesson
by
Rebecca Cushman

1. I would like to be able to say that the reason I started visiting Bethany Frierson was because I wanted to show her love, but it wasn't. I would also like to be able to say that the reason for showing love to this little girl was not motivated by selfish ambition, but it was. Even though my motives for doing good were not rooted in the right place, God showed me through this needy and unloved girl what true love and happiness are.

2. It was my junior year of high school and I was looking for community service activities to boost my resume for colleges. When one of my adult friends suggested that I become a buddy with the Big Brothers/Big Sisters Buddy Program, the first thing that popped into my head was how impressive this activity would look on my college applications. All I had to do was fill out an application, take a personality test, and then they would match me with a girl in the elementary school of my choice. Before they matched me with a girl, they told me that I was only to visit her while she was in after school care and to visit her once a week. I began to gloat in my brilliance. This good deed I was about to begin would not be time consuming at all.

3. About two weeks later, I received a phone call from the Buddy Program coordinator. She told me that they had matched me with a kindergartner named Bethany Frierson. I had no more information on Bethany at that time. All I had was a mental picture of what our first encounter would be like. I had no idea if she was going to be black or white, rich or poor, talkative or quiet. I was prepared for any situation, but in the back of my mind I began to think that I had jumped into something I could not handle. The thought that kept me going was the idea that Bethany was a service project to help beef up my resume. I thought of her as a project, not a person.

4. The night before I was supposed to meet Bethany, my dad questioned me on my real motive for joining the Buddy Program. He told me to make sure that I was becoming a buddy so I could be there for Bethany, not so she could make me look better. Up until that point, I thought that I had hidden my true motive of the resume rather well, and that what people were seeing was my desire to do good for others. I had not realized that my selfish desires were so apparent. For the rest of the night, I questioned whether I should even go through with the meeting the next day. Why should I do something that would make me appear selfish?

5. After school I made my way over to the elementary school to meet my service project. I was greeted at the door by the Buddy Program coordinator and the school counselor. As we made our way to the counselor's office, we passed all of the kids in after school care as they were watching a movie. The counselor left me in the office with the coordinator while she went to get Bethany. The moment she left, I began to feel nervous. Was I really supposed to be doing this? Should I become a buddy if my first desire was not to be there for this child? If my desire is selfish, will I be able to show Bethany the love that she will most likely need? A wave of guiltiness swept over me, and I realized how self-centered I had been.

6. As the counselor escorted Bethany into the room, all of my doubts seemed to find an answer. She seemed to be just as nervous as I was, and she looked at me with a strange fascination. She had big beautiful brown eyes that held me in their gaze. I am not sure what she saw in me, but at that

moment I began to realize that Bethany Frierson was not a project for my selfish gain. She was a little girl who needed a friend.

7. Bethany's appearance reminded me of a rag doll. Her hair was pulled back into a messy ponytail, and her clothes were unclean. Although her rough outer appearance was overwhelming, her smile lit up the room. Her dark skin and white teeth were a beautiful contrast, and her laugh was joyful. As soon as I began talking to her, I knew that this was what I needed to be doing. I wanted to be there for this child, and I wanted to be her friend. I desired to show her love, and to do that, I knew that I could no longer look at her as a project, but as a child. I never totally dismissed the idea that visiting Bethany was community service, but I considered visiting her to be the most rewarding experience ever.

8. I was Bethany's buddy during her kindergarten and first grade years. We played together, read books together, and even cried together. My favorite time of each visit was when I arrived. She would run towards me, jump into my arms, and scream "Hello buddy! What are we going to do today?" I watched as she gained confidence in herself and her abilities. This little girl seemed to grow up before my eyes. Bethany showed me that a little attention and love could have a drastic effect on a child.

9. Bethany was not the only one affected by our time together. She grew more confident, while I matured as a person. She enabled me to realize that true happiness is not determined by our surroundings, but by our actions. The more love you give out, the more you will receive. True love for another person cannot be rooted in selfishness; it has to be rooted in selflessness. I will never forget how God used a kindergarten rag doll to show me true happiness.

Fearless and Experienced
by
Laura Wilson

1. Drew Lasater's bright red jeep looked like a shiny piece of candy. It was parked in a lot known as "the pit" and, in all the darkness, it appeared as the only thing to smile at. I could not believe that I was about to destroy this car by engulfing it in white toilet paper. My heart beat wildly as I glanced at my partners in crime.

2. Drew and several of his friends had been throwing Jolly Ranchers at our car all night. At first, we thought they were rocks and we were really mad. This deserved revenge. When we learned that it was just Jolly Ranchers, it was too late. The taste of crime was in our minds and we had to act. We bought supplies and headed to where we knew the car would be, waiting for us, beckoning us forward.

3. Lindsey Keith, Amy Rostek, and Bethany Pennington stood with me, armed with toilet paper and toothpaste. I was completely ecstatic. This was my first ever roll job and I had high expectations. All through high school I had heard about people rolling cars, houses, and yards but I had never been a part of it. Here I was, my first week in college, and I finally got my big chance to join in. That first Friday night with no curfew and no schedule to follow, I stood in front of a bright red Jeep Cherokee, anticipating my crime.

4. Lindsey, our fearless, experienced leader, led us to the car and began giving instructions. "Start rolling the paper around the car. Make sure you get the wheels too." I admired her for her experience. She did not panic when a car came; she just continued working. I, on the other hand, was very nervous about the entire ordeal. I jumped at the sight of headlights and hid from the sound of car engines as they passed by us.

5. The more toilet paper we put on, the more excited I became. The rush of adrenaline was strong and my face flushed with color. No part could go uncovered. We wrapped the entire car with special care, as though it was a present meant for some important person. After we finished with the toilet paper, we started on the toothpaste. I began to fill every window with little dots of toothpaste, as though tying a ribbon on our package to complete it. We wrote notes to Drew on the windshield and side windows. With every swab of toothpaste, our present came closer to being wrapped. For the final touch, we sprinkled Jolly Ranchers all over the car until they appeared to be confetti.

6. I smiled and laughed with my new friends. We were partners in crime and now we had inside jokes and nicknames. We were now the "Jolly Rollers" and that united us. Whenever we saw Drew's car we would smile and say, "Remember the time we...." I stopped for a moment and watched the others. I felt so special that I had been included, as though I belonged with them. As I stood there watching and feeling important, I noticed that we had left the back windshield blank. I called to the others and we looked at it together. Bethany spoke after a few moments of silence, "How about we write 'The War is On'," she said. "Yeah," we whispered in awe. It was perfect. If a war was on, that meant more chances for revenge and pranks. Our fun and glory did not have to end and we could look forward to more memories. I handed Bethany the toothpaste; it was only right that she do the honors.

7. When Bethany finished she put the toothpaste down and stepped back. We were finished. I looked at our masterpiece and beamed with pride. Several people walked by and praised our work of art. All of a sudden I was not nervous or scared. I loudly told them whose car it was and showed them our detailed work. As students commented on the Jeep covered with toilet paper I was quick to let them know who had done it.

8. Now, for the first time in my entire life, I had my very own story to tell. Not that I never had an influential or sentimental experience before, because I had. This was different. Not many people feel life-changing emotions while toilet papering a friend's car, but I did. I could tell my kids what I had done my first week in college. I would look back on this and know that it was the experience that changed me from an insecure girl to a college student. I felt as though I had become a fearless, experienced leader. Those emotions made the experience special and unique.

9. The rest of my group walked back to the dorm talking about other things, but I was still thinking about our crime. They talked about what we would do next weekend but I could still see our work of art in my head, and I was still smiling. I felt as though I had changed completely in a half an hour. I had friends and a new confidence in myself. Most of all I had one story, my very own story to tell.

10. That Friday night we covered Drew's bright red car with toilet paper until only the windshield was showing and every bit of red was gone. I went back the next morning to look at it again just to make sure I had not dreamed it all. There it was, still covered in toilet paper, toothpaste, and Jolly Ranchers. My heart pounded in my chest and my head filled with pride. I stood back and looked at the now white car with toothpaste on it, and I smiled. I thought Drew's car looked more beautiful white than it ever had looked red.

Reflection

Who's There?
by
Emily Curtin

1. It is a typical Sunday morning at the Waffle House. A lonely traveler stares at his coffee as if it will grant him the answers to his problems. He sits at the high counter, stroking the stubble on his chin in thought, and I watch as the dark circles around his eyes begin to fade into the shadows of the overcast early morning sky. I am suddenly awakened from my trance by the coarse voice of the old man sitting with his wife in the booth at the end of the building.

2. "Waitress!" he calls, and I sigh as I reach for the carafe containing the muddy looking sludge that is supposed to be coffee. Such were my Saturday and Sunday mornings for nearly a year at the Waffle House on Blankenbaker Road. I would rise in the morning at 5:30, put on a peppermint striped shirt and black work pants, and drive sixteen miles to be there at 6:30 to make sure the coffee was made and the salads were fresh. The only thing that would motivate me to be cheerful was the thought of money in my pocket and the chance to work and be around my boyfriend, Tommy. Not to say that I hated my job—actually, it was quite the opposite; I loved my job. It gave me the chance to do what I love to do: talk and meet new faces. The high speed, neck-bracing level of activity was physically tiring, but it would float the hours by nonetheless. At precisely two o'clock when the mopping was done and the last of the plates were cleaned I would collapse into my favorite chair at the low-counter, my hands smelling of detergent, my clothes smelling of waffle syrup and batter, and my ticket pouch filled with wads of bills. Those wads would make the whole day worthwhile, ranging anywhere from eighty to one hundred and ten dollars in ones and fives. Christmas was the plentiful season for tipping, and I counted on my customers' generosity to pay for my Christmas presents. Often times I would simply get something to eat at work, and then head straight for the shops to use the money that I had worked so hard for in the morning. This would save me the gas for the trip home and back out, the time to shower and change, and keep me from crashing as soon as I hit the door. However, there was a terrible downfall to Christmas shopping in my uniform. Simply by wearing the Waffle House garb, I would undergo a dramatic transformation. It's amazing how a stupid paisley bow tie and the smell of waffles could change an attractive, sixteen-year-old honors student into a single mother of six living in an Indiana trailer park. I was appalled at the repetitive number of sneers and cold shoulders I would get once I stepped out of my Waffle House bird cage and into the realm of our stereotypical world. What surprised me the most was not the way I was treated by the other shoppers, but the clerks themselves. Little did they know that I was making a lot more money than they were and that we were in the same position on the economic food chain. They would often stare as though I could not possibly afford to buy that pair of silk pajamas at Victoria's Secret or those pairs of pants at Brooks Brothers or Structure. They would only pay attention to me long enough to let me pay for my purchases and then I was no longer a distraction. I tried not to let their behavior get to me. The worst thing that I could do was cause a scene and further prove to people that I was nothing more than a distraction—a disruption to the middle and upper class families represented in the mall during Christmastime. Instead, I would treat everyone as I would want to be treated. On many occasions, I surprised those around me simply by being witty and conversational, an attitude that

did not necessarily match my outfit. It just goes to show that you cannot make assumptions about people. I did not want to be wearing that outfit any more than they wanted to talk to a girl who reeked of waffle batter and syrup. Once I even waited on a man who had the nerve to tell me that I must have three kids at home, no life, and a man around that I just used for money. I stared him straight in the face and told him that my name was Emily, I was a sixteen-year-old student at the Youth Performing Arts School, and unless he wanted to have his waffle surgically removed from his face, he would think twice before insulting a lady. With that I turned away from the table and waited on my other customers. Fifteen minutes later, I found a ten-dollar bill folded in a napkin documenting the man's apology for being so inconsiderate.

3. I no longer work at the Waffle House. The schedule began to take its toll on my body, and I was not getting enough rest to make the money worthwhile. However, my experience from working there has brought me to many conclusions about the misconceptions of people simply by their appearance. The object should not be to look at the uniform someone wears or his or her ethnic or religious background. Rather look at the way that they carry themselves and who they really are. Attitude speaks for itself. We have all experienced this in our lives at one time or another. John Schnauter, the founder of Papa John's Pizza, for instance, gets this kind of treatment all the time. He lives in my hometown of Anchorage, Kentucky, and when the delivery boys get behind he will actually go out and deliver pizzas himself. John Schnauter has not yet turned forty. He is an attractive dark-haired man who does not look a day over twenty-eight. However, because of his youthful appearance and casual stature, those whose pizzas are delivered by the founder himself often mistake him for a struggling twenty-eight-year-old delivery boy. Half of the time they don't even tip him. So the next time you make an assumption about someone from his or her appearance, tread lightly. The waitress you just stiffed at the Waffle House could be famous someday, and trust me she will remember you.

So Much Alike, Yet So Different
by
Amberly Crowe

1. I can still remember the occasion. It was a warm spring day, and I could hardly sit still in class. At the end of the day, the principal would announce the junior girl and boy who had been chosen Student of the Month. The teachers voted on this award and winning the award was considered a great honor. Everyone held you in highest esteem, not to mention the nice one hundred-dollar check that came with the honor. My sister Kimberly and I thought that one of us would receive the award because we were extremely outgoing and involved in numerous extracurricular activities ranging from class officers to cheerleaders. We also had the second and third highest grade point averages of all the girls in the junior class, and the girl with the highest grade point average had already received the Student of the Month honor for October, the only other month where juniors received the award. We knew one of us would get the award, the question was which one of us would be the winner.

2. As I was leaving physics class that day, Mr. Cashatt called me to his desk. He was a laid back easy-going guy who was quite humorous. I thought we would discuss the usual topic of how my softball team was playing. He was still smiling when he looked at me and said, "Amberly, I know that you have the highest grade in physics and probably deserve to be the Student of the Month more than anyone I know, but I did not want to choose between you and Kimberly so I voted for someone else. If one of you got it, the other one's feelings would be hurt."

3. At this very statement I was stunned. Had all of my teachers thought the same thing when they were voting? The award may not have seemed like a big deal to Mr. Cashatt, but it was to me. I had to know, so I tested my teachers. I said to my history teacher, who had become a friend to me, "I wonder why teachers will not choose between me and Kimberly when an award is at stake." He replied by telling me that he wanted to vote for one of us for Student of the Month, but he thought the one that did not get it would be upset. I even had a friend tell me that her math teacher was trying to choose between us, but finally gave up and voted for someone else. At that moment, I knew neither one of us would be chosen Student of the Month, but that is not what bothered me. What bothered me was that I realized I had been treated differently my entire life because I was a twin.

4. I came to many realizations as to why twins were treated differently. Many people think twins always have to be together. This is especially true for identical twins, like Kimberly and me. We are seen as inseparable. Where one of us is, the other one must be. A girl even told me that she saw me alone in the library one day and thought that Kimberly must be sick. She thought that her statement was funny, but it angered me. People see twins as one person. Seldom does anyone ever recognize the individuality that a twin possesses. Maybe I wanted to study that day and Kimberly wanted to watch television. Just because we consider ourselves best friends does not mean that we should always be together. We like many of the same things, but we also like different things. We have our own personalities and our own emotions. These differences are part of our individuality.

5. People often ask how they can tell us apart. Of course they are referring to physical differences, but my answer to them is get to know us. Look past the facial features and the facts that I have a freckle on my nose and my face is longer than Kimberly's, and look at what is on the inside. Look

at our personalities, our behavior, and our desires in life. Twins can look exactly the same but be totally opposite from each other. I am shy when I first meet people, while my sister can talk to anyone. I like sports; she likes shopping. I want to be a doctor, and she wants to be a lawyer. We even walk and talk differently. It irritates me when people call us "the twins" or the "Crowe twins." I want to hear the word, "Amberly," because I am not just a twin, I am an individual.

6. Not only are we treated as the same person, people are also afraid that we will get our feelings hurt if we do not get to do everything together or if one of us gets chosen for something. This assumption occurs in academics and social life. Like my physics teacher, many others have been scared that choosing between us would upset the one that did not get chosen. This is not true. As a twin, I would be overjoyed just to see my sister's happiness. My sister and I interviewed for a scholarship and I was asked, "How would you react if your sister got this scholarship and you didn't?" I told the interviewers that I would be happy for her. They kept asking, "Wouldn't you be upset?" How could I be upset if my family was getting money to help out with my sister's college tuition? Our friends often have extra tickets to a concert or game, but they do not ask one of us because they think the one that does not get asked might be upset. Twins are just as understanding as people who are not twins. We do not get upset because someone only has one ticket and can only take one other person. Twins just want an equal chance in life, whether it is in receiving awards or in social life.

7. People are totally amazed by twins. People think we can feel each other's pain and read each other's thoughts. The only pain of my sister's that I can feel is her emotional pain. But who does not feel the emotional pain of someone they care about? As to what she is thinking, I can only guess. Twins do not have magical powers and thinking that they do is absurd. When Kimberly and I pass people in the mall, we see pointing and whispering, and people smiling and saying, "Look, twins." If they are so amazed with us as twins, they will be even more amazed with us as individuals.

8. Twins only want to be treated as individuals. People have treated us as one person since elementary school where we dressed alike every day until fifth grade. Dressing alike does not make you the same person. Athletes dress alike, restaurant workers dress alike, and even amusement park ride operators dress alike. They may only be dressed like other people for a short period of time, but their individuality can be seen even in a uniform. Why can the individuality not be seen in twins? What I want is for people to take the time to get to know twins, call twins by their first names, and do not be afraid that twins get their feelings hurt when they are separated. It may take a lot of work, but in the end, twins will appreciate you for seeing them as individuals.

The Wrong Place At the Wrong Time?
by
Jennifer Weems

1. The spring break of my sophomore year in high school, my mother took my friend and me to Panama City Beach, Florida, the spring break headquarters of the South. One night of our vacation, we went to shop at a local bathing suit store. My friend and I found string bikinis to try on, just for laughs, and headed to the dressing rooms. After I tried on my red and black string bikini, I changed while my friend took our bathing suits back to the racks. When I walked out of the dressing room with no merchandise, I was stared at and briefly questioned by a clerk about what I had tried on. I explained the situation to the obviously inexperienced clerk, and I thought she believed me. Soon, however, my mother realized from the stares of the workers that I was suspected of stealing the swimsuit.

2. After this, I was stared at by every worker in the store, and finally questioned by the manager of the store. I assured him that I would never steal. I told him how I was extremely modest, and that I would never even wear a string bikini. I was particularly angered by the way I had been accused, and the manager only briefly apologized for taking my time. I felt like the victim of an injustice because I had been stereotyped a "typical spring break teenager", and because I had been accused so quickly without any real evidence.

3. Of course, this was not my first, or, I am sorry to say, my last encounter with feelings of injustice from adults. I cannot begin to name the countless times I have felt uncomfortable around adults, simply because I feared what they were thinking of me. When I go into a department store, I am often bombarded by suspicious and worried looks from the store's personnel. Many times, when at the beach or in a "teen-like" situation, I have been glared at rudely by adults and police officers because I was considered "another wild teen".

4. I am not just another wild teen. On the contrary, I have never caused harm to or seriously violated the rights of others. Furthermore, if these adults knew my "goodie-goodie" background, they would be embarrassed by their own false assumptions. I am always angered by the uncomfortable feelings I experience, but I remember my background and never react with the same disrespect that these adults show me. Sure, I may have had some crazy times in my life, but I have maintained my moral standards. And, if I do make mistakes, I accept my consequences. I believe that teens deserve the same respect that most adults expect to receive. If teenagers are expected to become adults, should they not be treated like adults as much as possible?

5. I have often thought about the circumstances surrounding my ordeal at the beach. Perhaps I should have looked a little more clean-cut, should have been more careful when returning the bikini, and should have addressed the issue immediately with the cashier. All the same, nothing I did can be considered an excuse for the workers' accusing behaviors. If the accusations had been made politely, I would have been understanding, but the workers acted as if they knew without any doubt that I had stolen their merchandise. The situation could have definitely been approached by the workers in a better way.

6. Even though I was angered and hurt that I was the suspect of a crime, I learned lessons from the incident. I will never again try on things that I just want to laugh at. For people to know that I tried

on a string bikini is embarrassing enough, but to be accused of stealing a string bikini is devastating. I believe that my incident was one those lifetime experiences that helps shape the way a person looks at people and feel in general. It taught me lessons in tolerance and taught me about people. I feel like it happened to toughen me up and get me ready for the real world, so I am not very bitter about the incident. At least *something* good came out of it.

7. Also, through the incident, I began to realize that in order to be treated with minimal respect as a teenager, I must be cautious at all times. It is a sad state that our world is in when people are required to be careful of their every action, even while shopping. Now, each time I go in a store, I make sure to smile at the cashiers, and I often get good responses. I always act polite and accept the help of the salespeople when they offer their services. I remember to take my tried-on clothes back to the racks, or I give them directly to a salesperson. I do anything I can in order to make myself feel comfortable and seem like the nice purchaser that I am.

8. When I get stopped by a policeman on a Saturday night, I turn down the radio, smile, and hope for the best. When elderly people look at me in condemnation for sitting at the town hang-out, I simply greet them when I see them and hope they do not talk about me too badly. I simply accept and ignore all the rude looks.

9. Even though I accept accusing looks and uncomfortable feelings, it is because I want to, not because I have to. No human should have to tolerate disrespect from another human being, but unfortunately in our society, we do not have the luxury of being respected all of the time. Should we fight this disrespect or let justice pass us by? Should teens get run over by injustice and humbly accept the stares and accusations that go along with the pains of growing up?

Observation

A Place That Saves Lives
by
Georg Pingen

1. Cream-colored walls that reach high into the sky are the first signs of the emergency room at the Jackson Madison County General Hospital. To me the building with its many dark windows and a huge parking deck, looked much more like a big factory or an old business building than a hospital. Coming closer, I saw three ambulances standing in front of the building and large, red signs with "Emergency" or "Emergency Entrance" written on them, but to me it still seemed more like a place where emergencies would happen and not where hurt people would find help. The peachy-cream building, where the emergency room was located, was five stories high and was part of a much larger hospital.

2. I entered the emergency room through two large swinging doors and saw seventeen people, whom I guessed were patients, sitting in the waiting room. After I registered at a desk, where two secretaries were sitting behind security glass, I became number eighteen in the waiting room. By looking at the other people for an extended period of time, I realized that no one there was injured and therefore assumed that they were family members of patients being seen. One woman with dark brown eyes and long brown hair was constantly tapping her foot, but most people sat in a cold stare. Were they scared of losing a loved one? Did they not know what to do? I imagined one man, wearing jeans and a white shirt, was to hear results about his wife. He shouted at his children who were playing in the waiting room and who did not seem to understand the seriousness of the situation. Seeing the fear in these people's eyes made me realize how fortunate I am because I have not yet encountered such a situation.

3. After fifteen minutes a man came to me and introduced himself as James Rhodes, a nurse in the emergency room. He was a very friendly man, whom I assumed to be in his early thirties, but he was not exactly what I imagined a nurse to be. I do not know what I was expecting but not a man like James, who weighed between 200 and 250 pounds. He was wearing light blue scrubs, a stethoscope around his neck, and glasses. He was about six feet tall and had short, spiked brown hair, which had begun to gray.

4. James decided to give me a short tour of the emergency room but could only show me the adult trauma room from the inside. On our way to the room, James explained to me that the Jackson emergency room has several rooms for minor injuries, several rooms to just lie down to rest, four orthopedic rooms, and four trauma rooms. The trauma rooms were split up into two minor trauma rooms, one pediatric major trauma room, and one adult major trauma room. The adult trauma room was the closest to the hospital's helicopter-landing pad; therefore, the patients could be taken care of as quickly as possible. While walking down the hallway to the adult trauma room, I saw many wheelchairs and crash-carts, all prepared for different emergencies.

5. Finally, we reached the adult trauma room where I was overwhelmed by the many machines and medical supplies. There was a stretcher in the center of the room. On one side was an infusion pump for IV fluids, and on the other side was a machine, which James called a defibrillator, used to revive a patient's heart. On one side of the room were several cabinets containing every imaginable medicine. Overall, the room was equipped for everything from the smallest headache to the worst gunshot wounds. It was also filled with the minty smell of the anti-bacterial antiseptic, and I could hear the doctors working in the other rooms.

6. James explained to me that during most emergencies two nurses, a primary and a secondary, work in one room. The primary nurse actually works on the patients, trying to get them to calm down so that they will be prepared for the operation. The secondary nurse stands at the drug cabinet, ready to pass whatever is needed to the primary nurse. James also told me that one of the hardest parts of his job is that he has to treat all patients as if they have a major disease. All nurses and doctors must wear scrubs, gloves, and a mask when they come in contact with the patients, in order that they do not risk infection with any of the countless possible diseases.

7. After seeing this first room, I thought that it must be a very exhausting and stressful job to work under such high pressure almost all day long. When I questioned James about this, his answer initially surprised me, for he said, "During the emergency there is not very much stress, there is just no time to think about stress." However, he further explained, "The times when this job gets really stressful are when I am alone after the crisis is over and must think about what just happened. It is also difficult when I have to tell bad news to a patient's family. I start thinking about what I could have done better; I start to question myself."

8. At that point I knew that I did not want to have the pressure of another person's life in my hands; I do not even like the pressures of school. When I asked James why he decided to live his life with this burden, he told me, "When I was in high school, I was driving on the interstate and saw the scene of a bad accident. A helicopter arrived and I saw several nurses who helped the victims. At that moment I just knew that I wanted to be able to help others in a situation like that." When I asked James about the worst part of his job, he told me that it would be to have a patient die. He told me the sad story of his first experience with this. It was a seventy-four year old woman, who grasped his arm as he worked over her and said, "Please don't let me die;" minutes later she died. After her death James often thought about her words and wondered if he could have saved this woman's life by doing something differently.

9. James does not mind working twelve-hour shifts on four days a week and having an additional job in a different part of the hospital on two other days. His main concerns are his patients, and he is willing to sacrifice much of his free time and a family life (which he says is impossible to have in his job) for them. I admire James for the work that he does and for the strong commitments that he has made. It was very easy for me to imagine James taking good care of his patients.

10. On the way back to the waiting room, I saw that James had to open one of the doors with a security code. It was just a normal hallway door, so I asked him why this was necessary. He answered, "It is very sad, but we have to lock ourselves in this place because there is a risk that we will be threatened with guns. Some of our patients are in such big trouble that people try to follow them into the emergency room to kill them." This really shocked me because I had never dreamed of having such a threat in an emergency room.

11. On the way outside I thanked James for giving me this wonderful opportunity to see an emergency room, and he apologized for not being able to let me see a real emergency situation. Back outside, I looked at the creamy walls of the building again; they still looked the same, but I had changed. I knew now that the emergency room, which was hidden behind the walls had nothing to do with a factory, but that it was a professionally run place that served to save lives. I do not look as much at the building or the ambulances anymore, but at the nurses who do their best to save as many lives as possible.

Zoos: The Inside Story
by
Derek Cavnar

1. Sounds of children blowing on whistles, sights of pink flamingos in front of a tropical background, and smells of nature combined with the aroma of the animals filled my senses as I entered the Birmingham Zoo. A feeling of excitement rushed through me as I anticipated the displays that I would encounter during the rest of that hot, muggy September day. As I began to walk along the boardwalk paths, I noticed the smiling faces of the crowd. A child begged his parents to buy him a zoo souvenir. A couple laughed as they observed the Japanese Macaque monkeys. A look of disgust appeared on the face of a lady as a giraffe ate food pellets from her hand. Overall, it was apparent that almost everyone was having a splendid time. However, I noticed that one group of living things were not having such a great day. At the expense of the human beings' entertainment, some of the animals had to be kept in smaller cages in an environment that was not natural to them. I then began to realize that the world's entertainment is not worth the destructive effect placed on the animals of the zoo.

2. As the day progressed, my enjoyment and anticipation quickly turned into anger and grief. The more I looked at the caged animals, the more I thought about the unfairness of captivity to them. In particular, the environments of the primates were ridiculously small. One type of monkey, the white-handed gibbon, looked like he had lost the will to live. To try to free himself from the boredom, the monkey jumped up and down on a rope in the small cage. As an ignorant monkey, he probably did not know the difference between captivity and wildlife since he had been born and raised within a zoo. However, as a human being, I found the condition of his environment repulsive. After viewing the smaller monkeys, I moved on to the lowland gorilla. Although his cage was suitable for his size, it was in a very messy condition. Trash and droppings covered a large portion of the gorilla's cage. Was it too much for the zookeepers to make sure that his cage was clean? Clean and suitable living conditions are the least the animals deserve. After all, zoos have already taken away their freedom. The gorilla had few movements at all. Since he was alone, the only entertainment for the gorilla was two small ropes. I could almost see the tears drop from his face. Do the zookeepers know the harm done to the animals caused by boredom?

3. Situations of boredom, such as the primates', are not commonly found in the wild. The acquisition of food is the animal's most natural and vital act in the wild. Since the zoo feeds the animals every day, the animals have lost most of their reasons to live. Animals of the wild spend most of their day seeking out food to eat. For example, it has been found that bears spend up to eighteen hours a day in the pursuit of meat (Harris 68). Without these quests for food, an animal is left in his cage with nothing more than a rope or possibly a toy for entertainment. Many zoologists have argued that the boredom that the animals experience is worth the safety that they have in the zoos. Does this protection really recompense for the apathy of the captive animal? According to zookeeper Stephen Bostock, "No matter how well the animals are cared for, they didn't ask to be rescued, and the protection cannot compensate for a life of dullness and boredom" (O'Connell 44). Once again, something that looks like a perfect solution to a problem usually has a negative counterpart. Since the animals cannot decide for themselves, the world must decide whether zoos have more negative or positive effects.

4. Many zoologists have found that the animals, as a result of boredom, begin to exhibit abnormal, psychotic behaviors in the zoos. During the day, I noticed a chimpanzee chewing on his feet and hands as if they were his supper. Such examples of self-mutilation have been found in zoos across America. Other uncommon behaviors such as an elephant attacking his trainer, a panther pacing constantly in his cage, or a gorilla becoming overly aggressive to his mate have also been discovered (Harris 68). These reactions to captivity are rarely found in the wild. Therefore, the animals that we examine at the zoos are not identical to the animals of the wild. Michael Fox, vice president of farm-animal protection for the Humane Society of the United States, says, "When you take an animal out of its environment and put it into an artificial one, you finish up with a virtual animal" (Harris 68). Education is one of the main reasons a zoo exists, but who wants to learn false information? With these false replicas, having a zoo for education reasons is meaningless. Fox also thinks that zoos are motivated less by the desire to sustain wildlife species, and more by entertainment appeal and gate receipts.

5. While I was observing the disturbing characteristics of the zoo, I noticed many signs explaining the zoo's effort to save certain species from extinction. At first, I was relieved that I finally found something positive about the zoo. However, I began to think about the concept. What was the zoo doing to save any animals from extinction?

6. Zoos across America have begun to participate in captive breeding. Captive breeding is a process that begins with the breeding of an endangered species, and finishes with the release of the animal when it has been prepared to take on the obstacles of the wild. Although this plan may seem ideal, zoologists have found that several problems exist in this method. First, studies have shown that many of the animals created by captive breeding do not survive the rugged life of the wild. In 1991 49 blackfooted ferrets were set free in the wild after they were bred within the zoo. Within a month, most of the ferrets died (Luoma 50). Zoologists found that the endangered species had either become victims of coyotes, or suffered from starvation or disorientation. Why did this devastating event occur? The ferrets were not prepared enough to endure the trials of nature. Without responsible training from the caretaker, the animals did not have certain survival skills such as navigation and protection. An animal should not be released until it proves that it can acquire food while securing himself. What good is it to breed animals if they are just going to die the next month? It is obvious that this method has no advantage at all if the proper procedures do not take place. Therefore, in order to ensure survival, the caretaker must be sure that he or she has properly prepared the endangered species. Unfortunately, this does not always happen.

7. In addition to the survival problem of captive-bred animals, the costs to implement the procedure are expensive. For instance, Wyoming's effort to save the black-footed ferrets cost millions of dollars to attempt (Luoma 50). With this factor, not many animals can be rescued from extinction. In result, only the highly acclaimed species will be saved. Also, the species formed from the captive breeding method usually do not turn out exactly like the original animal. Genetic flaws and adaptation to the caged environments can cause the animals to act abnormal to their normal characteristics. Are the zoos really accomplishing anything, or are they just showing off their new technology? Although captive breeding has been successful in a few cases, it is not worth the money and effort of the zoo since they do not efficiently execute the method properly. The money and time spent on this project could be used to protect the endangered species already living naturally in the wild. The world already knows that they can function properly on their own.

8. As I exited through the gates of the Birmingham Zoo, I noted that my views of the zoo had changed drastically. Although the zoo seems entertaining and exciting to the public, the animals think differently about this matter. The humans do not have to look through bars all day, watching people acting like monkeys themselves. However, it is obvious that humans are beginning to view animals with emotions and feelings. Even though the conditions of zoos are not fully suitable for the animals of today, zoos have improved within the past years. In the past, animals were confined to small, lonely cages. Today, zoos have begun to create larger, open areas that will prevent the animals from being alone. At this rate, the zoos may reach the solution for a perfect, natural environment for the animals in the future. Until then, zoologists must continue trying to improve the zoos from the negative condition that they are in now. Curby Simerson, animal care manager for mammals at the San Diego Zoo, says that "zoos have to educate people more and show a willingness to develop better relationships between people and animals" (Ettorre 281). If zoologists can find a way to do this, then zoos will have a positive revolution in the future.

Works Cited

Ettorre, Barbara. "A Day in the Life: The Wild Life of a Manager." *Management Review* 84.8

    (Aug. 1995): 28.

Harris, Mark. "Nature Behind Bars: Do Zoos Save Endangered Species or Exploit Them?" *Vegetarian*

    Times Feb. 1996: 68.

Luoma, Jon R. "Born to be Wild: Problems with Captive Breeding to Prevent Species Extinction."

    Audubon 94.1 (Jan. 1992): 50.

O'Connell, Sanjida. "Zoos and Animal Rights: The Ethics of Keeping Animals." *New Scientist* 140.1895

    (16 Oct. 1993): 44.

Stagoll, Clifford S., and Kelly A. Waples. "Ethical Issues in the Release of Animals from Captivity."

    Bioscience 47.2 (Feb. 1997): 115–22.

Concept

Beyond the Realm of Existence
by
Glen Harris, Jr.

1. The clock on the console of John's sports car read 7:58 a.m. He had two minutes until he was late for work, and another tardy could jeopardize his job. He punched the accelerator and went to pass a school bus through double yellow lines in the road. Instantly, a large pickup appeared coming down the hill ahead. John tried to brake but his car began to skid. The large truck and John's sporty coupe met head on at over fifty-miles-per-hour. John was confused as he viewed the wreckage from above. He felt as if he were in a dream; he saw his own body hanging out of the window. He saw his mangled limbs hanging lifeless and the car's interior strewn with his own blood. However, John felt a great deal of peace and he experienced no pain. He was drawn by a comforting voice to a brilliant, golden light. This light was completely serene, it accepted him, and for the first time in John's life, or afterlife, he felt protected. Before he could bask in this ornate glow, a swoosh took him back into the cab of an ambulance. John was in absolute terror as the paramedics worked on his incapacitated body. Where had the light gone? Why was he back on earth? His life had been restored against his own will and John had another chance at living.

2. What John experienced is not all that uncommon to the population today. His encounter with the other side of life is classified as a near-death experience or NDE. Dr. Raymond Moody coined this term in his 1975 book *Life After Life*. An NDE is typically spawned by a traumatic event (heart attack, gunshot, etc.) followed by the person seeing himself or herself from an out-of-body view. The person may then visit a bright tunnel of celestial light or see a garden where deceased relatives reside. Some hear the voice of a heavenly being, and the voice draws them nearer. A mood of complete peace soon sets in and afterwards the person is swept back to the earthly body (Morse 10, 11). Although all NDEs share similar characteristics, studies have found that no two near-death experiences are alike.

3. Research into this phenomenon has just become popular in the last twenty-five years. Dr. Moody, a pioneer of NDE study, was one of the first scientists to find that patients often shared common experiences during an NDE (Morse 9). Those who actually underwent a near-death experience reported they had "an altered state of feeling. . . without pain, bodily sensations, or fear," they were "aware of another reality. . . moving rapidly through a tunnel," and saw "an inner world of preternatural beauty" (Rinpoche 163). In 1982, a statistical study by George Gallup concluded that 15% of all of the American public (23 million people) had some sort of close encounter with death. Of that number, about 8 million had what they considered to be a near-death experience (Bailey and Yates 7). That particular survey has sparked an interest by the public and scientific community to study this mystic experience.

4. Although the study of near-death experiences has become prevalent only in the last quarter century, records of this phenomenon trace back as far as the fifth century before Christ. Dr. Raymond Moody even found proof of NDEs in Plato's essay, "The Republic" (Bailey and Yates 7).

Furthermore, as Melvin Morse notes (10), even Paul of the New Testament recounts his knowledge of an NDE:

> I know a person in Christ who was fourteen years ago caught up to heaven—whether in the body or out of the body I do not know; God knows. And I know that such a person. . . was caught up to Paradise and heard things that are not to be told, that no mortal is permitted to repeat. (2 Corinthians 12:2-4)

5.   Carol Zaleski explored the medieval theories of NDEs in her book *Otherworld Journeys*. The medieval experience was typically a passageway into another world where the traveler's soul exited from the oral cavity and made the journey to the other side (45). Zaleski continued to describe the Zoroastrian tradition, in which the soul lingers around the body for three days to assure that resuscitation is not accomplished (221). This stage of the near-death experience is still common, 26% have had the out of body feeling (Moody 29). The witnessing of these events through a different set of eyes may be the basis of human curiosity with the subject.

6.   The out-of-body experience is possibly the most fascinating of the phases of an NDE. The environment around, as well as the body itself, can be viewed by the person (Rinpoche 167). The person is completely aware of what is happening, and sometimes he or she may even try to prevent medical care from being administered. The person is in spiritual form, so the "living" aren't cognizant of the surrounding soul. Subjects have even reported that they were free to move at will throughout their environment (Bailey and Yates 5). The soul's exit from the body is usually the first step in the near-death experience process. From this point, different people witness different aspects of the phenomenon.

7.   One of these aspects in the near-death experience is the visualization of a divine light or a tunnel of light. Survivors often explain this light to be "loving, caring, non-judgmental, and often an angel, Christ, or God" (Bailey and Yates 5). NDEs occur in all types of religions and practices, hinting that there are no relations between this light and being good or bad, from a moral standpoint. However, this experience can dramatically change the way life is lived afterwards ("Near-Death Experience" 2). Of the survivors, 14% were reported to have experienced this light phenomena (Moody 29). This light is what has made the NDE very interesting to the public. Often, the tunnel of light is directly associated with a near-death experience.

8.   Over the last twenty-five years, there has been a plethora of information documenting what happens during a near-death experience but several questions still remain unanswered. Several theories exist as to why they happen but no concrete scientific evidence has been yielded. Several scientists have speculated that the extreme shock occurred during traumatic pain can release a chemical, ketamine, which causes neurotoxicity. This brain poisoning can result in abnormal functioning of the cerebral cortex, frontal, and temporal lobes. These areas control memory, cognitive processing, and perception. The same type of dysfunction occurs during epilepsy when a person is having seizures that are often accompanied with hallucinations (Jensen 267–268). Also, there is no constant as to if certain cultural groups are more prone to an NDE than another. Researchers have found only one factor that determines who will have a near-death experience: the type of injury sustained. Bruce Greyson found that the "cognitive features of NDEs do seem to be related to the suddenness of death." He also concluded that anticipated deaths (i.e. terminal illness) produced fewer of the NDE characteristics. Furthermore, in sudden deaths, more "cognitive experiences," like life review, occurred (Bailey and Yates 8). Scientific research is still done to increase the knowledge about near-death experiences.

9. The phenomenon of a near-death experience doesn't always have those characteristics of comforting light and peace. Small populations of people witness a hellish environment during their NDE. According to Bruce Greyson and Nancy Evans Bush, some people experience a feeling of eternal void and nothingness accompanied by graphic entities and hellish landscapes (209). Many of these occurrences go unreported because they may represent a bad person or mean that the survivor will go to hell. Even through this anonymity, "enough contemporary reports have surfaced to confirm that they do, in fact, exist" (Greyson and Bush 211). Sometimes a negative experience changes the way a person lives their worldly life ("Near-Death Experience" 2). A hellish environment and an eternal emptiness may be enough to scare someone into changing.

10. A near-death experience can mean different things for different people. Some see the incident as a reason to live life to the fullest while it is still there, yet there are those who turn their lives around, seeing the experience as a message from God. Whatever the case may be, the NDE is a remarkable phenomenon that may be the link between this world and the next. An explanation is not certain but theories do exist. The knowledge about this subject grows each day and reasoning may be found in the soon future. Whatever the outcome, an NDE can be seen as an earthly purgatory to the next world, an option to live for today or live for tomorrow.

Works Cited

Bailey, Lee W. and Jenny Yates, editors. Introduction. *The Near-Death Experience: A Reader.* New York: Routledge, 1996. 1–23.

Greyson, Bruce and Nancy Bush. "Distressing Near-Death Experiences." *The Near-Death Experience: A Reader.* Ed. Lee W. Bailey and Jenny Yates. New York: Routledge, 1996. 207–230.

Jansen, Karl. "Neuroscience, Ketamine, and the Near-Death Experience." *The Near-Death Experience: A Reader.* Ed. Lee W. Bailey and Jenny Yates. New York: Routledge, 1996. 265–282.

Moody, Raymond. "The Light Beyond." *The Near-Death Experience: A Reader.* Ed. Lee W. Bailey and Jenny Yates. New York: Routledge, 1996. 25–37.

Morse, Melvin. *Closer to the Light.* New York: Random House, 1990.

"Near-Death Experience." Yahoo.com. Online. 9 November 1998. Available: www.iands.org/nde.html

The New Oxford Annotated Bible. Ed. Bruce M. Metzger and Roland E. Murphy. New York: Oxford UP, 1989.

Rinpoche, Sogyal. "The Near Death Experience." *The Near-Death Experience: A Reader.* Ed. Lee W. Bailey and Jenny Yates. New York: Routledge, 1996. 157–177

Zaleski, Carol. *Otherworld Journeys: Accounts of Near-Death Experience in Medieval and Modern Times.* New York: Oxford UP, 1987.

The History and Resurrection of Herbalism
by
Derek Cavnar

1. Daily in households across America, miracle foods are being secretly served to consumers. One may ask, how could a mundane serving of salad, or even a slice of pizza, contain any medical significance? Although many may not be aware of this fact, herbal remedies often reside within the foods of which many individuals partake. Herbalists today include some vegetables, in addition to herbal spices and extracts, as part of the herbal world. For example, a carrot tossed into a salad, a piece of asparagus (often left unconsumed), or an onion found on a pizza are all herbs that can prevent diseases or fortify the immune system. Medicinal benefits can be obtained from these herbs which are eaten every day. However, there are many other herbs that are not commonly found on the dinner table. How have people discovered the many different types of herbs and how have they developed methods to use them medically? Even today, interest in herbal medicine continues to grow. As a result, modern physicians often look at herbalism as an effective method of healing in much the same manner as other cultures have throughout history.

2. Before investigating herbal medicine, one must be familiar with the definition of the word, "herb." By definition, an herb is a plant used for its "medicinal, savory, or aromatic qualities" (Mindell 19). Out of the 380,000 species of plants, 260,000 are capable of use in herbal treatments. However, only ten percent of these potential healers have been examined for medical value (Mindell 19–20). With many herbs left uninvestigated, the popularity of herbalism can only grow in the future.

3. Herbs and plants have been used for medical purposes for countless generations. However, man was not the first to realize the medical significance of herbs. In fact, according to Dr. Earl Mindell, there is a possibility that humans learned about the medicinal properties of herbs through the observation of animals. For example, many pet owners have noticed their dog consuming large amounts of grass. Early animal behaviorists thought this tendency to be the dog's way of allaying his indigestion. Therefore, perhaps the first herbalists became aware of the therapeutic use of plants by "mimicking" the animals' behaviors (Mindell 28–29). After being recognized as a source of natural remedies, herbal medicine began to grow in popularity in early civilizations.

4. Although it may seem surprising, the use of herbs came into existence during the early years of the cavemen. Paintings of medical herbs have been found to exist in the Upper Paleolithic cave at Lascaux, France. These paintings, which were sketched around 18,000 B.C., have led archaeologists to believe that many cavemen perceived herbs as having magical powers (Fleming 8). During early civilization, around 3,000 B.C., the first written guide of medicinal herbals was developed by the Sumerians. Herbs, such as caraway and thyme, were thought of throughout the Sumerian culture to either cure a person or make him stronger (Mindell 29). For example, thyme was given to the knights of the Middle Ages to prepare them for battle (Mindell 184). Caraway, on the other hand, was used primarily for healing. Caraway has been found to ease digestion, decrease nausea, or even increase the amount of breast milk in nursing mothers (Mindell 63–64). The herbal treatments used by early civilizations are closely related to some methods of herbal medicine used today.

5. While the Sumerians were developing their system of herbal healing, the people of Ancient Egypt were also using large quantities of herbs. As early as 2,800 B.C., herbal prescriptions written in

hieroglyphics began to appear in papyruses (Mindell 29). Examples of these medical documents include the Ebers Papyrus, the Edwin Smith Papyrus, and the Kahun Medical Papyrus. Herbs such as senna, thyme, frankincense, aloe, garlic, peppermint, manna, and sycamore were included in the early medical papyruses (Hobbs, par 1). Many of the herbs used in Ancient Egypt are just as commonly used today.

6. At the same time as the Egyptians, the Chinese were also making advances in herbal medicine. Richard Hyatt, author of *Chinese Herbal Medicine*, seems to think that renowned emperors heavily influenced the origin of herbal medicine in China. Before the end of his reign in 2697 B.C., Shen Nung became known as "the father of agriculture and herbal medicine" in China. Nung would venture out into the fields and forests to do research processes of trial and error on herbs and plants. He would sometimes even test them orally. Although he was poisoned many times each day, he would use his medical expertise to restore himself. As a result of his experiments, Nung published the first native herbal book, *Shen Nung's Herbal* (Hyatt 18). With the increasing research in herbal medicine came the increasing amount of herbal practice throughout China. Around 1500 B.C., I-Yin, an emperor's cook, began to serve herbal broth to the court. The customers were impressed, not only with the great taste, but with the broth's medical significance as well. The idea of serving herbs in broth soon spread around the world. Since then, I-Yin has been remembered as the founder of herb teas and soups (Hyatt 19). Today, one can find the same type of herbal teas or soups at a deli or grocery store.

7. As the centuries passed, the popularity of herbalism began to increase in most areas of the world. Susan Fleming, author of the book *Herbs*, states that during the fifth century B.C., herbalism underwent some of its most productive stages in Ancient Greece. The Greek doctor, Hippocrates, carried out many studies to disprove the theory that diseases were caused by evil spirits and sin. As a result of his experiments, Hippocrates derived the theory that diseases were caused by imbalances in the body, which had to be diagnosed through reason and specified observation. Hippocrates also wrote many books that collectively reported close to 400 herbal remedies. After he founded his own school of medicine, it was certain that Hippocrates would be known as the "father of medicine" (Fleming 8–9). During the first century A.D., another Greek naturalist, Dioscorides. would have a large impact on herbal medicine throughout the world. Not only was Dioscorides a Greek naturalist, but he was also a physician for the Roman army. While traveling with the army, Dioscorides gathered hundreds of plant samples. He later recorded his observations in the book *De Materia Medica*. One example of Dioscorides' findings was the use of the bark and leaves of the white willow tree to relieve aches associated with colds and fevers. Salacin, the active compound in the white willow bark, is closely related to the active ingredient found in today's synthetic aspirin (Fleming 9). Other drugs today, just like aspirin, are closely related to their herbal ancestors of the past.

8. After the advancements in herbalism during the time of the Greek and Roman civilizations, herbal practices continued during the following generations. During the Middle Ages, villages had a "wise woman" that people would see to receive herbal treatments (Fleming 9). For people who thought the women were witches, doctors were available with homemade herbal remedies (Mindeli 29). Besides the doctors and women, there were relatively few places to find herbal treatments. However, the exercise of herbalism during the Middle Age was enough to keep people's interest in herbal medicine.

9. Progression in herbalism continued through the fifteenth, sixteenth, and seventeenth centuries. After the discovery of America, several new methods of herbal medicine were presented (Fleming 10). The Europeans began sharing their knowledge with Native Americans. In return, the Native Americans gave Europeans new herbs that would later be shipped back to Europe (Mindell 30). For example, the Native Americans introduced echinacea to the European settlers. Since it has been discovered to boost the immune system, to promote faster healing of skin wounds, and to fight bacterial infections, echinacea remains popular today (Mindell 83–84). During the sixteenth century, the invention of the printing press also benefited the development of the field of herbal medicine. For the first time, herbal information could be available at the same time throughout different parts of the world. Books, such as John Gerard's *The Herball*, expanded the amount of available herbal information (Fleming 10). With the spread of herbal information around the world, herbal medicine began to reach the zenith of its popularity.

10. Although technology usually improves the processes of life, it can also sometimes negatively affect beneficial, traditional activities. Being a traditional method, herbalism lost much of its intrigue after the Industrial Revolution. With new technology came cheaper and easier forms of medicine. Instead of having to mix and create their own solutions, consumers soon realized that they could just visit their local pharmacy. As pharmaceutical findings increased, the practice of herbal medicine within Europe and America began to disappear (Fleming 117). The patent drug industry took over what was once a strong tradition.

11. Today, the practice of herbal medicine still exists around the world. In fact, 80% of the world's population uses herbal medicine as their main source of healthcare (Mindell 30). In the United States a renewed interest in herbalism has grown during the past few years. Herbal stores, drinks that contain herbs, and herbal books are commonly found in most cities. Sales of herbal supplements in the United States now surpass $1.2 billion per year (Jellin 1). What has caused this renewed interest in herbs during the past few years? According to Dr. Earl Mindell, one reason is the discovery of the uncomfortable and dangerous side effects of today's synthetic and over-the-counter drugs (14). Many consumers feel safer taking a more natural remedy. Also, Mindell also states that people use herbs extensively for preventive medicine. Like vitamins, herbs can help maintain good health. Physicians have also found that different types of herbs can reduce cholesterol, improve circulation, or prevent diseases such as cancer (Mindell 15). People are now also taking herbs such as Ginkgo and St. John's Wort to make them feel better and think more clearly. For example, St. John's Wort is now becoming a safer alternative to the prescription drug Prozac. Information has been discovered that St John's Wort can calm the body, promote faster healing, and relieve anxiety (Mindell 154–155). Because of the advantages of herbal treatments, people are trying herbal medicine once again.

12. Along with the advantages of herbal medicine come some disadvantages also. Since the U. S. Food and Drug Administration has a difficult time monitoring all of the different types of herbal drugs, false labeling often occurs (Tyler 1). Since the recent rebirth of herbal medicine in the United States, many people have been more "enthusiastic than knowledgeable" (Tyler 1). Therefore, people have jumped to conclusions about what each herb can actually prevent or cure. Dr. Varra Tyler, author of *The Honest Herbal*, comments that many herbal writings are "so comprehensive and so indiscriminate that they appear to recommend everything for anything" (2). People often think that natural drugs cannot cause harm to human beings. However, many types of herbal medicine have been harming people throughout herbalism's history. For example, Socrates drank the herb hemlock to carry out his execution (Tyler 2). Today, people with insomnia or large

amounts of stress often take kava kava to relieve their tension. However, the consumer often does not realize that large amounts of kava kava can cause liver damage (Mindell 124). Like kava kava, many other herbal remedies can also have negative effects on the body. Therefore, one must do large amounts of research and consult with herbal experts to avoid danger.

13. Herbalism has existed in the world since the beginning of civilization. In many countries of the world, herbal treatments are still the primary source of healthcare. However, today in the United States herbal medicine is often referred to as an alternative medicine even though the roots of herbalism strongly influenced present-day pharmacology. Despite the United States' reliance on synthetic medicine, many pharmacists are increasingly working more with herbal sources. With the renewed interest in herbs and their effects on the human body, the methods of herbalism have a strong and exciting potential for the next millenium.

Works Cited

Fleming, Susan. *Herbs: A Connoisseur's Guide*. New York: Crescent Books, 1993.

Hobbs, Christopher. "An Outline of the History of Herbalism." Online. Internet. 4 Nov. 1998. Available:

    http://www.healthworld.com/LIBRARY/Articles/Hobbs/HISTORYO.htm.

Hyatt, Richard. *Chinese Herbal Medicine: Ancient Art and Modern Science*. New York: Schocken

    Books, 1978.

"Pharmacist's Letter: Continuing Education #97-005." Ed. Jeff M. Jellin. Stockton CA: Therapeutic

    Research Center, 1998.

Mindell, Earl. *Earl Mindell's Herb Bible*. New York: Simon & Schuster, 1992.

Tyler, Varro E. *The Honest Herbal: A Sensible Guide to the Use of Herbs and Related Remedies*.

    New York: Pharmaceutical Products Press, 1993.

Evaluation

Reinterpreting the Past
by
Mary Louise Hendley

1. Few films reveal a more heart warming story than the tale of *Little Women*, successfully adapted from the equally entertaining novel by Louisa May Alcott. Depicting the life of a lower class family during the harsh times of the Civil War, this ageless classic paints a picture of friendships and family togetherness. The film contains three aspects which aid in the development of the plot and the overall entertainment value of the motion picture. The effective use of lighting, the excellent choice of cast members, and the memorable musical score are features which set this film apart from other average, family-oriented movies.

2. The characters' emotions, captured by the excellent lighting techniques, are evident throughout the entire film. In the first scene, for example, the camera skims the winter landscape, including the snow-covered fields and split-rail fences. The dull gray color of this scene leaves the audience with a chilly feeling. However, as the camera begins to focus on the March family household, the cold, bland color changes to a yellowish orange tint that penetrates through the big windows of the house. As Marmee opens the front door, the warm light from within cuts through the chilly winter evening and seems to melt the snow from her shoes. She is greeted by her daughters in the foyer, and the lighting reflects a golden glow onto the girls' faces as they smile with anticipation. By using this method of warm and cold light, this form of lighting communicates each character's emotions throughout the film.

3. Another aspect of the lighting is the use of shadow in this movie. When bad news reaches the household, the scenery usually appears darker. In these instances, Jo March retreats to a dark corner of the house, usually the attic or a staircase, and only a dim light reflects onto her face. In another memorable scene, where the snow descends upon the thick forest, where the sun pierces through the tree branches, where the children frolic on the iced pond, Amy falls through some thin ice into the freezing water. As Jo and Laurie skate to her rescue, the light immediately grows dimmer, and a shadow is cast on Amy's side of the pond. Also, the expressions on her rescuers' faces seem to reflect the colder atmosphere as opposed to the lighter scenery just seconds before the incident. These effective lighting techniques enhance the characters' overall emotional performance and "give the movie a precise but unforced period look" (Jahiel 1).

4. Along with the excellent use of light, the choice of talented actors and actresses for *Little Women* wonderfully match each character's description from the novel. Roger Ebert, commenting on these remarkable acting talents, writes, "...we gradually get to know them, we sense their personalities"(1). Winona Ryder, who plays the part of Jo March, does an excellent job as both the main character and narrator of this movie. Ryder takes the same approach in portraying Jo as she does in many of her other movie roles by being the center of attention. Her stage presence seizes the viewer's attention so that one can never take his or her eyes from Jo. Ryder's humorous expressions and gestures when making fun of Meg's suitor, Mr. Brooke, for example, add comedy to the plot. Although her misbehaving and improper conduct often get her into trouble, these qualities seem to warm the audience to her opaque personality.

5.   The many supporting roles in *Little Women* mix in key ingredients needed to complete the cast of this great film. I was pleasantly surprised with actress Susan Sarandon, who portrayed the character of Marmee, the girls' loving and nurturing mother. A seasoned actress, Sarandon's long list of acting credentials depict her as a more colorful and racy character in such movies as *Thelma and Louise* and *The Rocky Horror Picture Show*. In these types of movies her character becomes the epitome of sexiness. In sharp contrast, her nurturing mother role as Marmee in *Little Women* showcases Sarandon as an accomplished actress, able to act the part of a variety of different roles. *Little Women* would not be as commendable if not for the great acting talent of its lead and supporting characters.

6.   The musical score also makes this film truly a masterpiece. The movie begins with a soft melody played by a single clarinet while the full orchestra is gradually added. The overall effect gives the viewer a Christmasy feeling that reflects the togetherness the March family feels around this holiday season. This first piece of music, laced throughout the film, also varies with the different scenes and events that take place within the March family. With the more dark and somber settings, the music is played at a slower tempo as opposed to a faster tempo accompanying the lighter, happier scenes.

7.   The music also conveys to the audience the mental state of the characters. Like the different lighting techniques discussed earlier, the music conveys the characters' feelings and emotions. For example, when the March family receives a telegram saying that their father has been wounded in the war, the viewer can sense the tension in the household as Marmee reads the telegram to everyone. The music immediately becomes more staccato and quicker in tempo as Marmee prepares for the long train ride to help her ailing husband. Without even glancing at the characters' faces, we can feel the strained emotions of the girls as they help their mother.

8.   These examples dramatically illustrate the unique features of *Little Women*. I would have to give this quality film interpretation of a classic novel a very high score. The lighting techniques, along with the excellent cast of characters, and the memorable musical score make this film an outstanding motion picture suitable for all ages. In a world where family values seem to be rapidly diminishing, this movie takes us back to a time when the importance of family togetherness prevailed, and we long for that commonality. As *Time* magazine states, "*Little Women* gently but firmly asks us to penetrate its 19th century disguises and discover something of ourselves hiding in the dim past" (Schickel 1).

Works Cited

Ebert, Roger. "Little Women." *Chicago Sun-Times* 21 December 1994.

        <http://www.suntimes.com/ebert/ebert_reviews/1994/12/957013.html>.

Jahiel, Edwin. <http://www.prairienet.org/%7Eejahiel/litlwomn.htm>.

Schickel, Richard. "Transcendental Meditation." *Time* 19 December 1994. <http://www.

        pathfinder.coin/time/magazine/domestic/ 1994/941219/941219.cinema. Iittlewomen.html>.

A Woman's Place?
by
Rebecca Behan

1. The influence of advertising on women and the perception of women has been profound. Advertisements affect every area of life, and consequently the portrayal of women in advertising thwarts society's view of the female race. Throughout the years, women have most often been stereotyped as "a combination sex object, wife, and mother who achieves fulfillment by looking beautiful for men" (Kang 3). Because a natural discrepancy arises between the reality of women and their role in society and the role advertisements would have the consumer believe a woman possesses, evaluative criteria must be used when viewing any advertisement. Of the many questions one should ask are: "What is being sold?" "How are women pictured?" and "What is the response of the consumer to the advertisement?"

2. Determining the product offered to a consumer is not difficult, but determining what form of manipulation is used to sell a given product requires an in-depth approach to advertising. Advertisements often picture women smiling happily next to a cleaning product or actively involved in some domestic duty, but this is rarely the true purpose of the advertisement. Barbara Lippert explains in the October 1996 issue of *Brandweek* magazine that advertisers are not just selling a product. Instead, advertisers provide emotions for the consumer to identify with the product (1). Unnatural portrayals of perfection such as the super-skinny model or completely composed housewife become the ideal for many women. From advertisements, men and women in America form judgments about a woman's role in society. The world of advertising, while attempting to mirror real life, falls far short and instead becomes an alternate reality broken into easily understood contexts. These contexts are simply scenes which have been pulled from real life and manipulated to convey a message about the product and about life in general. In an advertisement picturing an American family, for example, the man will be taller and larger than the wife. She will be smiling at either the husband or her children who will most likely be behaving somewhat mischievously. In the background, a pet of some sort is usually present to appeal to consumers who own an animal. This advertisement tells the consumer that the product offered is stable and dependable, much like the theorized "typical American family." Consumers fail to discern that advertisements are simply these manipulated forms of reality. Without realizing the conclusions drawn from a highly stereotypical scene like the one described above, consumers often swallow the lies advertisers actively feed them.

3. In the 1990s, however, obvious stereotypes like a woman whose sole purpose is to remove stains from the carpet are not the most dangerous. Instead, it is in the more elusive area of body language that stereotypes can subtly influence the way an individual perceives him/herself and the world around him/herself. Advertisements present situations as fact, when they actually "depict for [society] not necessarily how [people] behave as men and women but how [people] think men and women behave" (Gornick XII). Therefore, how a woman is portrayed is of utmost importance. In 1979, Erving Goffman, author of what can be considered the definitive work on gender stereotyping in advertisements, outlines five observable phenomenon in gender-based advertising: feminine touch, function ranking, ritualization of subordination, relative size, and licensed withdrawal.

4. Feminine touch creates the illusion that a woman is fragile. This is achieved by gently caressing one's own body or objects. Men, on the other hand, often place their hands together in confident positions to grasp objects firmly (Kang 6). According to a study of randomly-chosen advertisements from leading women's magazines conducted in 1991, this form of stereotyping has undergone no significant change since Goffman's original study in 1979 (Kang 10). In an advertisement for Prada a woman is pictured gently sliding her hair behind her ears with a somewhat confused expression. The implication from the photograph is that this woman is thinking about something much too difficult for her. The gentle motion of her hands reiterates the frailness of her condition.

5. Function ranking also contributes to the idea of men as more capable counterparts. In advertisements featuring this form of stereotyping, men always perform the executive role, while women remain peripheral players in the scene (Kang 6). In an ad for this type a woman is seen speaking to a man cozily seated in a train station. Once again, her body language reveals the problem. Because she is looking up to this man, it seems as though she is asking him a question which only he can answer. In the nineteen years since Goffman's original study, women have made many in-roads in America concerning men and their positions of power. Advertising does not reflect these advancements, however. Basically the same percentage of advertisements feature function ranking today as in 1979 (Kang 10).

6. Also prevalent in today's society is ritualization of subordination. This form of stereotyping can be defined as an act or action depleting one's self-worth. This is accomplished through the use of submissive body posture. Common activities such as head lowering and/or the physical lowering of a woman in a man's presence, especially by kneeling, sitting, or lying all force the participant into a subordinate position (Kang 6). In the Prada ad, the woman pictured has her knee slightly bent, a position usually occupied by nervous children or adopted in the presence of royalty. Her eyes are also lowered, an obvious sign of submission. This woman lacks the confidence to look another in the eye, instead choosing to defer to the wishes of those around her.

7. Relative size involves the height and girth of men in relation to women in an advertisement. This area often comes under attack by many people who state that men are naturally taller than women. What these critics fail to take into account is that while men usually are taller, in advertisements height and girth are largely equated with social rank (Kang 6). Therefore, by creating a picture with a man in the foreground of an advertisement, making him larger, the woman behind him becomes of lesser importance. Unfortunately, this area has undergone little to no change in the twelve years since Goffman's original study (Kang 10).

8. Contrary to the other areas of gender stereotyping rampant in the print advertising genre, the area of licensed withdrawal has undergone change in the years since Goffman's study. Unfortunately, this change is moving the advertising world away from positive gender roles. Licensed withdrawal, which depicts women removing themselves psychologically from situations by withdrawing their gaze from the given situation, is now more prevalent than the pre-eighties study (Kang 11). If one is to believe advertisements, women are frequently plunged into the throws of ecstasy by a perfume, a cigarette, or a cellular phone. In these stereotypes, a woman will stare glassy eyed off into space as confident men in the picture dominate the scene. Also, the lips of models in advertisements are often parted with a lipstick, cigarette, or popsicle near or in the mouth. These are obvious phallic symbols relying on the supposition that sex sells. All of these portrayals lead a consumer to believe that women are petty creatures who focus on the sensual pleasures material possessions may bring.

9. The reader's response to these negative characterizations is subtle. Because they are so constant and manipulative, most people do not even realize that this information is present. Visual images do have meaning behind them and it is this meaning which is so insidious. To believe the picture of women in advertising is to believe that the female race is composed of "weak, childish, dependent, domestic, irrational, subordinate creatures, the producers of children and little else compared with men" (Kang 3). This is not just the attitude given to one small uneducated segment of society but is rather unconsciously accepted as truth by both men and women alike. The meaning of advertisements seeps "into the belief systems of the society" to which it is exposed (Kang 2). An independent study published in 1986 "found that exposure to advertisements employing stereotypical sex roles for women resulted in significantly lower perceptions of women's managerial abilities than exposure to advertisements depicting women in professional type roles requiring such abilities" (Kang 4). Obviously, advertisements do affect what people think about women and, unfortunately, these thoughts are often acted out in real life.

Works Cited

Goffman, Erving. *Gender Advertisements*. New York: Harper and Row, 1979.

Gornick, Vivian. Introduction. *Gender Advertisements*. By Erving Goffman. New York: Harper and Row, 1979. vii–ix.

Kang, Mee-Eun. "The Portrayal of Women's Images in Magazine Advertisements: Goffman's Gender Analysis Revisited." *Sex Roles: A Journal of Research*. 11–12. 979. Online. Internet. Dec. 1997. Available: web7.searchbank.com/infotrac.

Lipper, Barbara. "Attitude Unbecoming: Why Aggressive, In-Your-Face Ads are the Vogue of the Moment." *Brandweek*. 39. S36(4). Online. Internet. 7 Oct. 1996. Available: web7.searchbank.com/infotrac.

Their Side of the Story
by
Zane Birdwell

1. Believe it or not, there was a time when the filmmakers and actors of the adult film industry took a certain amount of pride in their work. Before the invention of the video camera, adult films took as much money, time, and effort to produce as any other major motion picture. For years, the price of filming, developing, synching, acting, and distributing resulted in the production of only a few adult films. Today, anyone with a few shameless "actors" and a camcorder can make a buck shooting their own torrid fantasy in his or her backyard. We are reminded of the assumed superiority of quality over quantity as *Boogie Nights*, the disco-laced first major film from director Paul Thomas Anderson roars into theaters, challenging and amazing its viewers with unbridled flare and intelligence.

2. What makes *Boogie Nights* work as well as it does is hard to pinpoint. First, make no mistake, *Boogie Nights* is a film about family, not about pornography. Just as Scorsese's *Raging Bull* was a film about one man's triumph over his own mental dysfunction, with the sport of boxing a mere backdrop with which to set the tone of the film, Anderson's new film works in much the same way. *Boogie Nights* works so well because it utilizes many different aspects of great filmmaking that are co-dependent. The cinematography, acting, and craftsmanship of the film are all incredible, yet none of these things alone are enough to hold the movie together.

3. In *Boogie Nights*, we are given the story of a young man named Eddie Addams (Mark Wahlberg) who believes that "everyone is blessed with one special thing." At the young age of seventeen, Eddie has already developed a keen interest in risky behavior, working late at a rather seedy nightclub outside of Los Angeles. In Eddie's case, his "special thing" happens to be the abnormally large size of his genitalia. Eddie is interested in focusing his special gift toward an area where it may be utilized to the fullest extent. So, after a scuffle with his parents, whose interests and ideals are also questionable, Eddie decides to head to the comfort of newfound friend and ironically enough, adult film director, Jack Horner (Burt Reynolds). Under the wing of Jack Horner, Eddie finds himself setting sail on a ship of dreams called porn stardom. With more "talent" than anyone else in the industry, Eddie is as valuable as crude oil. Slapped with a new screen name, Dirk Diggler, Eddie is well on his way to fame.

4. As the plot thickens, we meet more and more interesting characters and superbly cast actors. Heather Graham plays another teenage film star named Rollergirl, whose real name in the film is never mentioned. This could possibly be due to a recurring theme of escaping one's past, a facet of time that all the characters in the film want to run from. Rollergirl is another lost soul, just like Eddie, who wants fame and fortune at any price, including the sacrifice of pride. Eddie's confidante and mother figure in the film is a woman named Amber Waves, played by Julianne Moore. Amber is constantly at Eddie's side, coaching and aiding him throughout the course of the film. The bond between the characters of the film and the depth that the director gives to each of them do an incredible job of holding together a movie that would otherwise be thought of as a waste of time and money. Even the director himself says, "They are a family, comically dysfunctional in many ways, but a family nonetheless (Production)."

5. For the first half of the epic-length film, director Paul Thomas Anderson is intent on celebrating the good times of the era. Disco music, funny clothes, and a heady brew of nostalgic dancing accompany the wild nights that fall between showing all for the camera. Anderson tells his wild story, completely devoid of the inherent consequences that acts such as drug use and promiscuous sex will inevitably bring. At times in the film, even with the awareness of the 1990s, we feel almost as carefree as the actors we are watching on screen. Naturally, Anderson does this for no other reason than to have you right where he wants you, waiting for the perfect moment to make you own up to all the debauchery that preceded. This moment of realization comes at the end of the seventies with a surprise twist that takes the direction the movie is heading and reverses it almost instantly. In the blink of an eye, the good times of the seventies are forgotten and we are suddenly thrust into a new decade of addiction, disease, and moral indirection. This is quite possibly the greatest trick in a series of magic acts that make the movie what it is.

6. From this point on, *Boogie Nights* is no longer a comedy; it is now a soul-searching drama, where the actors who once were kings of the hill now walk the earth like zombies, trying to convince themselves that the way they make their living is worthwhile and noble. With the invention of the video camera, porn movies are a dime a dozen. The word "actor" in an adult film is scarce and even pointless. People who watch these disgusting movies don't want actors; they simply want an erotic thrill. The characters in *Boogie Nights* realize this and have a lot of difficulty dealing with a truth that holds their fate in the balance. The only answer to such a dilemma is to roll with the punches, to adapt, and this is what the characters in the film end up doing.

7. *Boogie Nights* is a movie about family, not a family movie. Families are not always like the ones we watch on television sitcoms. They are real people and people cannot be categorized. The one thing that holds the stars of this film together is the bond that at least if they are not sure what they are doing is the correct way to live, at least they are doing it together. There is a centrifugal force at work in *Boogie Nights* that teaches us why people behave the way they do and why lost souls stick with each other. People are so used to passing off the stars of adult films as classless, tasteless beggars who make their living off of carnal sin, we forget that these are real people with real lives.

8. As the majority of people who will view *Boogie Nights* will probably have a hard time accepting a movie so controversial in its nature, it is important to remember a few things. Pornography is used to help exemplify the freedom and carelessness of the disco era. Because the film is set against the backdrop of the adult entertainment industry, necessary evils such as the use of drugs, profanity, and violence are less shocking than they would otherwise be. Also, it is important to remember that in reality, some people do use drugs and are sometimes violent. Why then not tell the story from the point-of-view of a drug cartel or a group of gangsters? Because we know that would-be good people sometimes get involved in bad things such as drugs and violence. Bad deeds don't necessarily add up to bad individuals. Paul Thomas Anderson feels that maybe it is time to tell the story from another medium, one less commonly used; his answer is the adult entertainment industry.

9. One could easily be disgusted, overwhelmed, or shocked senseless by *Boogie Nights'* courage if that is what you would like to call it. During the world premiere of the film, Mark Wahlberg's mother began crying at the sight of her son portraying such a character (Comments). But don't think that Anderson didn't count on the angst of the viewer; he did. One cannot however ignore the masterful way the story is told, the film's excellence in nearly every aspect of filmmaking and its close attention to detail. If anyone sits down to view this film expecting to get an erotic thrill out of it, that person will be thoroughly disappointed, as well as set back a few dollars. The film's focus

isn't on the adult films themselves, but on the lives of the people who made them. During an era when nothing seemed to matter except having a good time, the stars of the adult film industry were the gurus of their day, setting the standard by not questioning their actions and just enjoying the ride. At the end of the seventies, all that changed and whatever respect the adult film industry once thought it possessed was lost, leaving nothing but a muddy puddle of confused faces and indecision. *Boogie Nights* recounts this transition, not from the side of those who were screaming, "I told you so, I told you so!" throughout the midst of the hoopla, but from the side of the people who were riding the crest of the tidal wave when it finally reached the shore and broke.

Works Cited

Production Notes on *"Boogie Nights"* Oct. 1997. 6 Feb. 1999

      <http://www.markymark.com/movies/boogie/comments.htm

Comments from Mark Wahlberg on Dirk Diggler Oct. 1997 6 Feb. 1999

      <http://www.markymark.com/movies/boogie/notes.htm

Proposal

No Need for the Rush
by
Azurae Willis

1. The McWhorter School of Pharmacy is a prestigious college within the gates of Samford University. Awarding the Doctorate of Pharmacy (Pharm.D.) to its graduates after four years of intense study in the school, the graduates are "ready" to conquer the world of medicine. Have they truly had enough time to develop as educated students? Instead of being rushed through the program, which is designed to be completed in six years, students need to obtain a degree before applying to pharmacy school. This will not only enhance their study skills, confidence, and qualifications, but also provide them with a more wide range of experiences to ensure they want to be in school for another four years of intense study.

2. The new Pharm.D. program, which has been implemented across the country as the standard for a practicing pharmacist, is a six-year program in which students do two years of pre-requisites prior to their four years of pharmacy school. Samford is one of the many universities that has switched to this program. Opinions differ as to the quality of this new program that began to be a part of pharmacy schools nationwide in 1994. According to an article by Paul Larrat from Brown University, "The Pharm.D. degree will be the sole entry level degree for the profession, requires six or seven years to complete (with pre-requisites), and features a curriculum that heavily emphasizes applied clinical work. These pharmacists should graduate with greater clinical skills that could be applied readily to geriatric (older) populations" (para. 3). Opposing this perspective in *American Druggist* was Victor Ostrowidzki. He explained that there was no concrete evidence to support the idea that the extra year(s) would provide any more important knowledge for the students, just a greater cost of time and money (para. 5). Pharmacists must have a Pharm.D. in order to have a practice; therefore these years of school are inevitable.

3. Currently Samford University offers the pre-requisites for entrance into pharmacy school in a plan laid out course-by-course that begins with eighteen hours in the student's first semester of college. Having to balance Samford's core classes, which require a lot of reading and writing, with difficult math and science courses that students normally take in their later college years, provides great stress and anxiety on the student's behalf. There is also a struggle to balance the intense studying required, with the "college experience". The next three semesters are very similar, requiring students to take at least sixteen hours. This rigorous schedule leaves the student without any room for flexibility or other opportunities. According to one pre-pharmacy student, "I wish I could just take some other types of classes and explore what else is out there!" Because of constraints such as chemistry labs students are unable to study abroad. They must also begin the application process for admission to the Pharmacy School in the first semester of their sophomore year. Can a twenty-year-old truly be prepared for graduate school? Not at the rate that is required of them at Samford.

4. Though most pharmacy schools have similar requirements for their pharmacy schools, each one has a slightly different process. Auburn University has a program that is very similar to Samford's in that the first two years serve the sole purpose of getting the student accepted into pharmacy school (para. 3).

5. Pre-pharmacy students at the University of Florida have a bit more say in the courses that they take. Though there are courses that are recommended, the student has a choice. For example, he/she must have six to nine credits of humanities as well as social and behavioral sciences. These courses, which can be selected by the student, give them opportunities to explore other interests that they may have (para. 6). While there are certain pre-pharmacy courses that they must take, students at Florida must also obtain an Associate of Arts degree prior to admission to pharmacy school (para. 1). Students who wish to continue their education at Florida's pharmacy school must also take the PCAT (Pharmacy College Admission Test) (para. 9). Academic process is also tracked over the course of the two years to make sure that the student is doing well enough to be accepted into Pharmacy School (para. 15). These are each very important in that the student has an accredited degree, proves they have been educated enough to pass the PCAT, and are informed of their academic progress in relation to the pharmacy school's requirements. Samford does none of these things.

6. "Students at The Ohio State University typically pursue Doctor of Pharmacy education after the completion of the bachelor's degree" (Entry, para. 4). Ohio State is one of the few universities that still recommend that students receive a degree before applying to pharmacy school. Though they do allow students who complete the pre-requisites in three years to go ahead and apply, they give preference to the students with a bachelor's degree (para. 4). Ohio State also requires a PCAT score.

7. "I love that I have to take at least three, if not four years to do my pre-requisites here. My classes are difficult, but they are also more spread out. I feel like I am actually learning instead of just making the grades to get into pharmacy school like I was at Samford. I am also taking a class or two in conjunction with the pharmacy school at Ohio State to make sure that is where I want to spend another four years of school," explained Nancy Henricks, a recently transferred pharmacy student from Samford to Ohio State.

8. So where does this leave Samford in the mix? Students need more time. The two years that pre-pharmacy students spend working hard to get into school help them do just that and it ends there. No degree is received, not even an Associate of Arts. Mary Bolus, a Registered Nurse and Registered Dietician, found Samford's pharmacy school very difficult and decided to stop after her third year. "Because I did not receive any type of degree prior to my entrance into pharmacy school, I had to go back and basically pick up where I left off. Basically, I was in school for five years, but had not received any type degree!" she explained. This is important, because in the event that a pharmacy student realizes pharmacy school is not for him/her, he/she will need to have something to fall back on. Going backwards and taking courses just to obtain a degree is a waste of time and money for the student.

9. In order to eliminate this problem, Samford should offer courses that introduce this field of study more clearly so that students are more knowledgeable as to what they are jumping into. Possibly a course called "Intro to Pharmacy" where students learn not only of the numerous opportunities the field has to offer, but can also hear firsthand what is expected of them. This would be especially helpful for the students if a professor from the pharmacy school taught it.

10. Taking extra classes would require more years, which is why students should obtain a four-year degree prior to entering Samford's pharmacy school. At Ohio State University, applicants are not required to have a degree in a related pharmacy field. Any major is acceptable as long as the student takes the prerequisites for pharmacy school (para. 6). In pursuing a degree outside of a

pharmacy concentration (pharmaceutical sciences, chemistry), the student's mind is exposed to a variety of things that could be applied later on in his/her career. For example, a Spanish major who receives a degree and then goes through pharmacy school could be quite an asset in South Florida or even in Latin America. Biology major at Samford, Dave Kinsley, waited until his senior year to apply for pharmacy school. He will graduate with a degree in biology and then pursue a career in pharmacy. "There is no way that I would have made it if I tried to start in after my sophomore year. My study habits are much more secure, I am more confident in who I am, and I am ready for graduate school."

11. Being unprepared is the largest problem with the rush to begin pharmacy school. According to two current Samford pharmacy students I was introduced to by Dean Franklin who each graduated with degrees in chemistry and psychology from the University of Alabama at Birmingham, "The Samford students who enter the McWhorter School of Pharmacy in their third year of college, are not prepared for the work that lies ahead of them. They forget that this is no longer their junior year of college, it is their first year of graduate school!" By graduating with a four-year degree, a student shows that he/she is committed to his/her studies and ready for the next step. Also, should that student decide the extra four years of school required for their Pharm.D. is not for them, they have a degree to fall back on.

12. These are a number of reasons why Samford University's McWhorter School of Pharmacy needs to re-evaluate their process. Whatever the case may be pharmacy is not an easy profession. People put their lives into the hands of their pharmacists every time they have a prescription filled. We need dedicated people who are committed to what they do behind those counters, not students who were rushed through their college experience so they could start making big money.

Works Cited

An Introduction. *Au School of Pharmacy Homepage*. 21 Mar. 2000. <http://pharmacy.

auburn.edu/admin/intro_info.html>.

Bolus, Mary. Personal Interview. 15 Mar. 2000.

Henricks, Nancy. Personal Interview. 21 Mar. 2000.

Kinsley, Dave. Personal Interview. 13 Mar. 2000.

Larrat, Paul. "Improved pharmaceutical care will become more specialized." *Brown

University Long-Term Care Letter*. 12 Sept.1994. Vol. 6 Issue 17. 21 Mar. 2000.

<http://ehostvgw16.epnwt.com/print2.asp?r...eControl=loaded&est=&b

Citation=&x=28&y=9>.

Ostrowidzki, Victor. "Against Pharm.D." *American Druggist*. Apr. 1994. 21 Mar.

2000. <http://web7.infortrac.galegroup.com/itw/i...0_A15426621&dyn=7!ar_fmt?

sw_aep=naal_sam>.

Pharmacy: Entry-Level Program. *Ohio State University Pharmacy Homepage*. 21 Mar.

2000. <http://www.pharmacy.ohio-state.edu/homepage/pros_students/entry

level.html>.

Pharmacy Students. Personal Interview. Nov. 1999.

Pre-Pharmacy Course Requirements. *University of Florida Pharmacy Homepage*. 21

Mar. 2000. http://www.cop.ufl.edu/.

The New Plagiarism
by
Elizabeth Evans

1. We've all been there: it's three o'clock in the morning and you have a six-page paper due the next morning and you're only on page one, not having a clue about what you are writing. You could just quit and deal with the consequences of turning in your assignment late. But, hey, this is the age of technology. You don't have to write your own paper if you don't want to. This moment of decision comes as you remember that Internet web site your friend told you about where you could buy a paper on any topic. With your eyes shutting and your head about to fall on your computer screen, the possibility of soon being fast asleep in bed is quite tempting. All of your worries could end by typing in your credit card number.

2. Late-night moments of truth such as these are occurring all around college campuses these days. With Internet access being available to most students 24 hours a day through free university service, the temptation is always present for many students looking for an easy way out of their procrastination. Internet plagiarism is the fastest growing trend in cheating (Stebelman, par. 1). Since this form of taking someone else's work has not been available for very long, many universities still don't know how to deal with it. Internet plagiarism is different than traditional ways of cheating. It doesn't involve taking a selected passage from a book or periodical and passing the words off as your own; rather, it involves downloading an entire essay from the great reaches of the World Wide Web and passing the words off as your own.

3. Plagiarizing with the aid of the Internet gets easier every day. With the Web expanding every hour, the list of possible sites to get papers from is always expanding. John Hickman says, "The number of term-paper sites has swelled from 28 in the beginning of 1997 to 72 [in March of 1998]" (par. 3). The sites continue to grow. When I searched for such sites myself, I discovered overwhelming possible hits (Links). After finding just one web site with "sample essays" on it, I was linked to numerous related sites. In fact, I printed out a list three pages long of places to buy papers, and I am sure more sites like this can be found. Although most sites I investigated contained a disclaimer that the information on the site was for research purposes only, nothing can stop the student from downloading one of the sample essays and putting their name on it. Students are just a click away from having a free ride. One Princeton University freshman acknowledges she turned in a paper she found on the Internet because "it's just so easy, and the class was a waste of time, anyway" (qtd. in Hickman, par. 6). With even Ivy League students admitting to such immoral behavior, you begin to see the seriousness of the problem. Plagiarism is not just for the dumb kids anymore; through the aid of the Internet, it's for the smart kids too.

4. It's easy to see why this is a problem because of the numerous effects Internet plagiarism has on students. Dr. Bryan Johnson, a course coordinator for Samford University's Communication Arts classes, says that Internet plagiarism is "sort of like walking into Wal-Mart and buying something you could do for yourself. It's giving yourself a Wal-Mart education" (Johnson interview). By taking the easy way out through buying Internet papers, students merely go through the motions of schoolwork without actually learning what writing assignments are meant to teach them. For example, Joe Smith, a hypothetical pre-med student, bought his Biology research paper about the workings of the human heart from the Internet without being caught. He gleefully prides himself in his temporary success, but his laziness comes back to haunt him as he begins his first heart surgery in medical school. Because he plagiarized through the Internet, Joe has missed a piece in the puzzle of his education.

5. Not only does Internet plagiarism hurt the student who cheats, but it hurts the honest students who are striving to do their own work. Because some students are able to turn in sophisticated and scholarly writing, passing it off as their own, their hard-working and honorable classmates are penalized for not turning in something written at the doctorate level. Honest students are often put on the low end of the curve because their colleagues are cheating through the Internet (Roach, par. 28).

6. Professors are often put in a Catch-22 as well. Instead of focusing all of their time in leading students in academic pursuits, teachers have to decide if they will become like "Ken Starr" by investigating suspected dishonest students (Johnson interview). Teachers are forced to invent creative ways of preventing the growth of Internet plagiarism. Because a professor's time has to be used in some way to make decisions about how to deal with cheaters, the good students are cheated of time that could have been theirs.

7. How can this cycle end? Ultimately the goal is to teach students "that no difference exists between plagiarizing a printed essay and one that appears on the Web" (Stebelman, par. 6). I propose that first the problem needs to be better understood by professors. If they don't care about the issue and take measures to stop it, who will? In continuing education seminars, professors need to be better informed about the seriousness of the issue. One way of doing this would be to hold teacher workshops and have them look at such popular sites as "Evil House of Cheat" or "Term Paper 911" to see what kind of papers are out there on the Web. In these sites, various types of essays are found on almost every topic imaginable. Ungraded papers can be bought for five to twelve dollars a page (Ivy). Through education on the issue, Dr. Johnson described to me a change that has occurred in his attitude about cheating. He says his personal awareness of the problem made him decide to take steps to correct it. He feels some personal responsibility in preventing occurrences of plagiarism (Johnson interview). Although some professors' apathy about Internet plagiarism will remain whether they are informed about it or not, such continuing education seminars have the ability to open the eyes of those who had no idea such Web sites existed.

8. Next, instead of ignoring the issue or just saying, "Do your own work," professors should confront the problem head-on with their students. They need to show they are smarter than their students. To do this, all freshman composition courses need to have a field trip down to the computer labs at least once during the semester. During this time, the instructor needs to take students to some of the numerous "sample essay" sites to critique the quality of various papers. In doing this the students are, first, made aware that the professor knows of potential plagiarism sites, and second, the unscholarly nature of many papers can be studied as a teaching aid. Dr. William McHenry at Georgetown University advises professors: "Let's not pretend these sites don't exist... [let the] Buyer Beware" (quoted in Roach, par. 19).

9. If time constraints don't allow for the entire class to go to a computer lab, my proposal still can be implemented. Professors themselves can go to the web sites and photocopy sample essays to be used in class discussions. Scott Stebelman points to this solution when he advises that "Faculty should visit term paper mill sites ... and inform students of the investigative activity" (par. 19). Dr. Johnson has found much success in this approach in battling student reliance on *Cliffs Notes*. During the weeks before a paper is due in one of his literature classes, he finds it helpful to bring photocopies of selected interpretations from *Cliffs Notes* to discuss the explanations found. "By doing this," he says, "I am able to encourage students to think originally and show I know what's out there" (Johnson interview). Through this approach to the problem, honest and dishonest

students alike can gain benefits. The potential cheaters can have their consciences softened, while those who would never think of cheating can sharpen their minds through exercises of critique.

10. One reason why Internet plagiarism is so easy is because teachers continue to give students the same assignments year after year, so with general topics late-night procrastinators have no trouble finding a paper to buy on their topic. Professors should create topics for their writing assignments which are unique to a specific idea or theory while avoiding popular subjects such as AIDS (Stebelman, par.22). In doing this, teachers limit the opportunities of students to cheat. Dr. Johnson echoed this when he described to me one of his recent writing assignments. In this assignment, he gave students a list of novels to read and then write a theme analysis paper on one work. The students which he suspected plagiarized were those who read novels which have had much written about them. The other novels on the list were those which were not as popular or well known, so he did not find students plagiarizing in their papers. When teachers' assignments encourage students to stay away from Internet plagiarism because it is not possible, the problem is eliminated. Through taking preventive measures to decrease the amount of plagiarism that is possible, professors will have to do less amounts of investigative work on their students. If students don't cheat in the first place, honest students will not be penalized for turning in their own work.

11. I realize that my solution to Internet plagiarism just touches the tip of the iceberg of the problem. Dishonest individuals will always find a way to cheat, and because of the Constitution's first amendment, plagiarism-friendly web sites will continue to grow. There is no doubt about this. However, if professors are more aware of the magnitude of this problem and have specific steps to take in dealing with it, students might think twice about clicking on a "sample essay" site for their next assignment.

12. Just as you begin to type in the last three numbers of your credit card, you remember the handout your professor brought to class the day before from the "AAA Guide to Cheating." The quality of the essay was repulsive, and after all, Dr. Jones knew about this easy way out. On top of that, the essay you are about to buy is not really on the topic of how Oedipus' hubris brings his downfall in *Oedipus the King* anyway; it's just a glorified plot summary. So, you disconnect from the Web and with your cup of coffee in one hand you begin to type once more.

Works Cited

Hickman, John N. "Cybercheats: Term-Paper Shopping Online." *The New Republic*. 23 March 1998.

Infotrac.

Johnson, Bryan. Personal Interview. 7 April 1999.

Roach, Ronald. "High-Tech Cheating." *Black Issues in Higher Education*. 24 December 1998. Infotrac.

Stebelman, Scott. "Cybercheating: Dishonesty Goes Digital." *American Libraries*. September 1998.

Infotrac.

"Ivy Essays to Buy" n. pag. Online. Internet. 30 March 1999. Available: http://www.ivyessays.com

"Links Database for Erin Carlson's Web Pages." n. pag. Online. Internet. 30 March 1999. Available:

http:// www.csc.calpoly.edu/~ercarlso/links/index.html

Cause/Effect

A Long Time Ago in a Galaxy Far, Far Away
by
John Ragsdale

1. "May the Force be with you." It has become "a buzz-phrase uttered in place of 'good luck' or 'Godspeed'" (Woods 57). The three *Star Wars* films, *A New Hope, The Empire Strikes Back,* and *The Return of the Jedi*, have become a significant part of our film culture. With the *Star Wars* trilogy, George Lucas created "a language, a world, an entire cultural system, that has entered our own" (Cone 4). It was immensely popular at its release and continues to remain so today. When the first movie came out, it was "the highest-grossing film of all time" (Handy 69). It earned $2.8 million in its first week of limited release (Woods 52). With the re-releases, the original 35-screen opening in 1977 had grown to a 2,104-screen opening in 1997 (Handy 69). And, its popularity does not stop with the movies themselves. USA spent $5 million to $7 million for the five-year rights to *Star Wars* ("'Star' Buy" 18). In addition to this, PepsiCo launched a $2 billion promotion campaign in May of 1996 in conjunction with the re-release of the films (Vaz 20). Corporations are willing to spend large amounts of money on these motion pictures because they know the popularity of the films exists. As if these numbers are not impressive enough, the films, along with the products based on them, have earned more than $4 billion (Woods 52). The popularity of *Star Wars* is undoubtedly immense. This popularity, though often as mysterious as the Force itself, has definite causes. Among these are its themes, characters, and technology.

2. The themes in *Star Wars* were not new to film or even science fiction. In the words of the creator George Lucas, "it's based on ideas and themes that have been around for two to three thousand years" (Handy 74). Though not new, the themes that the trilogy presents are ones which are relevant to the average person. These are issues with which everyone must deal and to which everyone can relate. They are universal themes. The largest among these is the theme of maturation. The main character, Luke Skywalker, goes from being a naive farm boy to a Jedi master and leader of the Rebellion. The movies, in essence, are a narrative of his development. The training he receives in the Force represents the much larger education everyone receives in life and formally. He must learn to deal with pain, love, hate, and frustration to fully become a master of the Force. This journey is often painful. As everyone must deal with the process of growth, the films involve one in Luke's maturation, seeing aspects of his/her own. Another theme involved in maturation, independence, is also evident. Luke is forced to deal, as each person is, with leaving his parents. For him, this comes suddenly and unexpectedly as his aunt and uncle, who were caring for him, are killed by the Empire, but the issue is still the same. He no longer has any family ties and must therefore live his own life. So, he leaves the planet to fulfill his destiny as a leader in the Rebellion. Through this independence, Luke is able to search for his own identity. He is no longer forced to become a moisture farmer like his uncle, but, rather, he can become the person he wants to be. He can follow his dreams of piloting spaceships and going into the war against the Empire. All people must deal with this issue when coming to realize what they want for their own lives and refusing to allow others to decide for them. Part of what motivates Luke in his discovery of his identity is his desire to be part of something larger than himself. This is evident in his joining of the Rebellion and desire to learn the Force, which is present in all things. Somewhere, in all

people, is the same desire. Everyone has a need to feel that they are making a difference outside their individual lives. Furthermore, through Luke's becoming a part of something greater than himself, the larger universe in which he lives is revealed. One of his teachers, Obi-Wan Kenobi, even says to him, "you've taken your first step into a larger world." In this universe, one is able to see many alien beings and cultures which are different from one another and from one's own world. These new and diverse worlds arouse the curiosity in each person to explore that which is not known. In addition to this theme, another theme which is present throughout the movie is the battle between good and evil. On a large scale, this is seen in the Rebellion going to war against the Empire over the corruption and injustice of the latter. On a smaller scale, this is evident in Luke's battles against Darth Vader, who places no value on human life and kills his commanders for disagreeing. The good versus evil theme is one which is present throughout life. People are forced to take a stand against inequality and unfairness. Countries must go to war to protect the rights of their citizens. In addition to presenting this battle, the popularity of the trilogy also results from the fact that good prevails. In the films, the virtuous side, the Rebellion, triumphs initially, in the first movie, and finally, in the last movie. People feel more secure seeing the side prevail which upholds goodness, even if that is not always what happens in life. Finally, another universal theme present in the films is the parent-child conflict. In *Star Wars*, this occurs between Luke and Darth Vader, who he learns is his real father. The conflict is physical (light saber duels) at times and psychological (trying to convert one another to his own side) at other times. Whether paternal or maternal, everyone must deal with parental conflict in his/her life. Andrew Lewis Conn in "*Star Wars*: Always" says, 'I also remember beginning to come to terms with certain dualities that until [I saw *Star Wars*] I couldn't approach in my father" (3). In summation, the themes of maturation, independence, self-discovery, assimilation, opposing forces, and parental conflict are universal and present in *Star Wars*. By being universal, they are relevant to many different people. This relevance to people's lives is responsible for much of the popularity of the *Star Wars* trilogy.

3. The characters in Star Wars have personalities that draw the audience into the movies. Each of them has an individuality which contributes to the films in its own way. This is especially evident in the two main droids (i.e. robots) of the films, C-3PO and R2-D2. C-3P0 is intelligent and precise. R2-D2 is excitable and determined. Together, these two produce a unique comical team built on their disagreement and bantering. The two are called "the hottest comedy duo since Laurel and Hardy" (Woods 53). C-3PO's need to be accepted (Spelling 57) and R2-D2's independent nature provide for much amusement as the two are juxtaposed. Such engaging personalities as these are part of the reason for the success of the trilogy. As another example, Han Solo is a rebellious character who lives outside the law. He is sought by bounty hunters and routinely smuggles goods into forbidden territories. He appeals to the natural desire to live dangerously. Princess Leia is a determined character who will not be told what to do. Much of her popularity comes from the fact that the heroine is portrayed as independent rather than helpless. David S. Meyer calls her "a post-feminist princess who wields her own blaster and makes decisions" (101). Yoda, the Jedi master who teaches Luke the ways of the Force, is liked for being both wise and humorous. Obi-Wan Kenobi's sense of self-sacrifice and devotion to Luke (even through Luke's obstinacy) endear him to audiences. Part of the appeal of many of the characters lies in their uniqueness. Among these are Chewbacca (an oversized ape), R2-D2 (a robotic "trash can"), Jabba the Hutt (a monstrous slug), the Ewoks (aboriginal "teddy bears"), and Yoda (a nine hundred-year-old reptile). Finally, Luke Skywalker's appeal comes from his relevance rather than his peculiarity. In him, many people find characteristics with which they can identify. He is primarily an adventurous dreamer. He is restless and wants to explore new worlds. This can be seen very well in the first movie when Luke looks longingly to the horizon as his planet Tatooine's twin suns are setting. He has just argued with his uncle about leaving their farm to pursue his dreams. All people have hopes and feel a need to explore. He is also passionate about what matters to him. He leaves

his Jedi training against the advice of his teacher Yoda to save his friends from danger. Everyone has a cause which matters to him/her and about which he/she becomes very impassioned. As a part of his dreams, Luke also desires adventure. He, as every person does, wants to move beyond his mundane life and find excitement. Through the distinct personalities and relevance of the various characters, much of the popularity of *Star Wars* can be seen.

4. Much of the technology used in *Star Wars* was developed for the films. When current technology did not allow for a certain effect, a method was developed by Lucas' company Industrial Light and Magic to perform it. In addition to forwarding general movie-making technology, this allowed for unique special effects in the *Star Wars* films. Audiences were dazzled by the destruction of whole planets and the glow of light sabers. In addition to the effects, the imaginary worlds of the films were also made real by the technology. The Mos Eisley spaceport seemed to be an actual place on a real planet called Tatooine. One might wonder if there were truly a planet in some far-off galaxy being orbited by a Death Star. The creatures which inhabited these places were brought alive by the technology. The puppet Yoda and the three-person costume of Jabba the Hutt seem as lifelike as any of the actors. In addition to making the effects, places, and creatures seem real, the technology also allowed for a convincingly "futuristic" setting. Though *Star Wars* is set "a long time ago in a galaxy far, far way," the majority of its scientific knowledge is considerably more advanced than Earth's. This creates an imaginary universe where the audience can dream and ask, "what if?" It has been compared to "the futuristic tales of Buck Rogers and Flash Gordon" (Woods 55). Overall, the technology in *Star Wars* allows for development of special effects, imaginary worlds, and lifelike creatures, all in a "futuristic" setting.

5. The popularity of the *Star Wars* trilogy can be traced back to its relevant themes (i.e. maturation, independence, self-discovery, assimilation, opposing forces, and parental conflict), its varied characters (with distinct personalities and pertinence), and its pioneering technology (allowing for special effects, imaginary worlds, and lifelike creatures). Essentially, *Star Wars* has everything a popular movie should; it has romance, humor, mystery, sadness, and, above all, action. It is a fairy tale of epic proportions. In the words of Mark Hamill, the actor who played Luke Skywalker, "it was kind of a fresh take on elements that have been part of entertainment since the beginning of time" (Mandharan 44). Basically, *Star Wars* is "a grand story with compelling characters that ultimately captivated the world" (Vaz 10). And, the world will likely be captivated again in 1999 with the release of the next installment in the *Star Wars* series. In the words of C-3PO, "here we go again."

Works Cited

Conn, Andrew Lewis. "*Star Wars*: Always." *Film Comment* May-June 1997: 2–4.

Handy, Bruce. "The Force is Back." *Time* 10 Feb. 1997: 69–74.

Mandharan, Raj and Marc Shapiro. "Back from the Wars." *Starlog* March 1997: 4347.

Meyer, Davis S. "Star Wars, Star Wars, and American Political Culture." *Journal of Popular Culture* Fall 1992: 99–115.

Spelling, Ian. "Being Threepio." *Starlog* March 1997: 55–58.

"'Star' Buy." *Broadcasting* 18 Nov. 1991: 18.

Vaz, Mark Cotta. "Launching the Rebellion." *Star Wars 20th Anniversary Magazine* 1997: 19–20.

Woods, Bob. "It Took the World by Force." *Star Wars 20th Anniversary Magazine* 1997: 52–59.

The Effects of Violent Media Content on Children

by

Rebecca Pounds

1. The question of the effects of negative media content on children plagues today's society in a way that was unimaginable even twenty years ago. Over the years, even in the past decade, the amount of crudeness, vulgarity, profanity, sexual explicitness, and violence in television has drastically increased. At the same time, and possibly consequently, aggressive and violent behavior and lower academic performance have increased in today's children. This correlation is alarming, and this matter is not one to be taken lightly. Evidence shows that negative media content produces negative effects in society, specifically that violence in television produces negative results when viewed by children.

2. The media, specifically television, has a tremendous influence on society. Ninety-eight percent of American households own at least one television set, and that set is turned on for nearly seven hours per day. The average American child watches approximately twenty-one hours of television per week, excluding rented movies, music videos, and video games ("TV" 68). The typical American preschooler views over twenty-seven hours of television each week, thus receiving more personal interaction with the television than with teachers and parents combined (Grossman 54). According to Leslie Prawd, by the time today's children graduate from high school, they will have spent nearly 11,000 hours in the classroom setting and over 15,000 hours watching television (225). By the time that same child reaches the age of seventy, he or she will have spent from seven to ten years of his or her life watching television (Shelov 786). Television has a colossal influence on the average American household, but more importantly, on the average American child.

3. According to the National Association for the Education of Young Children, media violence in children's television programs has drastically increased since 1980, and it continues to increase. In 1982, war cartoons occupied 1.5 hours per week of air-time, while that number grew to forty-three per week by 1986 (Smith 35). This increase can be viewed in the graph below.

Figure 1
Air-Time for War Cartoons Per Week

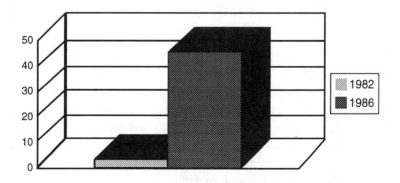

Source: Smith, Marilyn E. "Television Violence and Behavior: A Research Summary." *Emergency Librarian* Nov./Dec. 1996:34

4. In 1980, children's programs consisted of 18.6 violent acts per hour, while they now have over twenty-six per hour. At this rate, by the time a child completes elementary school, he or she will have viewed 8,000 murders and over 100,000 other violent acts (Smith 35). By the time he or she reaches the age of eighteen, he or she will have witnessed at least 16,000 murders. This world viewed on television becomes the real world for some children (Shelov 786).

5. This exposure to violence and other negative media content affects the behavior of children. Experts conclude that people learn by emulating what they see, and that children are especially receptive to this type of learning. According to Louis H. Primavera, scholarly researcher for the *International Journal of Instructional Media,* "the majority of studies point to the conclusion that viewing violence does increase interpersonal aggression, particularly in young children" (137). Marilyn E. Smith reports that "there is a sensitive period between the ages of eight and twelve during which children are particularly susceptible to influence of television violence" (34) due to the fact that during this time, "identification with a [television] character substantially increases the likelihood that the character's aggressive behavior will be modeled" (34). The probability of television influence is most likely due to the manner in which the violence is depicted. There is often praise or lack of castigation for the perpetrator of the violence, and the violence is often justified. In addition, the violence relates to the type of violence conceivably experienced in real life. Notable relationships have been discovered between children's notion that television violence is authentic, their combative conduct, and the amount of violence they view through the media (Smith 35).

6. There are three main areas of consideration concerning children's exposure to television violence and its effect on children. According to the National Association for the Education of Young Children, exposure to media violence may result in a desensitization to the affliction and pain of others, aggressive and harmful behavior, and fear of the world in which they live (Smith 36). Various studies indicate that "television mayhem may contribute to paranoia and aggressive behavior in [children]" ("TV" 68). With such great evidence that children's viewing of violence on television results in such negative effects, measures must be taken to ensure that children are not exposed to it. There is a debate over whether parents or the government are responsible for protecting children from this exposure, or whether it is the obligation of the television industry or independent organizations (Walsh). Regardless of whose duty or responsibility it is, measures must be taken to prevent a continuing rise in child violence due to the violence in the media. Parents should determine rigid limits on how much television children watch since violence is so abundant in the programs. The American Academy of Pediatrics recommends that children live in "media free" bedrooms to decrease their exposure to violence ("TV" 68). In addition to regulating the amount of television their children watch, parents should also instill in their children the ability to discern what is wholesome and beneficial to watch so that they will be able to make wise viewing decisions.

7. As the amount of negative media content, specifically violence in television, continues to rise, aggressive and violent behavior in children also increased. Although media violence is not solely responsible for this result, it is a key factor. The relationship is frightful, and preventive action must be taken. It is possible that society is not reflecting the vulgarity, crudeness, profanity, and violence in the media, but rather that the media is reflecting the deterioration of values of society. Regardless of whether the media reflects society or society reflects the media, or if the two reflect each other, steps must be take to ensure that children are not exposed to negative media content. We owe it to the children, and we owe it to society.

Works Cited

Grossman, Dave. "We Are Training Our Kids to Kill." *Saturday Evening Post* Sept./Oct. 1999: 54–49.

Prawd, Leslie. "The Negative Effects of Television on Children." *International Journal of Instructional Media* 22 (1995): 255+

Primavera, Louis H., and William G. Herron. "The Effect of Viewing Television Violence on Aggression." *International Journal of Instructional Media* 23 (1996): 137+

Shelov, Steven P., and Miriam Bar-on. "Children, Adolescents, and Television." *Pediatrics* 96 (1995): 786+

Smith, Marilyn E. "Television Violence and Behavior: A Research Summary." *Emergency Librarian* Nov./Dec. 1996: 34–37.

"TV Guide." *Newsweek* 16 Aug. 1999: 68.

Walsh, Ann D., et al. "Mothers' Preferences for Regulating Children's Television." *Journal of Advertising* 27.3 (1998): 23–37.

Affirmative Discrimination
by
Ruffin Flowers

1. "That teacher was selected for affirmative action reasons." This is where Ernest Pasour, a student, first heard the term used—implying a lack of ability on the part of a teacher at his school. Affirmative action was first coined in the context of Executive Order No.10925 issued by President John Kennedy in 1961, dealing with racial discrimination. This order indicated that federal contractors should take affirmative action to ensure that everyone in the job field was to be treated "without regard to their race, creed, color, or national origin"(Pasour 1). Since Kennedy issued this order in 1961, the system has evolved to become a perversion of the original intent. Kennedy's order insinuated equal access and nothing else.

2. The shift in emphasis from the equality of good opportunity to the goal of seeing statistical results was already under way by the time Congress debated the Civil Rights Act of 1964. The pressure for minorities and women to have a "correct" percentage of their population in the job force has since become a hot topic of debate for civil rights activists. The application of affirmative action used now is detrimental to the operation of the job market, to white males, and other groups.

3. Racial discrimination has been acknowledged ever since the founding of America. The Civil War was fought, and the United States was torn apart due to it. Though slaves were freed and laws were drafted, the underlying tensions and bigotry continue to be evident. Due to this hatred and tension coming to a climax around the time John F. Kennedy became President, he saw the need to help find a cure for racial discrimination. This was why he issued Executive Order 10925 mentioned in the above paragraphs. Also during this time, the Civil Rights Movement surfaced. Due to many people's beliefs in the statement that all men were created equal, many acts and bills were passed to help blacks and other minorities gain the rights they deserved. The Civil Rights Act of 1964 restated and broadened the application of affirmative action that JFK had presented. Title VI stated that:

   > No person in the United States shall, on the ground of race, color or national origin, be excluded from participation in, be denied the benefits of, or be subjected to discrimination under any program or activity receiving Federal financial assistance (Cahn xi).

4. A year after this act went into effect, President Johnson stated that equality would take more than a commitment to impartial treatment. Several months later he issued Executive Order 11246 that stated:

   > It is the policy of the Government of the United States to provide equal opportunity in Federal employment for all qualified persons, to prohibit discrimination in employment because of race, creed, color or national origin, and to promote the full realization of equal employment opportunity through a positive, continuing program in each department and agency (xii).

   The order was amended two years later to prohibit discrimination on the basis of sex.

5. In 1971, during the Nixon Administration, the Department of Labor issued Revised Order No.4. It required contractors to develop, "an affirmative actions program," including:

   > An analysis of areas within which the contractor is deficient in the utilization of minority groups and women, and further, goals and timetables to which the contractor's good faith efforts must be directed to correct the deficiencies (Cahn xii).

   The term utilization meant "having fewer minorities or women in a particular job classification that would reasonably be expected by their availability" (xii). This preferential treatment has opened up many doors for debate. The application of affirmative action may benefit the minorities and females in employment, education and contracting decisions, but it oftentimes hurts and has many effects on the white male.

6. Many philosophers, social theorists, legal scholars, and judges have produced many opinions, which argue that affirmative action policy violates the equal protection clause stated in the Fourteenth Amendment. They think that it actually destroys the meaning and cause of the civil rights movement by replacing racial quotas for the sake of color blindness. Also, it has been contended that the economics of affirmative action require hindrance with the running of the market that will eventually diminish the material opportunities of African Americans. Finally, many have asserted that affirmative action has psychological effects on the self-image of an individual.

7. Tim Fay, in a special advisory report on affirmative action related to post traumatic stress, reported a connection between discrimination and PTS (post traumatic stress). Fay quotes that:

   > Symptoms such as profound shock, anxiety and despair are often manifested in victims who have been denied employment, education, or government contracting opportunities simply because they are *not* protected by preferential government and private sector programs which specify that persons of the *correct* race (non-whites) be given preference in hiring, promotions, and contracting (Fay 2).

8. Many educational and employment services are hurt due to the promotion of hiring less skilled workers. Affirmative action sometimes forces employers to hire the best of the minority workers they can find, regardless of their job skills. For example, in 1993, Duke University was required to hire at least one new black teacher for each department. However, in all of the United States, only six blacks received Ph.D.s in 1987, for mathematics. This proves that it would be impossible to hire enough well qualified black professors to sufficiently educate students (Pasour 2).

9. Some students seeking an education are also robbed because of affirmative action. Many colleges and universities have quotas making it necessary to admit minorities to "round out" their freshman class. At Berkeley, only 40% of the entering class was admitted on the basis of academic performance. Whites need a 3.7 GPA in high school to be admitted, but most minority candidates are admitted with a much lower GPA (2).

10. Promotions are also oftentimes denied to those who deserve it more. A study done by The Male Class, a group of USDA Forest Service Employees shows that the promotion percent of females to males since 1988 has been drastically higher than the promotion percent of males.

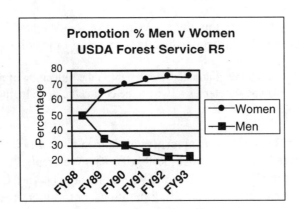

11. While many will agree that affirmative action helps minorities gain jobs that they would normally not get, it angers and hinders others, including white males. This creates more racial tension and hostility. Reverse discrimination against white males is equal to the discrimination found against minorities. Due to the racial tensions affirmative action brings up, many minorities and women say that, "Its benefits are no longer worth its side effect: the perception of their success is unearned" (Froomkin 2). Its original intentions have gone out of focus, and its counter-productivity has gotten out of hand. With affirmative action, true civil rights may never be achieved for everyone.

Position

Give a Child a Family
by
Kerrie Lambert

1. When a mission team from south Florida arrived in Camp Haiti, they saw what to them was the most poverty stricken land on earth. Some of the men were literally ill at the sight of the filth in the rivers, on the land, and covering the children. Because Haiti is one of the poorest nations in the world, families do not even have enough to provide for their children, and many of them are left to fend for themselves. The mission team witnessed them bathing in polluted waters and scrounging for non-existent food. I asked one member of this mission team if adoption was a possibility for any of these kids. His response was enthusiastic and emotional. I witnessed first hand for months his diligent efforts to rescue at least one Haitian child from a hopeless life. However, in his efforts, my father was faced with an issue aside from the finances and legalities of the adoption procedure. Many questioned if it was ethical for our family to adopt a child from a different culture. Our answer was simple. Yes, international adoption is logical and ethical.

2. Two main reasons why so many Americans are seeking foreign adoptions are humanitarianism and frustration with the laws and policies in domestic adoption (Kleiman). Critics of international adoption argue that Americans should not look elsewhere for children when there are so many needy ones right here in our country. However, there are more families seeking children than there are children who need homes. Over the past thirty years there has been a decline of domestic adoptions by 47 percent (Fulton 2). Some reasons that there are fewer children being placed for adoption are the early introduction of sex education in public schools and the easy access of birth control diminishing unwanted pregnancies (Hibbs 266). Also, America has become more accepting and supportive of unwed mothers, encouraging them to keep their babies. Still another reason why fewer children are available for adoption is the legalization of abortion. While these are not all necessarily negative reasons, they still are a discouragement to families desiring a child. Because there are so few children placed for adoption, the current waiting list is seven years or more (Fulton 2). International adoptions, however, can take as little as four months (Jeffreys 9), and at most one year (Fulton 2). Also, the adoption process itself is much simpler when dealing internationally. There are fewer restrictive eligibility requirements: a home study by a social worker, police records clearing the perspective parents of past wrong-doing, financial statements, a marriage certificate, proof of citizenship, medical histories, and reference letters (Fulton 3). The applicants may work through specific orphanages, adoption agencies, or their personal attorney. International laws state that agencies must be non-profit organizations and may not operate on the basis of region or creed (Hibbs 211). This extends the possibility of adoption to a greater economical and sociological group.

3. Two reasons that there is such an abundance of homeless children in foreign countries are poverty and overpopulation. For instance, because China houses nearly one fourth of the world's population, they have set a one child-per-family law (Fulton 3). This forces the Chinese people to discard their daughters so that they might have a son who will carry on the family name. Chinese girls are left in parks, railway stations, and any convenient dumping place (*Economist*). Susan

Parisella, adoptive mother of one of these girls, has this to say about the situation in China: "We're talking about China. They are poor. We are talking about tens of thousands of little girls who are abandoned every year. Why don't we get in there and give them a chance at a life" (Fulton 7)? These girls are in situations where 90 percent of the time they are undernourished and deprived of any parental figures (Hibbs 281). They are so neglected that in China and Korea they spend their days in high chairs and are not free to roam about, which may cause a hindrance in their physical and psychological growth (Jeffreys 11). If they are ill, orphanage attendants do not even always report it so that they may be treated. There are known cases in China where workers purposely let unwanted children die (*Economist*). This kind of neglect may cause trauma associated with the living conditions in the child's native country (Jeffreys 7). One Chinese toddler adopted by an American had a lung infection, her nose was encrusted, she was coughing and scratching, covered in filth and sores, and crawling with lice (Fulton 7). She was later diagnosed as also having Hepatitis B. When she returned to the orphanage for final paper work, she clung to her new mother in terror. The mother said that all the babies looked like they were going to die. The conditions in many of these facilities are unsanitary. Jeffreys described an orphanage in China as an "incubator for infection and disease" (9). He also states that "urine and flies surround Chinese children daily in the dirt-poor conditions." This kind of environment poses many health problems including Parasitosis, Hepatitis B, Tuberculosis, Anemia, and Ringworm to name a few (1). Health screening shows a large number of intestinal parasites, and many children have multiple parasites (9). Medical screenings also show that 67 percent of foreign-born adoptees have infectious disease, which is out of the 63 percent that prior screenings deemed healthy (12). Because of these poor living conditions and insufficient health attention, many Americans believe that they could provide "vastly better opportunities for the children's welfare than would be available in most Third World countries (Feigelman 85)." Americans also feel that these children would not have made it in their own countries because they arrived physically and emotionally deprived (Hibbs 279).

4. Many people feel that it is not "rescuing" a child to remove him or her from his or her own country. Critics of inter-country adoption call it "kidnapping" and "cultural genocide" (Feigelman 85). They argue that Third World people are "taken from their homelands and stripped of connection to their community and culture," and that it is "psychologically crippling to the children involved, leaving them in cultural no-man's land." Feigelman and Silverman combat this argument with a solution that is actually already in progress. They say that parents should emphasize the child's culture and consider it an important part of his or her life (77). Children, too, should take part in their background and develop pride for it. Sixty-three percent of inter-country children say that they identify themselves with their native culture and the backgrounds of their American families, giving them the best of both worlds (Brodzinsky 196).

5. Critics also claim that the cultural and racial differences can have a devastating effect on the child's emotional stability. However, self-esteem tests on inter-cultural blacks resulted the same as non-adopted white children (197). The reason for this is that insecurity and low self-esteem are universal. They are not based on race, ethnicity, or place of residence. Oddly enough, there is more concern for the adjustment of blacks by those who oppose international adoption than the larger number of Asian adoptees (198). This concern is unnecessary because studies show that the adjustment is the same all across the board. Paul is a twelve-year-old black boy from Europe who was adopted by white Americans (Feigelman 78). He has positive feelings about himself and gets along well with his siblings and friends who are predominantly white. Paul says that he does not feel like he is missing out by not having more contact with blacks and that he is very happy and content with his present friends and family. Inter-country adoptees show no more interest and pride in their birth culture, and no greater sense of shame or discomfort about their race and appearance than children adopted among their own ethnic background.

6. Another argument by those against international adoption is that the child will face much racial prejudice and feelings of unbelonging. But of those polled, only nine percent said they had faced some negative attitudes, but that they are rare occurrences (Feigelman 133).

7. All of this shows that most transcultural adoptees adapt well to their American homes and that most of their emotional and developmental problems can be traced to their pre-adoption experiences.

8. Hundreds of thousands of children are trapped today in pools of filth and orphanages. These children are without hope and have no future. If we adopt a child, then we are in essence saving a life otherwise lost to sickness and poverty. We do not need to play "police-men of the world," but we can show Christian compassion and love by providing for a special and cherished life. The cultural differences have little value when considering that the problems they face where they now remain are much more real, powerful, and detrimental to their development. My father still prays to break the walls for Haitian adoptions to be made as freely as other countries, but until then we can only do all in our power to help the children across the world who need a family. Katherine Jones, co-founder of the quarterly magazine, *Adoption Helper*, once stated that "family is the single most important thing in life. There are other things-careers, interests, pursuits-but without family none of that really means anything (Fulton 5)." Would you be willing to give a lost child a family?

Works Cited

Brodzinsky, Dr. David M., and Marshall D. Schechter. *The Psychology of Adoption*. New York: Oxford University Press, 1990.

Feigelman, William, and Arnold R. Silverman. *Chosen Children*. New York: Praeger Publishers, 1983.

Fulton, Kaye E., and Sharon Doyle Driedger, and Rae Corelli. *"Bringing Home Baby."* Maclean's 21 August 1995 34–39.

"Give Me Your Squalling Masses: Coming to America." *The Economist*. 3 Feb. 1996: 22–23.

Hibbs, Dr. Euthymia D. Adoption International Perspectives. Madison International University Press, 1991.

Jeffreys, Darya P. "Intercountry Adoption: A Need for Mandatory Medical Screening." *Journal of Law and Health*. Spring-Summer 1996: 243–270.

Kleiman, Erika Lynn. "Caring For Our Own Why: American Adoption Law Must Change." *Columbia Journal of Law and Social Problems*. Winter 1997: 30.

Late Classical Style: From Technical Precision to Passionate Emotion
by
Rebecca Pounds

1. Thousands of years ago a magnificent and flourishing civilization existed. The men and women of this civilization esteemed the human mind, soul, and body, and they valued thought as well as sport. They recognized the importance of order and beauty in life, and this order and beauty is reflected in every aspect of their culture, including their art (Schoder 2-3). This civilization is known as Ancient Greece, and out of this society sprung amazing works of art that have since been considered classics. The art produced during this era can be classified as one of two styles—the High Classical style or the Late Classical style. Although one may assert that the High Classical Style is the epitome of the ideal, and the Late Classical style is a devaluation of the ideal, neither style is greater than the other. Instead, the Late Classical style is a development of the High Classical style, and both styles should be equally esteemed.

2. The High Classical style was the result of thousands of years of artistic metamorphosis. Greek art originated as very naturalistic in the Mycenaen Age, beginning in 1600 BC, and progressively became more realistic during the Geometric Interlude, where the human figure first appeared in art (Schoder 4–6). In the sixth and seventh centuries, known as the Archaic Period, artistic techniques became more refined, and the human figure became more representative. As in Egyptian art, humans were depicted as rigid, youthful figures standing with clenched fists that were connected to straight arms. The oval head with embellished features sat atop a neck connected to broad shoulders. A narrow waist, implied muscles, and meticulous hair completed these early artistic representations (Schoder 7).

3. Finally, in the "Golden Age," an era lasting from 530 BC to around 470 BC, the High Classical style began to emerge (Rayner 17). Critic Edwin Rayner states that, "The whole trend of sculpture in Greece was toward the typical figure, the figure that was free from any momentary expression or individual defect. Its purpose was to suggest an agelessness, a freedom from limits of time or place that would result in the portrayal, not of a man, but of Man" (17). There was freedom of posture of the body and more refined traits, and although everything from gesture and pose to facial expression and anatomical details was more natural, every aspect was idealized. This style reached its peak from 425 B.C. until roughly 375 B.C. (Schoder 8). The style was initially fairly severe and solemn, but it ultimately achieved the pinnacle of grace (Carpenter 100).

4. Polyclitus, an expert sculptor of the High Classical style, excelled during this time. He was an intellectual artist who was extremely interested in the dilemma of ideal proportions of the human figure in sculpture. For this reason, "his work possesses an internal firmness, and all later sculpture when portraying the human figure in its external appearance builds on his foundations" (Kjellberg 118-19). His *Doryphoros*, the "Spear Bearer," was authorized as the "Canon or Rule for sculpture" (Carpenter 100). Polyclitus mindfully determined the dimensions of the body, and the result was a perfectly proportioned statue. The body itself epitomizes the ancient ideal of the faultless man (Rayner 17). According to Raymond V. Schoder, the "ideal human figures by Polyclitus revealed the grandeur and inherent beauty of man-in whose image the Greeks imagined their gods" (9). What has come to be referred to as the "Polyclitan ideal" is a very recognizable stance. One foot of the figure is set back and only the toes are in contact with the ground. The figure is powerful and

muscular with a cubic head and short, curly hair. As a whole, the statue implies physical, as opposed to mental, strength (Chase 96). Critic Rhys Carpenter remarks that,

> Even with its canonic formula of modular measurement, its system of *symmetria*, still hidden from us, the *Doryphoros* remains a stylistic landmark in Greek sculpture by virtue of other and more instantly discernible qualities; for in addition to its obscurely calculated proportions it embodies an almost academic demonstrated of perfection in its studied pose and carefully pondered compositional balance (102).

The High Classical style is typified in the work of Polycitus, specifically in the *Doryphoros*.

5. Later in the fourth century, the late Classical style developed. The late Classical style was an evolvement of the techniques and expertise perfected during the High Classical style. At this time, humanism was prominent and the sculptures began to radiate warmth and beauty (Schoder 9). The distinctly contoured figure, which was evident in the works of sculptors like Polyclitus, was replaced with a figure possessing softer, more emotional, more sensuous appeal. The sculptor Praxiteles "introduced a new divine ideal. Gravity was replaced by charm. . . . The gods approached more closely to human beings. . ." (Kjellberg 133).

6 One distinctly Praxitelean trait, depicted in *Hermes and the Infant Dionysus*, is the "S-curve of Praxiteles," a curve created in the figure of the sculpture when one hip is thrust out. In addition to this characteristic, Praxiteles' works contained other elements representative of the Late Classical style. The figure has a high skull and long, narrow eyes that create an appearance of passive observation (Chase 115). The anatomy of figures of this style is "accurate and graceful, without excessive detail" (Schoder 9). The focus of the sculpture centers on the person rather than on the ideal. Richter describes it as follows:

> The intimate personal note in the conception, the relaxed attitude of the figure with its lovely curve, the gentle, dreamy expression of the face, the infinitely variegated and yet not sharply contrasted modeling, all help to create an impression of sensuous loveliness; and we delight in its exquisite appeal. (258)

7. These qualities are evident in the works of the Late Classical style, specifically in Praxiteles' *Hermes and the Infant Dionysus*. Praxiteles, the most famous ancient sculptor, achieved insurmountable proficiency in "expressing in marble the feelings of the soul" (qtd. in Chase 119). The passion and expressiveness are distinct features of Praxiteles' works. Praxiteles advanced Greek art by developing the systemic precision and technical perfection of the works of the High Classical style into works that express emotion and feeling.

8. Though one might maintain that Praxiteles, a sculptor of the Late Classical style, is inferior to Polycitus, a sculptor of the High Classical style, I contend that this is not the case. The two sculptors and their works are equal in eminence but different in technique and purpose. *Hermes and the Infant Dionysus*, by Praxiteles, is parallel in merit to Polycitus' *Doryphoros*, despite the fact that it emphasizes feeling and emotion as opposed to form and precision. The works created in the Late Classical style represent an outgrowth of the techniques and styles perfected in the High Classical style.

Works Cited

Carpenter, Rhys. *Greek Sculpture: A Critical Review*. Chicago: Chicago P, 1960.

Chase, George Henry, and Chandler Rathfon Post. *A History of Sculpture*. New York: Harper, 1925.

Kjellberg, Ernst, and Gosta Saflund. Greek and Roman Art: 3000 B.C. to A.D. 550. New York: Crowell,
  1968.

Rayner, Edwin. *Famous Statues and Their Stories*. New York: Grosset & Dunlap, 1936.

Richtler, Gisela M.A. *The Sculpture and Sculptors of the Greeks*. New Haven: Yale UP, 1969.

Schoder, Raymond V. *Masterpieces of Greek Art*. Greenwich, CT: New York Graphic Society, 1965.

The Medium is the Metaphor

from Neil Postman,
Amusing Ourselves to Death:
Public Discourse in the Age of Show Business

At different times in our history, different cities have been the focal point of a radiating American spirit. In the late eighteenth century, for example, Boston was the center of a political radicalism that ignited a shot heard round the world—a shot that could not have been fired any other place but the suburbs of Boston. At its report, all Americans, including Virginians, became Bostonians at heart. In the mid-nineteenth century, New York became the symbol of the idea of a melting-pot America—or at least a non-English one—as the wretched refuse from all over the world disembarked at Ellis Island and spread over the land their strange languages and even stranger ways. In the early twentieth century, Chicago, the city of big shoulders and heavy winds, came to symbolize the industrial energy and dynamism of America. If there is a statue of a hog butcher somewhere in Chicago, then it stands as a reminder of the time when America was railroads, cattle, steel mills and entrepreneurial adventures. If there is no such statue, there ought to be, just as there is a statute of a Minute Man to recall the Age of Boston, as the Statue of Liberty recalls the Age of New York.

Today, we must look to the city of Las Vegas, Nevada, as a metaphor of our national character and aspiration, its symbol a thirty-foot-high cardboard picture of a slot machine and a chorus girl. For Las Vegas is a city entirely devoted to the idea of entertainment, and as such proclaims the spirit of a culture in which all public discourse increasingly takes the form of entertainment. Our politics, religion, news, athletics, education and commerce have been transformed into congenial adjuncts of show business, largely without protest or even much popular notice. The result is that we are a people on the verge of amusing ourselves to death.

As I write, the President of the United States is a former Hollywood movie actor. One of his principal challengers in 1984 was once a featured player on television's most glamorous show of the 1960's, that is to say, an astronaut. Naturally, a movie has been made about his extraterrestrial adventure. Former nominee George McGovern has hosted the popular television show "Saturday Night Live." So has a candidate of more recent vintage, the Reverend Jesse Jackson.

Meanwhile, former President Richard Nixon, who once claimed he lost an election because he was sabotaged by make-up men, has offered Senator Edward Kennedy advice on how to make a serious run for the presidency; lose twenty pounds. Although the Constitution makes no mention of it, it would appear that fat people are now effectively excluded from running for high political office. Probably bald people as well. Almost certainly those whose looks are not significantly enhanced by the cosmetician's art. Indeed, we may have reached the point where cosmetics has replaced ideology as the field of expertise over which a politician must have competent control.

America's journalists, i.e., television newscasters, have not missed the point. Most spend more time with their hair dryers than with their scripts, with the result that they comprise the most glamorous group of people this side of Las Vegas. Although the Federal Communications Act makes no mention of it, those without camera appeal are excluded from addressing the public about what is called "the news of the day." Those with camera appeal can command salaries exceeding one million dollars a year.

American businessmen discovered, long before the rest of us, that the quality and usefulness of their goods are subordinate to the artifice of their display; that, in fact, half the principles of capitalism as praised by Adam Smith or condemned by Karl Marx are irrelevant. Even the Japanese, who are said to make better cars than the Americans, know that economics is less a science than a performing art, as Toyota's yearly advertising budget confirms.

Not long ago, I saw Billy Graham join with Shecky Green, Red Buttons, Dionne Warwick, Milton Berle and other theologians in a tribute to George Burns, who was celebrating himself for surviving eighty years in show business. The Reverend Graham exchanged one-liners with Burns about making preparations for Eternity. Although the Bible makes no mention of it, the Reverend Graham assured the audience that God loves those who make people laugh. It was an honest mistake. He merely mistook NBC for God.

Dr. Ruth Westheimer is a psychologist who has a popular radio program and a nightclub act in which she informs her audiences about sex in all of its infinite variety and in language once reserved for the bedroom and street corners. She is almost as entertaining as the Reverend Billy Graham, and has been quoted as saying, "I don't start out to be funny. But if it comes out that way, I use it. If they call me an entertainer, I say that's great. When a professor teaches with a sense of humor, people walk away remembering."[1] She did not say what they remember or of what use their remembering is. But she has a point: It's great to be an entertainer. Indeed, in America God favors all those who possess both a talent and a format to amuse, whether they be preachers, athletes, entrepreneurs, politicians, teachers or journalists. In America, the least amusing people are its professional entertainers.

Culture watchers and worriers—those of the type who read books like this one—will know that the examples above are not aberrations but, in fact, clichés. There is no shortage of critics who have observed and recorded the dissolution of public discourse in America and its conversion into the arts of show business. But most of them, I believe, have barely begun to tell the story of the origin and meaning of this descent into a vast triviality. Those who have written vigorously on the matter tell us, for example, that what is happening is the residue of the exhausted capitalism; or, on the contrary, that it is the tasteless fruit of the maturing of capitalism; or that it is the neurotic aftermath of the Age of Freud; or the retribution of our allowing God to perish; or that it all comes from the old stand-bys, greed and ambition.

I have attended carefully to these explanations, and I do not say there is nothing to learn from them. Marxists, Freudians, Levi-Straussians, even Creation Scientists are not to be taken lightly. And, in any case, I should be very surprised if the story I have to tell is anywhere near the whole truth. We are all, as Huxley says someplace, Great Abbreviators, meaning that none of us has the wit to know the whole truth, the time to tell it if we believed we did, or an audience so gullible as to accept it. But you *will* find an argument here that presumes a clearer grasp of the matter than many that have come before. Its value, such as it is, resides in the directness of its perspective, which has its origins in observations made 2,300 years ago by Plato. It is an argument that fixes its attention on the forms of human conversation, and postulates that how we are obliged to conduct such conversations will have the strongest possible influence on what ideas we can conveniently express. And what ideas are convenient to express inevitably become the important content of a culture.

I use the word "conversation" metaphorically to refer not only to speech but to all techniques and technologies that permit people of a particular culture to exchange messages. In this sense, all culture is a conversation or, more precisely, a corporation of conversations, conducted in a variety of symbolic modes. Our attention here is on how forms of public discourse regulate and even dictate what kind of content can issue from such forms.

To take a simple example of what this means, consider the primitive technology of smoke signals. While I do not know exactly what control was once carried in the smoke signals of American Indians, I can safely guess that it did not include philosophical argument. Puffs of smoke are insufficiently complex to express ideas on the nature of existence, and even if they were not, a Cherokee philosopher would run short of either wood or blankets long before he reached his second axiom. You cannot use smoke to do philosophy. Its form excludes the content.

To take an example closer to home: As I suggested earlier, it is implausible to imagine that anyone like our twenty-seventh President, the multi-chinned, three-hundred-pound William Howard Taft, could be put forward as a presidential candidate to today's world. The shape of a man's body is largely irrelevant to the shape of his ideas when he is addressing a public in writing or on the radio or, for that matter, in smoke signals. But it is quite relevant on television. The grossness of a three-hundred-pound image, even a talking one, would easily overwhelm any logical or spiritual subtleties conveyed by speech. For on television, discourse is conducted largely through visual imagery, which is to say that television gives us a conversation in images, not words. The emergence of the image-manager in the political arena and the concomitant decline of the speech writer attest to the fact that television demands a different kind of content from other media. You cannot do political philosophy on television. Its form works against the content.

To give still another example, one of more complexity: The information, the content, or, if you will, the "stuff" that makes up what is called "the news of the day" did not exist—could not exist—in a world that lacked the media to give it expression. I do not mean that things like fires, wars, murders and love affairs did not, ever and always, happen in places all over the world. I mean that lacking a technology to advertise them, people could not attend to them, could not include them in their daily business. Such information simply could not exist as part of the content of culture. This idea—that there is a content called "the news of the day"—was entirely created by the telegraph (and since amplified by newer media), which made it possible to move decontextualized information over vast spaces at incredible speed. The news of the day is a figment of our technological imagination. It is, quite precisely, a media event. We attend to fragments of events from all over the world because we have multiple media whose forms are well suited to fragmented conversation. Cultures without speed-of-light media—let us say, cultures in which smoke signals are the most efficient space-conquering tool available—do not have news of the day. Without a medium to create its form, the news of the day does not exist.

To say it, then, as plainly as I can, this book is an inquiry into and a lamentation about the most significant American cultural fact of the second half of the twentieth century; the decline of the Age of Typography and the ascendancy of the Age of Television. This change-over has dramatically and irreversibly shifted the content and meaning of public discourse, since two media so vastly different cannot accommodate the same ideas. As the influence of print wanes, the content of politics, religion, education, and anything else that comprises public business must change and be recast in terms that are most suitable to television.

If all of this sounds suspiciously like Marshall McLuhan's aphorism, the medium is the message, I will not disavow the association (although it is fashionable to do so among respectable scholars who, were it not for McLuhan, would today be mute). I met McLuhan thirty years ago when I was a graduate student and he an unknown English professor. I believed then, as I believe now, that he spoke in the tradition of Orwell and Huxley—that is, as a prophesier, and I have remained steadfast to his teaching that the clearest way to see through a culture is to attend to its tools for conversation. I might add that my interest in this point of view was first stirred by a prophet far more formidable than McLuhan, more ancient than Plato. In studying the Bible as a young man, I found intimations of the idea that forms of media favor particular kinds of content and therefore are capable of taking command of a culture. I refer specifically to the Decalogue, the Second Commandment of which prohibits the Israelites from making concrete images of anything. "Thou shalt not make unto thee any graven image, any likeness of any thing that is in heaven above, or that is in the earth beneath, or that is in the water beneath the earth." I wondered then, as so many other have, as to why the God of these people would have included instructions on how they were to symbolize, or not symbolize, their experience. It is a strange injunction to include as part of an ethical system *unless its author assumed a connection between forms of human communication and the quality of a culture.* We may hazard a guess that a people who are being asked to embrace an abstract, universal deity would be rendered unfit to do so by the habit of drawing pictures or making statues or depicting their ideas in any concrete, iconographic forms. The God of the Jews was to exist in the Word and through the Word, an unprecedented conception requiring the highest order of abstract thinking. Iconography thus became blasphemy so that a new kind of God could enter a culture. People like ourselves who are in the process of converting their culture from word-centered to image-centered might profit by reflecting on this Mosaic injunction. But even if I am wrong in these conjectures, it is, I believe, a wise and particularly relevant supposition that the media of communication available to a culture are a dominant influence on the formation of the culture's intellectual and social preoccupations.

Speech, of course, is the primal and indispensable medium. It made us human, keeps us human, and in fact defines what human means. This is not to say that if there were no other means of communication all humans would find it equally convenient to speak about the same things in the same way. We know enough about language to understand that variations in the structures of languages will result in variations in what may be called "world view." How people think about time and space, and about things and processes, will be greatly influence by the grammatical features of their language. We dare not suppose therefore that all human minds are unanimous in understanding how the world is put together. But how much more divergence there is in world view among different cultures can be imagined when we consider the great number and variety of tools for conversation that go beyond speech. For although culture is a creation of speech, it is recreated anew by every medium of communication—from painting to hieroglyphs to the alphabet to television. Each medium, like language itself, makes possible a unique mode of discourse by providing a new orientation for thought, for expression, for sensibility. Which, of course, is what McLuhan meant in saying the medium is the message. His aphorism, however, is in need of amendment because, as it stands, it may lead one to confuse a message with a metaphor. A message denotes a specific, concrete statement about the world. But the forms of our media, including the symbols through which they permit conversation, do not make such statements. They are rather like metaphors, working by unobtrusive but powerful implication to enforce their special definitions of reality. Whether we are experiencing the world through the lens of speech or the printed word or the television camera, our media-metaphors classify the world for us, sequence it, frame it, enlarge, it, reduce it, color it, argue a case for what the world is like. As Ernst Cassirer remarked:

> Physical reality seems to recede in proportion as man's symbolic activity advances. Instead of dealing with the things themselves man is in a sense constantly conversing with himself. He has so enveloped himself in linguistic forms, in artistic images, in mythical symbols or religious rites that he cannot see or know anything except by the interposition of [an] artificial medium.[2]

What is peculiar about such interpositions of media is that their role in directing what we will see or know is so rarely noticed. A person who reads a book or who watches television or who glances at his watch is not usually interested in how his mind is organized and controlled by these events, still less in what idea of the world is suggested by a book, television, or a watch. But there are men and women who have noticed these things, especially in our own times. Lewis Mumford, for example, has been one of our great noticers. He is not the sort of a man who looks at a clock merely to see what time it is. Not that he lacks interest in the content of clocks, which is of concern to everyone from moment to moment, but he is far more interested in how a clock creates the idea of "moment to moment." He attends to the philosophy of clocks, to clocks as metaphor, about which our education has had little to say and clock makers nothing at all. "The clock," Mumford has concluded, "is a piece of power machinery whose 'product' is seconds and minutes." In manufacturing such a product, the clock has the effect of disassociating time from human events and thus nourishes the belief in an independent world of mathematically measurable sequences. Moment to moment, it turns out, is not God's conception, or nature's. It is man conversing with himself about and through a piece of machinery he created.

In Mumford's great book *Technics and Civilization,* he shows how, beginning in the fourteenth century, the clock made us into time-keepers, and then time-savers, and now time-servers. In the process, we have learned irreverence toward the sun and the seasons, for in a world made up of seconds and minutes, the authority of nature is superseded. Indeed, as Mumford points out, with the invention of the clock, Eternity ceased to serve as the measure and focus of human events. And thus, though few would have imagined the connection, the inexorable ticking of the clock may have had more to do with the weakening of God's supremacy than all the treatises produced by the philosophers of the Enlightenment; that is to say, the clock introduced a new form of conversation between man and God, in which God appears to have been the loser. Perhaps Moses should have included another Commandment: Thou shalt not make mechanical representations of time.

That the alphabet introduced a new form of conversation between man and man is by now a commonplace among scholars. To be able to *see* one's utterances rather than only to hear them is no small matter, though our education, once again, has had little to say about this. Nonetheless, it is clear that phonetic writing created a new conception of knowledge, as well as a new sense of intelligence, of audience and of posterity, all of which Plato recognized at an early state in the development of tests. "No man of intelligence," he wrote in his Seventh Letter, "will venture to express his philosophical views in language, especially not in language that is unchangeable, which is true of that which is set down in written characters." This notwithstanding, he wrote voluminously and understood better than anyone else that the setting down of views in written characters would be the beginning of philosophy, not the end. Philosophy cannot exist without criticism, and writing makes it possible and convenient to subject thought to a continuous and concentrated scrutiny. Writing freezes speech and in so doing gives birth to the grammarian, the logician, the rhetorician, the historian, the scientist—all those who must hold language before them so that they can see what it means, where it errs, and where it is leading.

Plato knew all of this, which means that he knew that writing would bring about a perceptual revolution; a shift from the ear to the eye as an organ of language processing. Indeed, there is a legend that to encourage such a shift Plato insisted that his students study geometry before entering his Academy. If true, it was a sound idea, for as the great literary critic Northrop Frye has remarked, "the written word is far more powerful than simply a reminder; it re-creates the past in the present, and gives us, not the familiar remembered thing, but the glittering intensity of the summoned-up hallucination."[3]

All that Plato surmised about the consequences of writing is now well understood by anthrophologists, especially those who have studied cultures in which speech is the only source of complex conversation. Anthropologists know that the written word, as Northrop Frye meant to suggest, is not merely an echo of a speaking voice. It is another kind of voice altogether, a conjurer's trick of the first order. It must certainly have appeared that way to those who invented it, and that is why we should not be surprised that the Egyptian god Thoth, who is alleged to have brought writing to the King Thamus, was also the god of magic. People like ourselves may see nothing wondrous in writing, but our anthropologists know how strange and magical it appears to a purely oral people—a conversation with no one and yet with everyone. What could be stranger than the silence one encounters when addressing a question to a text? What could be more metaphysically puzzling than addressing an unseen audience, as every writer of books must do? And correcting oneself because one knows that an unknown reader will disapprove or misunderstand?

I bring all of this up because what my book is about is how our own tribe is undergoing a vast and trembling shift from the magic of writing to the magic of electronics. What I mean to point out here is that the introduction into a culture of a technique such as writing or a clock is not merely an extension of man's power to bind time but a transformation of his way of thinking—and, of course, of the content of his culture. And that is what I mean to say by calling a medium a metaphor. We are told in school, quite correctly, that a metaphor suggests what a thing is like by comparing it to something else. And by the power of its suggestion, it so fixes a conception in our minds that we cannot imagine the one thing without the other: Light is a wave; language, a tree; God, a wise and venerable man; the mind, a dark cavern illuminated by knowledge. And if these metaphors no longer serve us, we must, in the nature of the matter, find others that will. Light is a particle; language, a river; God (as Bertrand Russell proclaimed), a differential equation; the mind, a garden that yearns to be cultivated.

But our media-metaphors are not so explicit or so vivid as these, and they are far more complex. In understanding their metaphorical function, we must take into account the symbolic forms of their information, the source of their information, the quantity and speed of their information, the context in which their information is experienced. Thus, it takes some digging to get at them, to grasp, for example, that a clock recreates time as an independent, mathematically precise sequence; that writing recreates the mind as a tablet on which experience is written; that the telegraph recreates news as a commodity. And yet, such digging becomes easier if we start from the assumption that in every tool we create, an idea is embedded that goes beyond the function of the thing itself. It has been pointed out, for example, that the invention of eyeglasses in the twelfth century not only made it possible to improve defective vision but suggested the idea that human beings need not accept as final either the endowments of nature or the ravages of time. Eyeglasses refuted the belief that anatomy is destiny by putting forward the idea that our bodies as well as our minds are improvable. I do not think it goes too far to say that there is a link between the invention of eyeglasses in the twelfth century and gene-splitting research in the twentieth.

Even such an instrument as the microscope, hardly a tool of everyday use, had embedded within it a quite astonishing idea, not about biology but about psychology. By revealing a world hitherto hidden from view, the microscope suggested a possibility about the structure of the mind.

If things are not what they seem, if microbes lurk, unseen, on and under our skin, if the invisible controls the visible, then is it not possible that ids and egos and superegos also lurk somewhere unseen? What else is psychoanalysis but a microscope of the mind? Where do our notions of mind come from if not from metaphors generated by our tools? What does it mean to say that someone has an IQ of 126? There are no numbers in people's heads. Intelligence does not have quality or magnitude, except as we believe that it does. And why do we believe that it does? Because we have tools that imply that this is what the mind is like. Indeed, our tools for thought suggest to us what our bodies are like, as when someone refers to her "biological clock," or when we talk of our "genetic codes," or when we read someone's face like a book, or when our facial expressions telegraph our intentions.

When Galileo remarked that the language of nature is written in mathematics, he meant it only as a metaphor. Nature itself does not speak. Neither do our minds or our bodies or, more to the point of this book, our bodies politic. Our conversations about nature and about ourselves are conducted in whatever "languages" we find it possible and convenient to employ. We do not see nature or intelligence or human motivation or ideology as "it" is but only as our languages are. And our languages are our media. Our media are our metaphors. Our metaphors create the content of our culture.

Media as Epistemology

It is my intention in this book to show that a great media-metaphor shift has taken place in America, with the result that the content of much of our public discourse has become dangerous nonsense. With this in view, my task in the chapters ahead is straightforward. I must, first, demonstrate how, under the governance of the printing press, discourse in America was different from what it is now—generally coherent, serious and rational; and then how, under the governance of television, it has become shriveled and absurd. But to avoid the possibility that my analysis will be interpreted as standard-brand academic whimpering, a kind of elitist complaint against "junk" on television, I must first explain that my focus is on epistemology, not on aesthetics or literary criticism. Indeed, I appreciate junk as much as the next fellow, and I know full well that the printing press has generated enough of it to fill the Grand Canyon to overflowing. Television is not old enough to have matched printing's output of junk.

And so, I raise no objection to television's junk. The best things on television *are* its junk, and no one and nothing is seriously threatened by it. Besides, we do not measure a culture by its output of undisguised trivialities but by what it claims as significant. Therein is our problem, for television is at its most trivial and, therefore, most dangerous when its aspirations are high, when it presents itself as a carrier of important cultural conversations. The irony here is that this is what intellectuals and critics are constantly urging television to do. The trouble with such people is that they do not take television seriously enough. For, like the printing press, television is nothing less that a philosophy of rhetoric. To talk seriously about television, one must therefore talk of epistemology. All other commentary is in itself trivial.

Epistemology is a complex and usually opaque subject concerned with the origins and nature of knowledge. The part of its subject matter that is relevant here is the interest it takes in definitions of truth and the sources from which such definitions come. In particular, I want to show that definitions of truth are derived, at least in part, from the character of the media of communication through which information is conveyed. I want to discuss how media are implicated in our epistemologies.

In the hope of simplifying what I mean by the title of this chapter, media as epistemology, I find it helpful to borrow a word from Northrop Frye, who has made use of a principle he calls *resonance*. "Through resonance," he writes, "a particular statement in a particular context acquires a universal significance."[1] Frye offers as an opening example the phrase "the grapes of wrath," which first appears in Isaiah in the context of a celebration of a prospective massacre of Edomites. But the phrase, Frye continues, "has long ago flown away from this context into many new contexts, contexts that give dignity to the human situation instead of merely reflecting its bigotries."[2] Having said this, Frye extends the idea of resonance so that it goes beyond phrases and sentences. A character in a play or story—Hamlet, for example, or Lewis Carroll's Alice—may have resonance. Objects may have resonance, and so many countries: "The smallest details of the geography of two tiny chopped-up countries, Greece and Israel, have imposed themselves on our consciousness until they have become part of the map of our own imaginative world, whether we have ever seen these countries or not."[3]

In addressing the question of the source of resonance, Frye concludes that metaphor is the generative force—that is, the power of a phrase, a book, a character, or a history to unify and invest with meaning a variety of attitudes or experiences. Thus, Athens becomes a metaphor of intellectual excellence, wherever we find it; Hamlet, a metaphor of brooding indecisiveness; Alice's wanderings, a metaphor of a search for order in a world of semantic nonsense.

I now depart from Frye (who, I am certain, would raise no objection) but I take his word along with me. Every medium of communication, I am claiming, has resonance, for resonance is metaphor writ large. Whatever the original and limited context of its use may have been, a medium has the power to fly far beyond that context into new and unexpected ones. Because of the way it directs us to organize our minds and integrate our experience of the world, it imposes itself on our consciousness and social institutions in myriad forms. It sometimes has the power to become implicated in our concepts of piety, or goodness, or beauty. And it is always implicated in the ways we define and regulate our ideas of truth.

To explain how this happens—how the bias of a medium sits heavy, felt but unseen, over a culture—I offer three cases of truth-telling.

The first is drawn from a tribe in western Africa that has no writing system but whose rich oral tradition has given form to its ideas of civil war.[4] When a dispute arises, the complainants come before the chief of the tribe and state their grievances. With no written law to guide him, the task of the chief is to search through its vast repertoire of proverbs and sayings to find one that suits the situation and is equally satisfying to both complainants. That accomplished, all parties are agreed that justice has been done, that the truth has been served. You will recognize, or course, that this was largely the method of Jesus and other Biblical figures who, living in an essentially oral culture, drew upon all of the resources of speech, including mnemonic devices, formulaic expressions and parables, as a means of discovering and revealing truth. As Walter Ong points out, in oral cultures proverbs and sayings are not occasional devices: "They are incessant. They form the substance of thought itself. Thought in any extended form is impossible without them, for it consists in them."[5]

To people like ourselves any reliance on proverbs and sayings is reserved largely for resolving disputes among or with children. "Possession is nine-tenths of the law." "First come, first served." "Haste makes waste." These are forms of speech we pull out in small crises with our young but would think ridiculous to produce in a courtroom where "serious" matters are to be decided. Can you imagine a bailiff asking a jury if it has reached a decision and receiving the reply that "to err is human but to forgive is divine"? Or even better, "Let us render unto Caesar that which is Caesar's and to God that which is God's"? For the briefest moment, the judge might be charmed but if a "serious" language form is not immediately forthcoming, the jury may end up with a longer sentence than most guilty defendants.

Judges, lawyers and defendants do not regard proverbs or sayings as a relevant response to legal disputes. In this, they are separated from the tribal chief by a media-metaphor. For in a print-based courtroom, where law books, briefs, citations and other written materials define and organize the method of finding the truth, the oral tradition has lost much of its resonance—but not all of it. Testimony is expected to be given orally, on the assumption that the spoken, not the written, word is a truer reflection of the state of mind of a witness. Indeed, in many courtrooms jurors are not permitted to take notes, nor are they given written copies of the judge's explanation of the law. Jurors are expected to *hear* the truth, or its opposite, not to read it. Thus, we may say that there is a clash of resonances in our concept of legal truth. On the one hand, there is a residual belief in the power of speech, and speech alone, to carry the truth; on the other hand, here is a much stronger belief in the authenticity of writing and, in particular, printing. This second belief has little tolerance for poetry, proverbs, sayings, parables or any other expressions of oral wisdom. The law is what legislators and judges have written. In our culture, lawyers do not have to be wise; they need to be well briefed.

A similar paradox exists in universities, and with roughly the same distribution of resonances; that is to say, there are a few residual traditions based on the notion that speech is the primary carrier of truth. But for the most part, university conceptions of truth are tightly bound to the structure of logic of the printed word. To exemplify this point, I draw here on a personal experience that occurred during a still widely practiced medieval ritual known as a "doctoral oral." I use the word *medieval* literally, for in the Middle Ages students were always examined orally, and the tradition is carried forward in the assumption that a candidate must be able to talk completely about his written work. But, of course, the written work matters most.

In the case I have in mind, the issue of what is a legitimate form of truth-telling was raised to a level of consciousness rarely achieved. The candidate had included in his thesis a foot note, intended as documentation of a quotation, which read: "Told to the investigator at the Roosevelt Hotel on January 18, 1981, in the presence of Arthur Lingeman and Jerrold Gross." This citation drew the attention of no fewer than four of the five oral examiners, all of whom observed that it was hardly suitable as a form of documentation and that it ought to be replaced by a citation from a book or article. "You are not a journalist," one professor remarked. "You are supposed to be a scholar." Perhaps because the candidate knew of no published statement of what he was told at the Roosevelt Hotel, he defended himself vigorously on the grounds that there were witnesses to what he was told, that they were available to attest to the accuracy of the quotation, and that the form in which an idea is conveyed is irrelevant to its truth. Carried away on the wings of his eloquence, the candidate argued further that there were more than three hundred references to published works in his thesis and that is was extremely unlikely that any of them would be checked for accuracy by the examiners, by which he meant to raise the question. Why do you *assume* the accuracy of a print-referenced citation but not a speech-referenced one?

The answer he received took the following line: You are mistaken in believing that the form in which an idea is conveyed is irrelevant to its truth. In the academic world, the published word is invested with greater prestige and authenticity than the spoken word. What people say is assumed to be more casually uttered than what they write. The written word is assumed to have been reflected upon and revised by its author, reviewed by authorities and editors. It is easier to verify or refute, and it is invested with an impersonal and objective character, which is why, no doubt, you have referred to yourself in your thesis as "the investigator" and not by your name; that is to say, the written word is, by its nature, addressed to the world, not an individual. The written word endures, the spoken word disappears; and that is why writing is closer to the truth than speaking. Moreover, we are sure you would prefer that this commission produce a written statement that you have passed your examination (should you do so) than for us merely to tell you that you have, and leave it at that. Our written statement would represent the "truth." Our oral agreement would be only a rumor.

The candidate wisely said no more on the matter except to indicate that he would make whatever changes the commission suggested and that he profoundly wished that should he pass the "oral," a written document would attest to that fact. He did pass, and in time the proper words were written.

A third example of the influence of media on our epistemologies can be drawn from the trial of the great Socrates. At the opening of Socrates' defense, addressing a jury of five hundred, he apologizes for not having a well-prepared speech. He tells his Athenian brothers that he will falter, begs that they not interrupt him on that account, asks that they regard him as they would a stranger from another city, and promises that he will tell them the truth, without adornment or eloquence. Beginning this way was, or course, characteristic of Socrates, but it was not characteristic of the age in which he lived. For, as Socrates knew full well, his Athenian brothers did not regard the principles of rhetoric and the expression of truth to be independent of each other. People like ourselves find great appeal in Socrates' plea because we are accustomed to thinking of rhetoric as an ornament of speech—most often pretentious, superficial and unnecessary. But to the people who invented it, the Sophists of fifth-century B.C. Greece and their heirs, rhetoric was not merely an opportunity for dramatic performance but a near indispensable means of organizing evidence and proofs, and therefore of communicating truth.[6]

It was not only a key element in the education of Athenians (far more important than philosophy) but a preeminent art form. To the Greeks, rhetoric was a form of spoken writing. Though it always implied oral performance, its power to reveal the truth resided in the written word's power to display arguments in orderly progression. Although Plato himself disputed this conception of truth (as we might guess from Socrates' plea), his contemporaries believed that rhetoric was the proper means through which "right opinion" was to be both discovered and articulated. To disdain rhetorical rules, to speak one's thoughts in a random manner, without proper emphasis or appropriate passion, was considered demeaning to the audience's intelligence and suggestive of falsehood. Thus, we can assume that many of the 280 jurors who cast a guilty ballot against Socrates did so because his manner was not consistent with truthful matter, as they understood the connection.

The point I am leading to by this and the previous examples is that the concept of truth is intimately linked to the biases of forms of expression. Truth does not, and never has, come unadorned. It must appear in its proper clothing or it is not acknowledged, which is a way of saying that the "truth" is a kind of cultural prejudice. Each culture conceives of it as being most authentically expressed in certain symbolic forms that another culture may regard as trivial or irrelevant. Indeed, to the Greeks of Aristotle's time, and for two thousand years afterward, scientific truth was best discovered and expressed by deducing the nature of things from a set of self-evident premises, which accounts for Aristotle's believing that women have fewer teeth than men, and that babies are healthier if conceived when the wind is in the north. Aristotle was twice married but so far as we know, it did not occur to him to ask either of this wives if he could count her teeth. And as for his obstetric opinions, we are safe in assuming he used no questionnaires and hid behind no curtains. Such acts would have seemed to him both vulgar and unnecessary, for that was not the way to ascertain the truth of things. The language of deductive logic provided a surer road.

We must not be too hasty in mocking Aristotle's prejudices. We have enough of our own, as for example, the equation we moderns make of truth and quantification. In this prejudice, we come astonishingly close to the mystical beliefs of Pythagoras and his followers who attempted to submit all of life to the sovereignty of numbers. Many of our psychologists, sociologists, economists and other latter-day cabalists will have numbers to tell them the truth or they will have nothing. Can you imagine, for example, a modern economist articulating truths about our standard of living by reciting a poem? Or by telling what happened to him during a late-night walk through East St. Louis? Or by offering a series of proverbs and parables, beginning with the saying about a rich man, a camel, and the eye of a needle? The first would be regarded as irrelevant, the second merely anecdotal, the last childish. Yet these forms of language are certainly capable of expressing truths about economic relationships, as well as any other relationships, and indeed have been employed by various peoples. But to the modern mind, resonating with different media-metaphors, the truth in economics is believed to be best discovered and expressed in numbers. Perhaps it is. I will not argue the point. I mean only to call attention to the fact that there is a certain measure of arbitrariness in the forms that truth-telling may take. We must remember that Galileo merely said that the language of *nature* is written in mathematics. He did not say *everything* is. And even the truth about nature need not be expressed in mathematics. For most of human history, the language of nature has been the language of myth and ritual. These forms, one might add, had the virtues of leaving nature unthreatened and of encouraging the belief that human beings are part of it. It hardly befits a people who stand ready to blow up the planet to praise themselves too vigorously for having found the true way to talk about nature.

In saying this, I am not making a case for epistemological relativism. Some ways of truth-telling are better than others, and therefore have a healthier influence on the cultures that adopt them. Indeed, I hope to persuade you that the decline of a print-based epistemology and the accompanying rise of a television-based epistemology has had grave consequences for public life, that we are getting sillier by the minute. And that is why it is necessary for me to drive hard the point that the weight assigned to any form of truth-telling is a function of the influence of media of communications. "Seeing is believing" has always had a preeminent status as an epistemological axiom, but "saying is believing," "reading is believing." "counting is believing," "deducing is believing," and "feeling is believing" are others that have risen or fallen in importance as cultures have undergone media change. As a culture moves from orality to writing to printing to televising, its ideas of truth move with it. Every philosophy is the philosophy of a stage of life, Nietzsche remarked. To which we might add that every epistemology is the epistemology of a stage of media development. Truth, like time itself, is a product of a conversation man has with himself about and through the techniques of communication he has invented.

Since intelligence is primarily defined as one's capacity to grasp the truth of things, it follows that what a culture means by intelligence is derived from the character of its important forms of communication. In a purely oral culture, intelligence is often associated with aphoristic ingenuity, that is, the power to invent compact sayings of wide applicability. The wise Solomon, we are told in First Kings, knew three thousand proverbs. In a print culture, people with such a talent are thought to be quaint at best, more likely pompous bores. In a purely oral culture, a high value is always placed on the power to memorize, for where there are no written words, the human mind must function as a mobile library. To forget how something is to be said or done is a danger to the community and a gross form of stupidity. In a print culture, the memorization of a poem, a menu, a law or most anything else is merely charming. It is almost always functionally irrelevant and certainly not considered a sign of high intelligence.

Although the general character of print-intelligence would be known to anyone who would be reading this book, you may arrive at a reasonable detailed definition of it by simply considering what is demanded of you *as you read this book*. You are required, first of all, to remain more or less immobile for a fairly long time. If you cannot do this (with this or any other book), our culture may label you as anything from hyperkinetic to undisciplined; in any case, as suffering from some sort of intellectual deficiency. The printing press makes rather stringent demands of our bodies as well as our minds. Controlling your body is, however, only a minimal requirement. You must also have learned to pay no attention to the shapes of the letters on the page. You must see through them, so to speak, so that you can go directly to the meanings of the words they form. If you are preoccupied with the shapes of the letters, you will be an intolerably inefficient reader, likely to be thought stupid. If you have learned how to get to meanings without aesthetic distraction, you are required to assume an attitude of detachment and objectivity. This includes your bringing to the task what Bertrand Russell called an "immunity to eloquence," meaning that you are able to distinguish between the sensuous pleasure, or charm, or ingratiating tone (if such there be) of the words, and the logic of their argument. But at the same time, you must be able to tell from the tone of the language what is the author's attitude toward the subject and toward the reader. You must, in other words, know the difference between a joke and an argument. And in judging the quality of an argument, you must be able to do several things at once, including delaying a verdict until the entire argument is finished, holding in mind questions until you have determined where, when or if the text answers them, and bringing to bear on the text all of your relevant experience as a counterargument to what is being proposed. You must also be able to withhold those parts of your knowledge and experience which, in fact, do not have a bearing on the argument. And in preparing yourself to do all of this, you must have divested yourself of the belief that words are magical and, above all, have learned to negotiate the world of abstractions, for there are very few phrases and sentences in this book that require you to call forth concrete images. In a print-culture, we are apt to say of people who are not intelligent that we must "draw them pictures" so that they may understand. Intelligence implies that one can dwell comfortably without pictures, in a field of concepts and generalizations.

To be able to do all of these things, and more, constitutes a primary definition of intelligence in a culture whose notions of truth are organized around the printed word. In the next two chapters I want to show that in the eighteenth and nineteenth centuries, America was such a place, perhaps the most print-oriented culture ever to have existed. In subsequent chapters, I want to show that in the twentieth century, our notions of truth and our ideas of intelligence have changed as a result of new media displacing the old.

But I do not wish to oversimplify the matter more than is necessary. In particular, I want to conclude by making three points that may serve as a defense against certain counterarguments that careful readers may have already formed.

The first is that at no point do I care to claim that changes in media bring about changes in the structure of people's minds or changes in their cognitive capacities. There are some who make this claim, or come close to it (for example, Jerome Bruner, Jack Goody, Walter Ong, Marshall McLuhan, Julian Jaynes, and Eric Havelock).[7] I am inclined to think they are right, but my argument does not require it. Therefore, I will not burden myself with arguing the possibility, for example, that oral people are less developed intellectually, in some Piagetian sense, than writing people, or that "television" people are less developed intellectually than either. My argument is limited to saying that a major new medium changes the structure of discourse; it does so by encouraging certain uses of the intellect, by favoring certain definitions of intelligence and wisdom, and by demanding a certain kind of content—in a phrase, by creating new forms of truth telling. I will say once again that I am no relativist in this matter, and that I believe the epistemology created by television not only is inferior to a print-based epistemology but is dangerous and absurdist.

The second point is that the epistemological shift I have intimated, and will describe in detail, has not yet included (and perhaps never will include) everyone and everything. While some old media do, in fact, disappear (e.g., pictographic writing and illuminated manuscripts) and with them, the institutions and cognitive habits they favored, other forms of conversation will always remain. Speech, for example, and writing. Thus the epistemology of new forms such as television does not have an entirely unchallenged influence.

I find it useful to think of the situation in this way: Changes in the symbolic environments are like changes in the natural environment; they are both gradual and additive at first, and then, all at once, a critical mass is achieved, as the physicists say. A river that has slowly been polluted suddenly becomes toxic; most of the fish perish; swimming becomes a danger to health. But even then, the river may look the same and one may still take a boat ride on it. In other words, even when life has been taken from it, the river does not disappear, nor do all of its uses, but its value has been seriously diminished and its degraded condition will have harmful effects throughout the landscape. It is this way with our symbolic environment. We have reached, I believe, a critical mass in that electronic media have decisively and irreversibly changed the character of our symbolic environment. We are now a culture whose information, ideas and epistemology are given form by television, not by the printed word. To be sure, there are still readers and there are many books published, but the uses of print and reading are not the same as they once were; not even in schools, the last institutions where print was thought to be invincible. They delude themselves who believe that television and print coexist, for coexistence implies parity. There is no parity here. Print is now merely a residual epistemology, and it will remain so, aided to some extent by the computer, and newspapers and magazines that are made to look like television screens. Like the fish who survive a toxic river and the boatmen who sail on it, there still dwell among us those whose sense of things is largely influenced by older and clearer waters.

The third point is that in the analogy I have drawn above, the river refers largely to what we call public discourse—our political, religious, informational and commercial forms of conversation. I am arguing that a television-based epistemology pollutes public communication and its surrounding landscape, not that it pollutes everything. In the first place, I am constantly reminded of television's value as a source of comfort and pleasure to the elderly, the infirm and, indeed, all people who find themselves alone in motel rooms. I am also aware of television's potential for creating a theater for the masses (a subject which in my opinion has not been taken seriously enough). There are also claims that whatever power television might have to undermine rational discourse, its emotional power is so great that it could arouse sentiment against the Vietnam War or against more virulent forms of racism. These and other beneficial possibilities are not to be taken lightly.

But there is still another reason why I should not like to be understood as making a total assault on television. Anyone who is even slightly familiar with the history of communications knows that every new technology for thinking involves a tradeoff. It giveth and taketh away, although not quite in equal measure. Media change does not necessarily result in equilibrium. It sometimes creates more than it destroys. Sometimes, it is the other way around. We must be careful in praising or condemning because the future may hold surprises for us. The invention of the printing press itself is a paradigmatic example. Typography fostered the modern idea of individuality, but it destroyed the medieval sense of community and integration. Typography created prose but made poetry into an exotic and elitist form of expression. Typography made modern science possible but transformed religious sensibility into mere superstition. Typography assisted in the growth of the nation-state but thereby made patriotism into a sordid if not lethal emotion.

Obviously, my point of view is that the four-hundred-year imperial dominance of typography was of far greater benefit than deficit. Most of our modern ideas about the uses of the intellect were formed by the printed word, as were our ideas about education, knowledge, truth and information. I will try to demonstrate that as typography moves to the periphery of our culture and television takes its place at the center, the seriousness, clarity and, above all, value of public discourse dangerously declines. On what benefits may come from other directions, one must keep an open mind.

Chapter 1: The Medium Is the Metaphor
1. As quoted in the *Wisconsin State Journal*, August 24, 1983, Section 3, page 1.
2. Cassirer, p. 43
3. Frye, p. 227.

Chapter 2: Media as Epistemology
1. Frye, p. 217.
2. Frye, p. 218.
3. Frye, p. 218.
4. As quoted in Ong, "Literacy and the Future of Print," pp. 201–202.
5. Ong, *Orality*, p. 35
6. Ong, *Orality*, p. 109
7. Jerome Bruner, in *Studies in Cognitive Growth*, states that growth is "as much from the outside in as from inside out," and that "much of [cognitive growth] consists in a human being's becoming linked with culturally transmitted 'amplifiers' of motoric, sensory, and reflective capacities." (pp. 1–2)

    According to Goody, in *The Domestication of the Savage Mind*, "[writing] changes the nature of the representations of the world (cognitive processes) for those who cannot [read]." He continues: "The existence of the alphabet therefore changes the type of data that an individual is dealing with, and it changes the repertoire of programmes he has available for treating his data." (p. 110)

    Julian Jaynes, in *The Origins of Consciousness in the Breakdown of the Bicameral Mind*, states that the role of "writing in the breakdown of the bicameral voices is tremendously important." He claims that the written word served as a "replacement" for the hallucinogenic image, and took up the right hemispheric function of sorting out and fitting together data.

    Walter Ong, in *The Presence of the Word*, and Marshall McLughan, in *Underatanding Media*, stress media's effects on the variations in the ratio and balance anoumg the senses. One might add that as early as 1938, Alfred North Whitehead (in *Modes of Thought*) called attention to the need for a thorough study of the effects of changes in media on the organization of the sensorium.